ISLAMIC ARCHITECTURE IN CAIRO

ISLAMIC ARCHITECTURE IN CAIRO

AN INTRODUCTION

BY

DORIS BEHRENS-ABOUSEIF

THE AMERICAN UNIVERSITY IN CAIRO PRESS

First published in Egypt in 1989 by
The American University in Cairo Press
113 Sharia Kasr el Aini, Cairo, Egypt
420 Fifth Avenue, New York, NY 10018
www.aucpress.com

This edition published by arrangement with E.J. Brill, Leiden, The Netherlands

Dar el Kutub No. 3977/89
ISBN 978 977 424 203 8

6 7 8 9 10 11 12   16 15 14 13 12 11 10 09

Printed in Egypt

TO MY STUDENTS IN CAIRO

Especially,

Eyad, Jihane, Lamia, Mary and Tarek

CONTENTS

(The numbers in [ ] refer to the Index of Islamic Monuments in Cairo and the Map of the Survey Dept.)

PREFACE

As this book is in the first place an introduction, the bibliography does not include unpublished materials such as waqf deeds, though they might be referred to in the text. For the same reason unpublished theses, of which the universities of Cairo hold a large number of interest to this subject, have not been cited.

Some buildings are dealt with only in the first, general part and have not been studied individually, such as the sabīls of the Ottoman period or the buildings of ᶜAbd al-Raḥmān Katkhudā.

To locate the monuments studied in this book, their index numbers are indicated in the list of Contents and, with the help of the Survey Map of the Islamic Monuments of Cairo, these will guide the reader to the sites.

The photographs, unless otherwise indicated, are by Mr. Muhammad Yusuf, chief photographer at al-Ahram newspaper, and Mr. Martin Huth. A few are by the author.

The plans that accompany the text are the work of either K.A.C. Creswell or the ''Committee for the Preservation of the Islamic Monuments of Cairo'', whose material is now in the Department of Antiquities.

Drawings published in *The Mosques of Egypt*, Ministry of Waqfs, Cairo 1949, have been used among the illustrations, as well as drawings made by Mr. Vilmos Sipos.

LIST OF PLATES

Note: Dates are supplied only for buildings not dealt with in the text.

PART I

THE CITY

STYLISTIC EVOLUTION OF ISLAMIC ARCHITECTURE IN CAIRO

THE FATIMID PERIOD

THE AYYUBID PERIOD

THE BAḤRI MAMLUK PERIOD

THE CIRCASSIAN MAMLUK PERIOD

THE OTTOMAN PERIOD (UNTIL MUHAMMAD ᶜALI)

DOMESTIC ARCHITECTURE IN CAIRO

PART II

EARLY ISLAMIC ARCHITECTURE IN CAIRO

ARCHITECTURE OF THE FATIMID PERIOD

ARCHITECTURE OF THE AYYUBID PERIOD

ARCHITECTURE OF THE BAHRI MAMLUKS

ARCHITECTURE OF THE CIRCASSIAN MAMLUKS

ARCHITECTURE OF THE OTTOMAN PERIOD

LIST OF FIGURES

PART I

THE CITY

STYLISTIC EVOLUTION OF ISLAMIC ARCHITECTURE IN CAIRO

DOMESTIC ARCHITECTURE

PART II

EARLY ISLAMIC ARCHITECTURE IN CAIRO

ARCHITECTURE OF THE FATIMID PERIOD

ARCHITECTURE OF THE AYYUBID PERIOD

ARCHITECTURE THE BAHRI MAMLUKS

IMPORTANT EVENTS IN THE HISTORY OF CAIRO

632	Death of the Prophet Muḥammad in Medina
639-41	Conquest of Egypt by the Caliph ᶜUmar's general, ᶜAmr Ibn al-ᶜĀṣ
641	Capture of the old Roman fortress of Babylon
641	Egypt becomes a province of the Caliphate of Medina
641-2	Mosque of ᶜAmr built; foundation of al-Fusṭāṭ as city and capital
661-750	*Umayyad Dynasty, Damascus*
750-1258	*Abbasid Dynasty, Baghdad/Samarra*
751	Governor of Egypt moves residence to new quarter of al-ᶜAskar
868	Aḥmad Ibn Ṭūlūn becomes governor of Egypt
868-905	*Tulunid Period*
870	Ibn Ṭūlūn moves residence to al-Qaṭāʾiᶜ
879	Mosque of Ibn Ṭūlūn completed
934-969	*Ikhshidid period*
969-1169	*Fatimid period*
969	Fatimid armies from North Africa take al-Fusṭāṭ; foundation of the walled city of al-Qāhira
972	Al-Azhar mosque dedicated
1012	Al-Ḥākim mosque completed
1066-72	Catastrophes of drought and pestilence
1087-91	New walls and gates built by the Vizier Badr al-Jamālī
1096	First Crusade begins
1099	Jerusalem falls to the Franks
1163-68	Syrians and Franks battle for control of Egypt
1168	Fusṭāṭ burned to prevent it falling to the Franks
1169	Salāḥ al-Dīn al-Ayyūbī takes control of Egypt
1171-1250	*Ayyubid period*
1170-76	Walls of Cairo extended; building of the Citadel starts
c. 1175	Madrasa and khanqāh systems introduced in Cairo
c. 1240	Elite corps of Turkish (Bahri) Mamluks formed by Sultan al-Malik al-Ṣāliḥ
1250	First mausoleum attached to a madrasa (Shajarat al-Durr builds a tomb at her husband's foundation)
1250-1382	*Bahri Mamluk period*
1258	Mongols take Baghdad and murder the Abbasid caliph
1261	Sultan Baybars sets up an Abbasid survivor as caliph in Cairo
1277	Baybars defeats the Mongols at ᶜAyn Jālūt
1292	Last Crusade enclaves captured
1309-40	Reign of al-Nāṣir Muḥammad Ibn Qalāwūn, greatest Mamluk builder and patron (with two interregnums)
1382-1517	*Circassian Mamluk period*
1468-96	Reign of Sultan al-Ashraf Qāytbāy, apogee of Circassian Mamluk period
1501-16	Reign of Sultan Qānṣūh al-Ghūrī

1517-1914	*Ottoman period*
1517	Selim I, Ottoman Sultan of Turkey, conquers Egypt and makes it a province of the Ottoman Empire
1768	Amir ᶜAlī Bey revolts against the Ottomans, takes part of Arabia and tries to annex Syria
1772	Revolt of ᶜAlī Bey put down
1798	Napoleon defeats Egyptian forces at the Battle of the Pyramids
1801	French evacuate Egypt; control restored to Ottomans
1805	Muḥammad ᶜAlī expels the Ottoman governor and massacres the last Mamluks

PART I

INTRODUCTION

CHAPTER ONE

THE CITY

Cairo's architectural monuments rank among humanity's great achievements. Recognizing that their preservation is a matter of importance to the whole world, UNESCO has listed the Egyptian capital as one of the "Cities of Human Heritage." Such recognition is well justified, for few cities on earth display such a dense concentration of historic architectural treasures as does Cairo.

This concentration reflects the political situation of Islamic Egypt, which never had another capital outside the space occupied by the city we now call Cairo. Historians describe a series of capital cities—al-Fusṭāṭ, al-ᶜAskar, al-Qaṭāᵓiᶜ and al-Qāhira—but all of these were within sight of one another and eventually became a single city. Cairo has been the uninterrupted center of power in Egypt since the year 641.

Continuous, centralized power in one area distinguishes Egypt from other Islamic nations such as Syria, Iraq, Anatolia, Andalusia, and Persia, where different cities vied for supremacy in different epochs, sometimes simultaneously. Muslim Egypt was ruled from a single site, the area between the mosque of ᶜAmr in the south and Bāb al-Naṣr and Bāb al-Fūtūḥ to the north. Outside this area very few medieval buildings of interest have survived, while within it, a large number of Egypt's medieval and post-medieval monuments still stand, witnesses to more than eleven centuries of history.

Al-Fusṭāṭ, al-ᶜAskar, al-Qaṭāᵓiᶜ

What we today call Cairo, or al-Qāhira, is an agglomeration of four cities founded within the area. The name al-Qāhira did not exist until the last of these was created in 969 as capital of Egypt under the Fatimids. Before this city came a succession of capitals beginning with al-Fusṭāṭ (641), the Abbasid foundation of al-ᶜAskar (750), and the Tulunid establishment of al-Qaṭāᵓiᶜ (870).

Al-Fusṭāṭ was founded as the capital of Egypt just after the Arab conquest of Egypt. Its location was a strategic decision by the Caliph ᶜUmar Ibn al-Khaṭṭāb in Medina, for although Alexandria was capital of Egypt at the time of the conquest, the Caliph preferred to settle his troops in an area less remote from the Arabian Peninsula. ᶜAmr Ibn al-ᶜĀṣ, commander of the Caliph's troops in Egypt, thus abandoned his plans to settle in the former capital on the Mediterranean. The new capital, at the apex of the Nile Delta, was strategically situated near the Roman fortress town of Babylon. This site, at the junction of Upper and Lower Egypt, allowed easy communication with the Arabian Peninsula without crossing the Nile and its Delta branches. ᶜAmr Ibn al-ᶜĀṣ redug the ancient canal connecting the Nile with the Red Sea, further facilitating communication with the Caliphate in the Hejaz. Al-Fusṭāṭ soon eclipsed Alexandria as the commercial and industrial center of Egypt, receiving goods from Upper and Lower Egypt and from the Mediterranean at its Nile port. In the ninth century, however, the Khalīj or canal connecting the Nile with the Red Sea was partially filled in, and all that was left was a pond southeast of the Delta called Birkat al-Ḥājj, the first station on the caravan road to Mecca.

Al-Fusṭāṭ was typical of the garrison cities established in the early days of the Arab conquests. Like Kufa and Basra in Iraq and Qayrawan in Tunisia, it was an unplanned agglomeration that later crystallized into true urban form. At the center of al-Fusṭāṭ was the mosque of ᶜAmr, a simple construction for the religious needs of the troops and, adjacent to it, the commander's house. The mosque overlooked the Nile, whose channel was much closer to it than it is now. Al-Fusṭāṭ was originally divided into distinct quarters occupied by the various tribes of the conquering army. This garrison gradually developed into a large town engulfing the town of Babylon around the Roman fortress.

Al-Fusṭāṭ acquired its first satellite city after the Abbasids overthrew the Umayyad Caliphate of Damascus in 750 and established their new capital at Baghdad. In order to reinforce their grip on the Egyptian province, the new rulers immediately sent troops and founded a new capital, al-ᶜAskar ("the soldiers"),

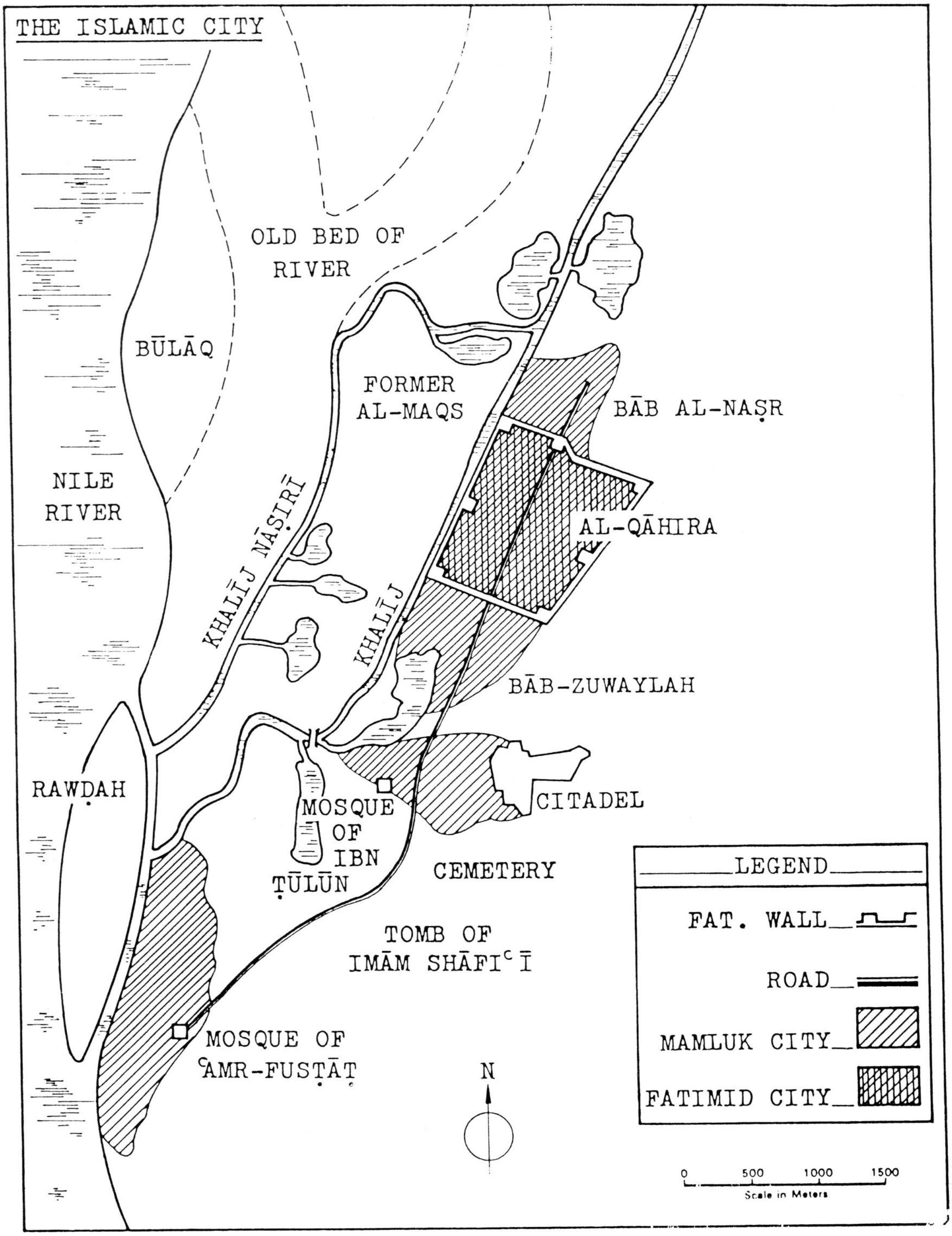

Fig. 1. Map of Cairo in the early Mamluk period.

with a new mosque and governor's palace, to the northeast of al-Fusṭāṭ. Despite the foundation of this satellite city, al-Fusṭāṭ continued for some time to be the administrative and commercial center. In the following period, the two communities of al-Fusṭāṭ and al-ʿAskar fused into a larger city designated simply as al-Fusṭāṭ, stretching to the Nile in the west and to the foot of the Muqaṭṭam hill to the east and north. The Great Mosque of al-ʿAskar had already disappeared in the Middle Ages, and Maqrīzī, the Egyptian historian of the early fifteenth century, mentions it only briefly.

Following the precedent set by the Abbasids in founding al-ʿAskar, later dynasties created for themselves new seats of power, each farther to the northeast, farther inland, and each more grandiose than the last. Aḥmad Ibn Tūlūn, sent to Egypt in 868 as the Abbasid Caliph's governor, soon asserted his independence, founding a new ruling dynasty (868-905) and a new capital, al-Qaṭāʾiʿ ("the wards"), northeast of the Fusṭāṭ-al-ʿAskar complex. The new city, standing on higher ground than al-ʿAskar, on the hill called Jabal Yashkur, the area today including the mosque of Ibn Ṭūlūn and the foot of the Citadel, was remote from the commercial and industrial center of al-Fusṭāṭ and its busy port. It was celebrated as a magnificent pleasure city, especially under the reign of Ibn Ṭūlūn's son Khumārawayh.

Ibn Ṭūlūn constructed a grand palace with vast gardens and a menagerie, as well as a hippodrome for horse races, polo, and other chivalric games. The hippodrome had a special triple gate, where Ibn Ṭūlūn entered alone through the middle arch flanked by his soldiers marching through the side arches. The Gate of Lions, another of the hippodrome's entrances, was surmounted by two lions in stucco and a belvedere or gallery for the ruler.

Ibn Ṭūlūn's son Khumārawayh embellished the works of his father in many ways. He furnished one of his belvederes, the Golden House, with statues of women painted and adorned with jewelry, representing his slaves and singers. Khumārawayh took special care of the garden of rare flowers and trees. Tree trunks were coated with gilded copper from which pipes trickled water into canals and fountains to irrigate the garden, and nearby was an aviary with singing birds. Most remarkable was a pool of mercury, where Khumārawayh, an insomniac, lay on an air mattress trying to rock himself to sleep. The entire complex, with its gardens, huge stables and menagerie of wild animals, did not overlook the Nile but rather the Birkat al-Fīl, a large pond connected to the Khalīj. In the surrounding area, luxury markets soon sprang up to serve the tastes of officers and notables.

The Tulunid age with all its luxurious trappings came to an end in 905 when the Abbasid troops once again marched on Egypt, this time to reestablish order and replace the dynasty whose sovereigns had lived so sumptuously. During this campaign, the entire city of al-Qaṭāʾiʿ was razed to the ground except for Ibn Ṭūlūn's aqueduct and his mosque, the oldest mosque in Egypt surviving in its original form.

Al-Qāhira

The fourth palatial satellite city was born with the conquest of Egypt by the Fatimids, an Ismāʿīlī Shīʿa dynasty originating in North Africa. The fourth Fatimid Caliph, al-Muʿizz li-Dīn Allāh, with his general Jawhar al-Ṣiqillī, overthrew the Ikhshidids who had ruled Egypt between 934 and 969. Egypt's status rose with that of its conquerors; it became the seat of a Caliphate.

Jawhar accordingly began construction on the walls which were to enclose the new caliphal residence. Al-Muʿizz first named the site al-Manṣūriyya after his father, the Caliph al-Manṣūr, but four years later renamed it al-Qāhira (The Victorious) after al-Qāhir, the planet Mars, in ascendance when the signal was given to break ground for the new capital. The new construction was completed in 971, with quarters for the various ethnic groups composing the Fatimid army: Greeks, other Europeans, Armenians, Berbers, Sudanese, and Turks.

Facing a huge esplanade for ceremonial activities, the palace complex of the Caliph stood midway along the artery that cut the city into two unequal parts on an approximate north-south axis. The residences occupied the heart of the new imperial city into which the Caliph al-Muʿizz made his triumphal entry in 974.

The Two Cities

Under the Fatimids, al-Qāhira became the seat of power, a ceremonial, residential center where the Caliph dwelt with his court and army, but al-Fusṭāṭ remained the productive and economic center of Egypt. The older city, by that time called simply Miṣr, had grown into a flourishing metropolis. Travelers visiting it from the tenth to the mid-eleventh centuries reported that it competed in grandeur and prosperity with the

Pl. 1. Tabbāna Street in the nineteenth century (Coste).

greatest Islamic cities of the time. Al-Muqaddasī in the tenth century described the highrise buildings of al-Fusṭāṭ as resembling minarets. According to Nāṣirī Khusraw, a Persian traveler of the early eleventh century, some of these buildings climbed as high as fourteen stories up to roof gardens complete with ox-drawn water wheels for irrigating them. Khusraw dedicates long descriptive passages to the city's thriving markets, and finally confesses, "I have seen so much wealth in al-Fusṭāṭ that if I tried to list or describe it, my words would not be believed. I found it impossible to count or estimate it."

Recent excavations at al-Fusṭāṭ have corroborated some of these contemporary descriptions. Eyewitnesses wrote that in the densest part of the city, around the mosque of ᶜAmr, merchants displayed goods from all over the world. Excavations have revealed Chinese wares of the most refined quality that found their way to al-Fusṭāṭ. The digs have also revealed considerable sophistication below the street level. The intricate sewerage system took advantage of differing altitudes of al-Fusṭāṭ's terrain to distribute water and eliminate wastes. According to other visitors' accounts, al-Fusṭāṭ also suffered, for all its glory and sophistication, from problems familiar to the inhabitants of modern cities. The physician Ibn Riḍwān (d. 1068) thought the streets were too narrow for their high buildings. The hills to the east and north prevented proper ventilation of the city so that the stagnant air became polluted, particularly with smoke from the furnaces of a multitude of steam baths. Dead animals thrown into the Nile contaminated the drinking water, and the congestion and dilapidation of the heart of al-Fusṭāṭ shocked some visitors. In the twelfth century Ibn Saᶜīd from Seville noted that the mosque of ᶜAmr had fallen victim to a traffic problem. The monument, its premises crowded

Pl. 2. Southern Cairo and the cemetery (Roberts).

with women, children and peddlers and its walls covered with graffiti, served the city's population as a short-cut between two streets.

Al-Qāhira, on the other hand, stood high above the problems of the mother city. Nāṣirī Khusraw, describing the Fatimid Caliph's city, refers to mansions and gardens of incredible beauty. Of the palace complex, dominating the center of town like a mountain, he writes:

> I saw a series of buildings, terraces and rooms. There were twelve adjoining pavilions, all of them square in shape. ... There was a throne in one of them that took up the entire width of the room. Three of its sides were made of gold on which were hunting scenes depicting riders racing their horses and other subjects; there were also inscriptions written in beautiful characters. The rugs and hangings were Greek satin and moire woven precisely to fit the spot where they were to be placed. A balustrade of golden lattice work surrounded the throne, whose beauty defies all description. Behind the throne were steps of silver. I saw a tree that looked like an orange tree, whose branches, leaves and fruits were made of sugar. A thousand statuettes and figurines also made of sugar were also placed there.

A French ambassador to Cairo, speaking of the palace in 1167, mentions floors of colored marble, grouted with gold, and a courtyard surrounded by magnificent colonnaded porticos. Water from a central fountain trickled through gold and silver pipes into channels and pools. There was a menagerie and an aviary filled with exotically colored birds from all over the world. Long passages of Maqrīzī's account tell of the different treasure halls of the Fatimid palaces and an academy with a vast library.

These accounts imply that by the end of the eleventh century, Egypt's two symbiotic capitals, Miṣr and al-Qāhira, physically manifested the separation between the indigenous people and the ruling elite. The larger one, Miṣr, supported the productive and mercantile population, while al-Qāhira was inhabited exclusively by the foreign rulers and their entourage. Commoners employed in the royal city returned to al-Fusṭāṭ (Miṣr) at the end of the working day. Each city had a port. That of al-Fusṭāṭ was close to its markets, while al-Maqs or Umm Dunayn (the pre-Islamic village of Tandunias) harbored the Fatimid fleet. This situation, however, did not survive the next century.

In the twelfth century a series of natural catastrophes, plague followed by famine and a violent earthquake, severely depopulated al-Fusṭāṭ and arrested its development. Al-Qaṭā'iʿ, on the northern outskirts, had not recovered from its destruction by Abbasid troops. The Fatimid vizier Badr al-Jamālī, responding to the situation, permitted the transfer of some markets to al-Qāhira and allowed wealthy citizens to build new houses in the formerly exclusive city. Al-Fusṭāṭ was thus already in decline when the French King Amaury (Amalric) and his Crusaders came from Jerusalem to attack Egypt. Nūr al-Dīn of Syria sent his armies to aid the Fatimids, and the Muslim troops, led by Shīrkūh and his nephew Ṣalāḥ al-Dīn, fought the Crusaders from 1164 to 1169. During these campaigns the Fatimid vizier Shawār is reported to have ordered the burning of al-Fusṭāṭ to stop the invaders. After his victory over the Franks, Ṣalāḥ al-Dīn became vizier under the last Fatimid Caliph, whom he overthrew in 1171, reestablishing the supremacy of the Sunni Caliphate of Baghdad and ending two centuries of Ismāʿīlī Shiʿite rule in Egypt.

These upheavals consolidated changes already in progress. Once opened to whoever wished to live there, al-Qāhira completely eclipsed al-Fusṭāṭ. The suburbs of the older city had decayed, leaving large empty spaces between al-Fusṭāṭ and al-Qāhira. Ṣalāḥ al-Dīn set out to enclose both cities and the intervening areas within one long set of walls. Undaunted by the enormity of the task, he also intended his wall to extend westward across the Khalīj to include the port of al-Maqs, and eastward to al-Muqaṭṭam, where he began his Citadel in the Syrian tradition of hilltop fortifications. He died before these projects were completed, and the walls of Cairo were never continued. The Citadel, however, designed not only as a fortress but also as the residence of sultans, was enlarged and embellished with new buildings throughout its history.

Pl. 3. Nineteenth century houses along the canal of Cairo (Coste).

The Outskirts

The city expanded on all sides under subsequent rulers. Under the Mamluks there was extensive development along the road leading from Bāb Zuwayla to the Citadel and its royal palaces. Natural forces played a part as well. The Nile's course shifted to the west in the fourteenth century, transforming the island of Būlāq into a port on the eastern bank and leaving al-Maqs, which Ṣalāḥ al-Dīn had planned to fortify, far inland. On the eastern edge of al-Qāhira the cemetery founded by al-Nāṣir Muḥammad, like that of Fusṭāṭ farther to the south, expanded into the desert and soon became the site of important religious foundations.

The Khalīj, which for centuries had formed the western border of the city, fed a number of ponds in the western, northern and southern outskirts. The Nile flooded these ponds in summer, leaving their beds green with vegetation when the waters receded. The beauty of these ponds made them the summer resorts of Cairenes, and many princely residences were built near them, particularly the Birkat al-Fīl in the south. The pond of Azbakiyya came into vogue during the late Mamluk period and remained fashionable under the Ottomans. Orchards and pleasure buildings on the western bank of the Khalīj gradually gave way to urbanization during the Ottoman period (1517-1914), as the city's northern areas expanded toward the Nile.

The Names of Cairo

The word Cairo is derived from the Arabic al-Qāhira, which is not, however, the name commonly used by Egyptians to designate their capital. They have always called it Maṣr (the popular form of Miṣr, meaning Egypt). Al-Qāhira is the official term used in written Arabic today.

Egyptian medieval historians make a clear distinction between Miṣr and Al-Qāhira. Al-Qāhira is the name of that part of the capital established in 969 by the Fatimid dynasty as its residential city. Miṣr is the abbreviation of Fusṭāṭ-Miṣr, or Fusṭāṭ of Egypt, designating the first Muslim capital of Egypt founded by the Arab general ᶜAmr Ibn al-ᶜĀṣ in 641-42.

There are two interpretations of the word Fusṭāṭ. While European scholars usually derive it from the Greek and Latin *fossatum* meaning trench, which could be a pre-Islamic local toponym, Arab scholars prefer to interpret it as the Arabic *fusṭāṭ*, meaning tent. According to legend, the name originated when the Arab troops on their way to Alexandria left the tent of ᶜAmr Ibn al-ᶜĀṣ behind in order not to disturb a dove that had built a nest in it. In time, people dropped the word al-Fusṭāṭ, and the area of the early Arab foundation was once again known as Miṣr. The term Miṣr was later extended to refer to the whole capital, composed of both al-Fusṭāṭ and al-Qāhira. Ottoman coins from Egypt are inscribed, *ḍuriba fī miṣr*, "struck in Miṣr", and Ottoman coins always refer to the city rather than to the province where they were struck. The mint was at the Citadel, in al-Qāhira. In the Ottoman period al-Fusṭāṭ (or Miṣr) itself was called Miṣr al-ᶜAtīqa, referring to the part of the city today called Miṣr al-Qadīma, meaning Old Miṣr. Many people still call it Miṣr al-ᶜAtīqa.

The habit of calling the entire Egyptian capital Cairo, or al-Qāhira, was begun by Europeans who visited Egypt. The name was reinforced by Napoleon's French scholars, who made a scholarly survey of the city which they called Le Kaire, translated by the British as Cairo. Cairo's traditional byname is Miṣr al-Maḥrūsa, or Cairo, the Protected City.

Despite its many losses, Cairo has been spared wholesale devastations by wars and other calamities, and today offers us a wealth of historic architecture.

CHAPTER TWO

STYLISTIC EVOLUTION OF ISLAMIC ARCHITECTURE IN CAIRO

THE FATIMID PERIOD (969-1167)

Not before the establishment of a Caliphate in Egypt under the Fatimids did an indigenous style in art and architecture crystallize. The mosque of Ibn Ṭūlūn, despite a few variations, is still a product of the Abbassid court art of Samarra.

While the arrival of a new dynasty need not automatically bring with it a change of style in arts and crafts, a new political system necessarily shapes the environment of the craftsman and thus brings new influences to bear upon his inherited methods and experience. The Fatimid reign promoted Egypt from a tribute-paying governorate within a Caliphate to a Caliphate itself, with Cairo the imperial capital.

Cairo's new status as seat of the Fatimid Caliphate led to the emergence of a new, individual style. The arts and architecture of the Fatimid period show an integrated use of Coptic, Byzantine and Samarran elements. Foreign forms in Fatimid architecture and decoration thus express not a provincial version of an imperial prototype, but a demonstration that the new imperial city had considerable attraction for craftsmen and artists from many traditions in and outside Egypt.

The Fatimid dynasty ruled Egypt between 969 and 1171. They came from North Africa, where they had established an empire prior to their conquest of Egypt. They were Shīᶜa Muslims of the Ismāᶜīlī branch, claiming descent from the Prophet through his daughter Fāṭima (hence their name) and his son-in-law, the Caliph ᶜAlī Ibn Abī Ṭālib, whom Shiᶜites especially venerate. The *shahāda*, or tenet of the Muslim faith, "There is no God but Allah and Muḥammad is the Prophet of Allāh," when spoken by Shiᶜites is supplemented by the phrase, *ᶜAlī waliyyu 'llāh*, "ᶜAli is the Protected of God." According to Shīᶜa doctrine, the only legitimate and authoritative religious leaders are the imāms, or descendants of ᶜAli through his sons from Fāṭima, al-Haṣan and al-Ḥusayn. The imāms, because of their ancestry, were considered by the Ismāᶜīlīs to be divinely inspired and therefore infallible. The Fatimid Caliphs were the imāms of the community.

Pl. 4. Trilobed arch at Bāb Zuwayla.

Under Fatimid Shīᶜa rule, most of the Egyptian population continued to be faithful to Sunnism, and were thus separated from their rulers by a religious barrier. This religious barrier might explain the building of a certain type of shrine, such as the Fatimid

Pl. 5. The base of the dome added by Caliph Al-Ḥāfiẓ li Dīn Allāh at al-Azhar; window grill inlaid with colored glass.

mashhads, memorial foundations dedicated to descendants of the Prophet Muḥammad who had died much earlier and most of whom had no connection with Egypt at all. These shrines, such as the shrines of Sayyida Nafīsa, Sayyida Zaynab, and al-Ḥusayn venerated by both Shīʿa and Sunni Muslims, are still venerated today, helped bridge the religious gap between rulers and subjects, and also enhanced the prestige of the Fatimid rulers, themselves descendants and relatives of the worshipped saints. Memorial buildings of this type were not peculiar to Egypt; they had appeared earlier in other parts of the Muslim world as well.

The Fatimid Caliphs were not buried in cemeteries, but within the confines of their own palaces. Their tombs and those of their ancestors were considered as shrines and visited on religious and official occasions. The outstanding architectural achievement of the Fatimid Caliphs, according to travelers' and historians' accounts, were their palaces. As nothing of these have survived except written descriptions, our visual experience of Fatimid architecture is restricted to a few surviving shrines, mosques, and the city gates. Though limited in number, these monuments show us the great creativity of Fatimid architecture and decoration, and the reasons for its long lasting influence in subsequent periods.

Fatimid mosques retained the hypostyle mosque plan, with column-supported arcades surrounding a courtyard. However, the keel arch was introduced, usually carried on pre-Islamic Corinthian capitals. An Islamic type of capital in the shape of a bell was used, and the shape was often repeated underneath the column to form its base, though set upside down. The piers of the mosque of Ibn Ṭūlūn already had such capitals and bases.

The prayer niche of a Fatimid mosque is always enhanced architecturally, either by a dome above it or by a transept (al-Azhar and al-Ḥākim have both), or by a widening of the aisle adjacent to the qibla wall (al-Aqmar mosque), or the aisle perpendicular to it (al-Ṣāliḥ Ṭalāʾiʿ mosque).

Aligning the facade of the mosque to the street, a feature characteristic of Cairene medieval architecture, appears for the first time in the Fatimid period. The al-Aqmar mosque is the earliest extant example, and is also the earliest extant example of an extensively decorated mosque facade. Facade decoration with recesses in which windows are placed is first seen at the mosque of al-Ṣāliḥ Ṭalāʾiʿ, and the location of a mosque above shops was also initiated during this period.

Fatimid minaret shapes show a clear evolution from al-Juyūshī to Abū'l-Ghadanfar toward the *mabkhara* shape, a term meaning "incense burner," which was used by Creswell to designate a rectangular shaft supporting an octagonal section with a ribbed helmet. This minaret shape, not, by the way, reminiscent of any known type of incense burner, was to become typical of minarets for the next two centuries.

It is known that marble was used for decoration, though none used in mosques has remained in place. Stucco, wood and stone carvings display floral designs, arabesques derived from Samarran and Byzantine motifs, and geometric patterns. Kufic inscription bands become increasingly ornate. Window grills have floral as well as geometric designs, and glass in stucco grills appears for the first time, a feature that was common from then on.

The Fatimid period introduced decorative features such as the keel-arched niche with fluted radiating hood, a variation on a late classic theme used widely in Coptic art. This fluted niche hood must have inspired architects to build fluted domes, a style continued in Mamluk architecture. The Fatimid use of inscription bands along the arches, however, was not continued, and is confined to the Fatimid period.

Although Samarran and Byzantine motifs inspired Fatimid decoration, these were further developed and modified into a complex and less repetitive treatment, emphasizing accommodation to the surface to be decorated.

Pl. 6. Prayer niche of al-Afḍal Shāhinshāh at the mosque of Ibn Ṭūlūn (drawing, "The Mosques of Egypt").

Pl. 7. The minaret of Abū'l-Ghadanfar, 1157.

THE AYYUBID PERIOD (1171-1250)

The Ayyubids, who adhered to the Shāfiʿī rite of Islamic law, allowed only one Friday mosque within an urban area, which explains why they did not build any new major mosques. They built instead a number of madrasas, of which only one has survived. Many of their madrasas were established in houses or palaces.

The madrasa was an institution sponsored by members of the ruling class for teaching theology and law according to an officially approved curriculum. Teaching in mosques was common since the beginning of Islamic history, but these early teaching institutions were private initiatives not subject to state control. The Shiʿites were the first to found official teaching institutions for the propagation of their own doctrine, as at al-Azhar. The Sunnis therefore emulated the system, promoting the madrasas to counteract Shīʿa propaganda.

In a madrasa, the student acquired a higher education in law and theology to enable him to undertake scholarly or administrative duties. He was given food, lodging, clothing, and even a stipend. The khanqāh was for the Sufis, who espoused the mystic, esoteric approach to religion, in which seclusion and ascetism played important roles. In the early khanqāh, the Sufis led a monastic life according to their own strict regulations and were also sponsored in the same manner as the students of the madrasa.

Imam Shāfiʿī, founder of the rite known by his

name, who lived and died in Egypt, was especially revered by the Ayyubids. The first madrasa in Egypt was built by Ṣalāḥ al-Dīn near the tomb of Imām Shāfiʿī at the cemetery of al-Fusṭāṭ. Ṣalāḥ al-Dīn also sponsored a magnificent wooden cenotaph on the Imām's grave, still in place today. Nothing of the madrasa has survived.

The first khanqāh of Egypt, also introduced by Ṣalāḥ al-Dīn, was established on the premises of a Fatimid palace in the center of al-Qāhira. It too has not survived, but throughout the medieval period it was one of the most important khanqāhs of Cairo. Originally, it was exclusively for Sufis from outside Egypt.

Architecture

The break into the political and religious system introduced by Ayyubid rule in Egypt did not affect the arts to the same extent, although it led necessarily to innovations in the field of architecture, required by the establishment of new forms of religious institutions.

The madrasa and the khanqāh which were both planned to lodge their respective communities of students and Sufis, were necessarily built on a plan different from that of the traditional mosque. They had to include living units, a kitchen, sometimes a bath, a reception hall and stables which are elements of domestic architecture. Thus the īwān, which historians mention in an earlier residential context, was adopted in madrasa and khanqāh architecture. In its classic form, it was a hall open on one side and covered by a vault or a flat ceiling. In Cairo, early īwāns—Ayyubid and Bahri Mamluk—were vaulted; in the later Mamluk period they were often covered with a wooden ceiling. At the madrasa of al-Ṣāliḥ Najm al-Dīn, two īwāns face each other across a courtyard with the living units on the lateral sides built on several stories. At the end of the thirteenth century, the so-called cruciform plan was adopted with four unequal īwāns framing the courtyard and the living quarters occupying the corners of the courtyard.

In funerary architecture, the mausoleum of Imām Shāfiʿī continued the shrine tradition established by the Fatimids, on a superlative scale and with new meaning. The Imām Shāfiʿī dome, like that of al-Ṣāliḥ Najm al-Dīn, has a feature alien to Fatimid domes: its profile curves near the springing of the dome. This dome, however, was restored several times, and it is possible that its shape was remodeled, in which case the dome

Pl. 8. Minaret base from the Ayyubid period at the shrine of al-Ḥusayn.

of al-Ṣāliḥ Najm al-Dīn would be the earliest extant example of this type of dome profile.

The facade of the madrasa of al-Ṣāliḥ Najm al-Dīn follows the pattern introduced at the mosque of al-Ṣāliḥ Ṭalāʾiʿ, with windows in recessed panels along the whole length of the facade.

The minaret of al-Ṣāliḥ Najm al-Dīn is of the mabkhara type decorated with stalactites. The earliest mabkhara minaret, that of Abū'l-Ghadanfar (1157), is without stalactites.

There are two undated buildings attributed by Creswell to the late Ayyubid decade that could also have been built in the first Mamluk decade. In either case, they deserve some mention here, as they represent a further step in the evolution of Cairo architecture of the mid-thirteenth century.

The Minaret of Zāwiyat al-Hunūd

One of these is a minaret known by its later designation as the minaret of Zāwiyat al-Hunūd. It is a mabkhara minaret which has retained more decorations than that of al-Ṣāliḥ, with lozenges and keel arches and more stalactites. Its silhouette is more slender and elongated, and it therefore might well have been built around 1250, as Creswell suggests.

The Mausoleum of the Abbasid Caliphs

The other building is known as the mausoleum of the Abbasid Caliphs, as several Abbasid Caliphs were buried there after Sultan al-Ẓāhir Baybars founded a nominal Abbasid Caliphate in Cairo following the sack of Baghdad by the Mongols. It adjoins the shrine of Sayyida Nafīsa in the cemetery of Fusṭāṭ and is undated.

The mausoleum includes several cenotaphs, the earliest of which is that of an ambassador of the Abbasid court named Naḍla, who died in Egypt in 1243. There are also two sons of the Mamluk Sultan al-Ẓāhir Baybars buried under the same dome and other later Caliphs' cenotaphs. The cenotaphs of course do not date the mausoleum itself; it might be older or later than the tombs. Creswell identifies it as having been built originally for Naḍla, the ambassador of the Abbasid Caliph, in 1243. Other arguments, such as the extraordinarily lavish decoration, favor its attribution to Sultan al-Ẓāhir Baybars who would have built it for his sons in the 1260's, especially since the enclosure in which the mausoleum stands axially is assigned to al-Ẓāhir Baybars.

The mausoleum of the Abbasid Caliphs is one of the most finely decorated buildings of medieval Cairo. Its dome's interior is covered with exquisitely carved stucco and painted medallions. It has a band of braided, painted Kufic script in its lower part, the only example in Cairene architectural decoration. The architec-

Pl. 9. The minaret of Zāwiyat al-Hunūd, ca. 1250 (Department of Antiquities).

Pl. 10. Keel-arched niche at the mausoleum of the Abbasid Caliphs, mid-thirteenth century.

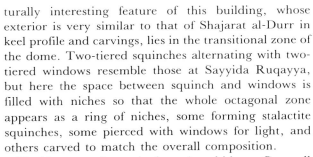

Pl. 11. The transitional zone of the dome of the Abbasid Caliphs, mid-thirteenth century.

turally interesting feature of this building, whose exterior is very similar to that of Shajarat al-Durr in keel profile and carvings, lies in the transitional zone of the dome. Two-tiered squinches alternating with two-tiered windows resemble those at Sayyida Ruqayya, but here the space between squinch and windows is filled with niches so that the whole octagonal zone appears as a ring of niches, some forming stalactite squinches, some pierced with windows for light, and others carved to match the overall composition.

If this mausoleum is late Ayyubid as Creswell assumes (1242/3), this would be the first use of this device, a year earlier than in al-Ṣāliḥ's dome (1243/4). This treatment of the transitional zone was subsequently adopted in all domes with squinches.

Decoration

Ayyubid decoration is quite distinct from that used by the Fatimids. The arabesques are more abstract and more intricate, to the extent that the basic design is concealed behind the densely carved curves very minutely and extremely delicately executed. Their basic arrangement, however, follows the usual geometric rules.

Indeed, the stuccos resemble lace, a prominent example being on the base of a minaret added in 1237 to the shrine of al-Ḥusayn whose original top has not survived. The decoration of Shajarat al-Durr's dome gives the same impression. Stucco window grills are no longer treated geometrically; arabesques are used instead. Work in stone and wood follows the same trend. The woodwork of the cenotaphs of Imām Shāfiʿī and the one added to the shrine of al-Ḥusayn (now in the Islamic Museum) are perhaps the most beautiful in Cairo's history. They are carved in deep relief in floral and geometric patterns and use both Kufic and naskhī scripts. The use of naskhī increases in Ayyubid decoration and is applied along with Kufic to decorate architecture and other artistic objects as well. Samarran and Byzantine styles were fully supplanted in the Ayyubid period by Islamic decorative art forms.

THE BAHRI MAMLUK PERIOD (1250-1382)

Cairo's legacy of Bahri Mamluk monuments is for the art historian a source of both delight and despair owing to the variety of forms and patterns adopted during this period, greater by far than that found in later periods.

The architecture of the Bahri Mamluks is primarily Cairene, based on the Fatimid and Ayyubid traditions that evolved into an indigenous Cairo art without, however, ever being closed to outside inspiration.

Functions

The mosque of ᶜAmr at Fusṭāṭ was the congregational mosque of the city, which means that it was the mosque where the Friday sermon was held, first by ᶜAmr himself, and subsequently by his successors, the first governors of Egypt and spiritual heads of the Muslim community. Of course it was not the only mosque of the city, for there were a multitude of others for the five daily prayers. The congregational mosque was called *masjid jāmiᶜ* and abreviated as *jāmiᶜ*, meaning congregational. The ordinary mosque was called *masjid*, which is the origin of the word "mosque". Today, this terminological distinction no longer exists.

Every medieval urban agglomeration had its own congregational mosque. When, however, the cities and their Muslim communities grew, the number of Friday mosques increased. The cities of al-ᶜAskar and al-Qaṭāʾiᶜ each had a Friday mosque. Al-Qāhira had the al-Azhar and al-Ḥākim mosques. The Fatimid Caliph, in his position as both political and spiritual leader, held prayer each Friday in the four mosques of ᶜAmr, Ibn Ṭūlūn, al-Azhar, and al-Ḥākim. Under the Ayyubids, the only congregational mosque of Cairo was that of al-Ḥākim, no doubt because it was the largest in the city. At Fusṭāṭ, the mosque of ᶜAmr continued to be the city's Friday mosque. The Mamluks increased the number of Friday mosques, and from the time of Sultan Ḥasan, madrasas and khanqāhs also became simultaneously Friday mosques so that by the fifteenth century, each quarter and sometimes even each street had its own. The sermon delivered by the shaykh had at that time only a spiritual, and not a political, function.

Plans

Creswell has demonstrated definitively that the madrasa plan called cruciform, consisting of a courtyard with four īwāns of unequal size and living units between them, developed in Egypt. The earliest known madrasas, those of al-Malik al-Kāmil and al-Malik al-Ṣāliḥ, had two iwāns facing each other across a courtyard, and at al-Ṣāliḥ's madrasa, this form was duplicated. We do not know exactly how the lateral sides were treated, but the madrasa of Sultan Qalāwūn is rather similar in plan. There, the lateral sides each have a small room in the form of a recess, rather than a true iwan. In later madrasas, these recesses become larger, forming small iwāns. This plan is very similar to the *qāᶜa*, or reception hall, of Mamluk and Ottoman residences, the only difference being that in the classic madrasa, the courtyard is not roofed or domed as it was in the residential qāᶜa.

Hypostyle mosques continued to be built in the Bahri Mamluk period, but were no longer free standing. In the already crowded urban setting, their plans generally lose their regularity. For example, the main entrance is no longer on the axis of the sanctuary.

With Shajarat al-Durr, who initiated the rule of the Bahri Mamluk sultans, it became traditional for the founder of a religious institution to add his own mausoleum to the building. The mausoleum dome was built to enhance the founder's prestige, and its location was therefore important. Ideally a mausoleum attached to a religious building had to be oriented to Mecca and at the same time accessible from the street. The formula succeeds at the mausoleums of Qalāwūn, al-Nāṣir Muḥammad, and all others located on the west side of the street. Where the Mecca orientation does not coincide with the street, the street orientation was given preference.

Mausoleums were given large windows with iron grills, where a shaykh sat and recited the Quran both for the soul of the dead and to attract the attention and blessings of passersby. Often, mausoleums were much more richly decorated than the buildings they were attached to, a good example being that of Baybars al-Jashankīr.

Facades

Mosques and madrasas since their earliest history had primary schools for boys (*maktab* or *kuttāb*) attached to them, which were usually dedicated to the education of orphans. Other boys could take private lessons with teachers who taught in shops within the city, as the tales of "The Schoolmaster" and "The Split-Mouth Schoolmaster" of the Arabian Nights tell us. Judging from the number of kuttābs that survived, most men in medieval Cairo must have been literate.

By the end of the Bahri Mamluk period, an architectural device was developed for such structures. A loggia occupying a corner with a double arch on each side surmounted the *sabīl* or water-house. The sabīl was another pious foundation that could be attached to a mosque. It was a place where the thirsty passerby could get a drink of water. A man especially employed for that purpose would serve him behind the large sabīl window. Since the madrasa of Amir Iljāy al-Yūsufī, the combination of a sabīl with a kuttāb became a standard feature of the facades, always at the corner, of religious foundations.

Bahri Mamluk facades standardize the panel-and-recess pattern begun at the mosque of al-Ṣāliḥ Ṭalāʾiʿ. The recesses are crowned with stalactites and have large rectangular lower windows with iron grills and higher arched or double arched windows with stucco grills and colored glass.

Portals

Various types of portals were used before the stalactite portal became typical during the mid-fourteenth century. The Qalāwūn complex has a round arch decorated in the spandrels with interlacing stripes of black and white marble. At the khanqāh of Baybars al-Jashankīr the portal is a round arch with cushion voussoir. At the mosques of al-Māridānī and Aqsunqur, pointed arches characterize the entrance recess. The mosques of Ulmās (1330) and Bashtāk (1336) have a rectangular recess with dripping stalactites above the entrance bay. The mosque of Amir Ḥusayn has a pointed arch with moldings radiating from a central point above the lintel and interlacing to form the voussoir of the arch. The northern portal of al-Nāṣir's mosque at the Citadel has a trilobed shallow recess.

Eventually, the stalactite portal composed of a half-dome resting on stalactites predominates, and later is used exclusively. Creswell traces its origins to Syria,

Pl. 12. The portal of the mosque of Amir Bashtāk, 1336.

where there are examples earlier than those in Egypt. This, however, is not a definitive argument, for many earlier buildings in Cairo that have not survived may have had this feature. The vestibules are almost always cross-vaulted.

Minarets

Minaret evolution is continuous from al-Juyūshī and Abū'l-Ghadanfar toward the more slender mabkhara type such as those of Sanjar and Sunqur al-Saᶜdī where the octagonal section above the rectangular first story increases proportionally. The minaret of al-Māridānī is the earliest surviving example of a new type of minaret with completely octagonal shaft and a top that is not a mabkhara, but a pavilion of eight columns, carrying above a crown of stalactites a pear-shaped bulb. This top is the standard for later Mamluk minarets, and the mabkhara top disappears in the second half of the fourteenth century. In later minarets, the rectangular shaft is supplanted by an octagonal first story.

Domes

Two types of dome profiles are used in the Bahri Mamluk period, those like Baybars al-Jashankīr's that curves near the base and are usually plain, and those like Sanjar's and Salār's that begin cylindrically and curve at a higher level and are often ribbed. Inscription bands carved in stucco decorate the drums of Bahri Mamluk domes.

In the domes' interiors are two main types of transitional zones. The earlier type has several-tiered squinches alternating with several-tiered windows and niches; windows, squinches and niches all have the same profile. Later, pendentives are used, first in wood as at al-Nāṣir Muḥammad's Citadel mosque, then in stone. In these, windows are arched instead of forming a pyramidal profile with several lights. There are also a few examples with stone squinches.

Domes are built higher, achieved primarily by increasing the height of the transitional zone. Stone domes make their first appearance under the Bahri Mamluks, but reach the height of their beauty under the Circassian Mamluks in the fifteenth century.

Decoration

In decoration, stucco is increasingly used on the exteriors of minarets and domes. Facades built of stone have carving and also inlaid marble, especially at the joggled lintels and in inscriptions above portals. Not much marble survives from pre-Mamluk times, but in the Mamluk period it was customary to panel walls with polychrome marble (dado), and marble gradually supplanted the stucco used in prayer niches. Panels with marbles and stones and mother of pearl inlaid in minute patterns characterize Bahri Mamluk wall and prayer-niche decoration. After Qalāwūn, use of square Kufic marble inlay decoration becomes widespread.

Voussoirs of arches are generally decorated with ablaq masonry, rather than the Fatimid style stucco inscription bands. In addition to the pre-Islamic and the Islamic bell-shaped capital, capitals sometimes have carved stalactites, as at Sultan Ḥasan's mosque. Stalactites on minarets decorated each ring of balcony, each

Pl. 13. The prayer niche at the madrasa of Ṭaybars attached to al-Azhar, 1309/10 (Creswell).

ring having a different pattern. Stalactites also adorn the recesses of facades, but in interiors, we see them mainly in the transitional zones of domes.

Window grills are no longer geometric, but floral patterned and quite intricate, often including colored glass. There are also several beautiful wooden grills.

Foreign Influence in Bahri Mamluk Architecture

Architecture has always been an international craft, and medieval architects moved to where there was most to be built and where patronage could be expected. Architectural styles thus reached far beyond political frontiers.

Foreign influences on Egyptian architecture under Islam came through several channels. The concept of the mosque came from Medina with the Arab conquerors, and as Islam spread, the various requirements of mosque building developed everywhere with substantial similarities. We see at the mosque of Ibn Ṭūlūn reflections of a style created in the imperial Abbasid capital of Samarra and imitated in Egypt at a time when a local Islamic style had not yet crystallized. The situation during Fatimid rule was quite different. When Egypt became a Caliphate, Egyptian architecture drew away from imitating the arts of the Abbasids.

Monks from Edessa coming as refugees from the Saljūq invasion demonstrated their skills in Badr al-Jamālī's fortified walls. The Persian artists who designed al-Juyūshī's and al-Afḍal's prayer niches might have been Shīʿa sympathizers or travelers eager to visit Fatimid Egypt. North African influences were continuous throughout the Fatimid and Bahri Mamluk periods. This is first seen at the mosque of al-Ḥākim, the minaret of al-Juyushi, and in various ornaments. In this case, craftsmen must have accompanied the Fatimid conquerors to Egypt; later ones may have visited in Egypt on their way to or from their Mecca pilgrimage.

The Andalusian style, obvious in the Imām Shāfiʿī mausoleum, the minaret of Lājīn, and several other buildings of the thirteenth and fourteenth centuries, could also have been brought by craftsmen on pilgrimage, or by refugees from the Spanish *Reconquista*, when Christian dominance must have diminished opportunities for artisans in Spain.

The mosque of al-Ẓāhir Baybars had a huge dome, the origins of which were in Saljūq Persia. The idea was adopted in eastern Anatolia, close to the Ayyubid and Mamluk sphere of power, and from there reached Cairo. According to Creswell, Syrian elements such as the stalactite portal and *ablaq* or striped masonry came to Cairo in a similar manner. In the thirteenth century, Mongol invasions pushed masses of people out of devastated countries, and Egypt received large numbers from Syria and Mesopotamia. Among them were craftsmen who introduced new arts and techniques. During the reign of al-Ẓāhir Baybars, thousands of Mongol refugees settled in Cairo.

Diplomatic exchanges often brought with them artistic imports, such as Qalāwūn's Byzantine and Sicilian elements and, under the reign of al-Nāṣir Muḥammad, Persian techniques and patterns in faience mosaic and stucco.

Battles with the Crusaders and the presence of Crusader prisoners also played a role in the arts in Cairo. War trophies were especially esteemed: the dome of al-Ẓāhir Baybars was made of captured materials; the portal of al-Nāṣir came from a church, and a number of western capitals can be seen in Cairo buildings such as the khanqāh of Baybars al-Jashankīr, the madrasa of Sunqur al-Saʿdī, the mosque of al-Nāṣir, and the madrasa of Sultan Ḥasan. If they were captured from the Crusaders, such trophies had, in addition to their material value, a symbolic importance. Creswell detects French craftsmanship in the iron window above Qalāwūn's entrance that may have been made by a Crusader artist.

Maqrīzī tells us that craftsmen from all over the world came for the building of the mosque of Sultan Ḥasan. Muslim and Christian Anatolian influences are obvious in the mosque's architecture and decoration. Even Chinese lotus and chrysanthemum patterns appear on its walls. The art objects Cairenes enjoyed importing from the Far East, such as porcelain and silks, thanks to the flourishing trade routes, brought many objects to Cairo that inspired local craftsmen.

The madrasa of Ṣarghitmish and the Sulṭāniyya mausoleums have double shell domes with high drums, a style totally alien to Cairo but familiar in eastern Islamic architecture. Not only were there foreign architects in Cairo, but the Mamluks themselves came from Central Asia, from the Caucasus, and even Europe. Al-Nāṣir Muḥammad had a Chinese mamlūk, Arghūnshāh, given to him as a present by the Mongol ruler of Iran. The madrasas and khanqāhs of Cairo housed large numbers of foreign students and Sufis, and priority was often given to foreigners. The madrasa of Ṣarghitmish, for example, was frequented primarily by foreigners.

This series of foreign elements in Cairo architecture by no means implies that the indigenous architecture was poor or provincial in comparison; on the contrary, the adapted elements made Cairo architecture cosmopolitan and innovative. Faience mosaics applied in a mosque no more made it Persian than a horseshoe arch made a building Andalusian. The mosque of Sultan Ḥasan is Mamluk in style in spite of importation of craftsmen "from all over the world." Mamluk here refers not to the ethnic origins of the Mamluk rulers, but to the Cairo Mamluks, and the architectural traditions that evolved in Cairo.

That foreign influence implies the opposite of cultural poverty is illustrated by Ibn Iyās, who wrote that the Ottomans, after they conquered a country, customarily took some of its craftsmen home, and at the same time introduced Turkish craftsmen to the new provinces. The prestige of a ruler was enhanced by collecting and sponsoring foreign art forms. Indeed, in the later Mamluk period, when Egypt's foreign relations were more limited and foreign influences no longer played a role in the arts, innovation also diminished and forms become comparatively static.

THE CIRCASSIAN MAMLUK PERIOD (1382-1517)

Functions

At the end of the fourteenth century, which corresponds to the beginning of the Circassian Mamluk period, a change had taken place in the function of religious institutions, the origins of which had already started under the Bahri Mamluks. This was the drawing together of various institutions into the multifunctional religious complex. The madrasa-jāmiᶜ combination has already been mentioned in connection with Sultan Ḥasan. Under Sultan al-Ẓāhir Barqūq, the complex included a khanqāh as well, thus forming a madrasa-khanqāh-jāmiᶜ. Later the functions of both the madrasa and the khanqāh were reduced, so that every Friday mosque is called a madrasa, even without a teaching curriculum, and they all—whether called madrasa, jāmiᶜ, or khanqāh—had Sufi rites, though the Sufis no longer had to live in them. The khanqāh had lost its monastic character. Already under the Bahri Mamluks, a madrasa commonly included Sufi activities and the khanqāh gave regular courses in Islamic law for its mystic community.

Living units no longer formed an integral part of the architecture of the religious complex. Rather, they were integrated into the commercial part of the complex, as a *rabᶜ*, an apartment complex for families, to be rented to persons of different professions by the endowment's administrator. This meant that the strict khanqāh and madrasa regulations were abandoned over time, and the original function of the mosque as a place open to all kinds of religious activities was revived. The main difference was that a multitude, instead of a few, congregational mosques now served the city. The architectural consequence of this development was the small covered mosque, instead of the hypostyle or the cruciform plan with living units around the courtyard.

Architecturally less known than the khanqāh and the madrasa was the *zāwiya*. This was a religious foundation of rather individual character, built by or for a shaykh to spread a particular form of Sufism or propagate a certain order (*ṭarīqa*). The shaykh generally lived in the zāwiya, sometimes along with disciples and visitors. When he died, he might be buried in the zāwiya; when that happened, the place then became a shrine. The zāwiyas and shrines continued to be the center of the Sufi community founded by the shaykh and were perpetuated by his successors, who may or may not be his descendants. The community enlarged and endowed the foundation. Sometimes rulers also contributed, for several Mamluk sultans shared the popular veneration of Sufi saints. A zāwiya might thus grow considerably, depending upon the importance of its members, and be repeatedly restored and embellished. For this reason, few zāwiyas have retained their original architectural features. Therefore, the zāwiya of Shaykh Zayn al-Dīn Yūsuf is of special interest, not only because it retained its original shape, but also because it shows that a shaykh could build like a sultan.

In the fifteenth century, Sufi shaykhs are often mentioned as sponsors of zāwiyas which are also referred to as madrasas and Friday mosques.

Plans

Two large mosques were built at the beginning of the fifteenth century, the khanqāh of Faraj Ibn Barqūq in the cemetery and the madrasa-khanqāh of Sultan al-Muʾayyad in the city. The mosque of al-Muʾayyad is the last mosque of this size to have been built within the confines of the crowded capital's walls.

As the number of religious foundations with Friday mosques increased, the size of the prayer hall was reduced. Even where space was available, as in the cemetery, or in the city center where a sultan could always contrive to get the land he desired, the space dedicated to the mosque proper remained quite small, though other structures, for example the living units attached to a religious foundation, increased in size. Since the reign of Barsbāy, these had acquired the character of duplex apartments, each with its own latrine.

Small mosques were usually covered. While the mosque of Barsbāy in the cemetery is an oblong hall with three aisles parallel to the prayer niche, the qā^{c}a plan became common in the second half of the fifteenth century. This is a reduced cruciform plan where the central courtyard is small, and covered. It is paved with marble, unlike the large open courtyards paved with stone and sometimes planted with trees. The covered cruciform plan resembled the reception halls, or qā^{c}as, in Mamluk and Ottoman palaces. The plan of the mosque of Barsbāy was repeated in other mosques such as the mosque of Sīdī Madyan (c. 1465) and the mosque of Jānim al-Bahlawān (1478-1510). In both cases, a wooden lantern protruding above the ceiling provided light to the interior.

In the reign of Sultan al-Ashraf Qāytbāy, several richly decorated mosques of the qā^{c}a type were built. They were often at the junction of two streets, with the sabīl-kuttāb at the corner of the building. Their facades are densely pierced with windows, as the mosques had no open courtyards to provide light. With the qā^{c}a plan, the ablution fountain is removed from the center of the mosque and adjoins the building outside. Also, there is no space for the bench called the *dikkat al-muballigh* in the qibla īwān; it becomes instead a balcony or loggia in the western īwān facing the prayer niche, reached by a staircase in the wall.

The reduced facades of the late Mamluk mosques have no space for the large inscription band along the upper part of the walls, common on earlier buildings; it is applied instead along the covered courtyard above the arches of the four īwāns. Moldings and keel arches, features that characterized either exterior or courtyard facades, are now found in the roofed central space of the qā^{c}a mosque.

Domes

Stone domes are a characteristic feature of Mamluk architecture in Egypt. They have no parallel elsewhere in the Muslim world. Stone domes, judging from the surviving evidence, seem to have begun their development in the first half of the fourteenth century and to have reached their zenith in the second half of the fifteenth century, declining soon afterward and disappearing shortly after the Ottoman conquest in 1517.

According to Christel Kessler, who studied the evolution of stone domes, the ribbed stone helmet of the mabkhara-style minaret of Amir Qūṣūn (1336) may have furnished the idea of repeating the same pattern on a larger scale as in a dome, since the architectural principle is the same.

The earliest surviving stone domes are small structures and are all ribbed, except for the unidentified one at the double mausoleum of Sanjar. The mason began by translating into stone what he had practiced with brick, at first without making much effort to adapt to the new material. For example, the early domes appear to have been coated with plaster to conceal the joints between the stone blocks. Later, however, the mason learned to conceal the joints in the spaces between the ribs, making plastering no longer necessary. With time and experience, the carving possibilities that stone offered introduced variations on the theme of ribbing. Instead of decorating the dome surface with rows of convex ribs, concave and convex ribs were alternated, a device applied earlier in the transition zone of Bashtāk's minaret (1336) on the stepped area and later on the transition zone of the domes of Faraj's khanqāh.

More variations followed, such as ribbing carved on oblique lines, as at Iljāy al-Yūsufī's and Aytimish al-Bajāsī's domes (1383/4). This pattern had been used earlier to decorate columns, as at the niches on the al-Aqmar mosque facade, the minaret of Ibn Ṭūlūn between the horseshoe arches, and at the corners of the facade of Sultan Ḥasan's mosque.

After ribbing, the zigzag, used earlier on minarets such as that of al-Nāṣir Muḥammad at the Citadel and several others, became fashionable. This pattern appeared on many domes, the most prominent examples being the domes of Faraj Ibn Barqūq's khanqāh. These are the largest Mamluk stone domes in Cairo and are only slightly smaller than the Imām Shāfi^{c}ī wooden dome. Faraj's domes are masterpieces of stone architecture that have elegantly resisted the effects of time.

Encouraged, the architects tried a more difficult device, adapting a geometric star pattern, usually used on flat surfaces, to the dome. The conch in the portal of the mosque of Aḥmad al-Mihmandār (1345) has a star pattern on the concave surface, but this presented

Pl. 14. The stone dome of Amir Aytimish al-Bajāsī, 1383.

no serious challenge, as the conch is quite small. On a large dome surface, the difficulty of adjusting the repetitive geometric star pattern to the diminishing area toward the apex, while keeping its rules of composition, is obvious.

The domes of Sultan Barsbāy

Sultan Barsbāy had four mausoleums built in his funerary complex, of which three are still standing. His own mausoleum, according to Kessler, appears to have been built first, judging from the execution of the work. The row of eight-pointed stars on the lower part of the dome change toward the top of the dome, to seven-pointed, then six-pointed, stars resulting in the appearance of a surface divided into three zones and lacking homogeneity.

The other two domes are treated differently. The one on the north side, that of Jānibak, has a row of halves of twelve-pointed stars radiating from the base of the dome, and ten-pointed stars above them. The ten-pointed stars do not exactly surmount the twelve pointed stars; rather the two types of stars are set in a zig-zag arrangement.

The dome on the east side of Barsbāy's mausoleum has eight-pointed instead of twelve-pointed star halves radiating from the base of the dome. Each star is surmounted by another twelve-pointed star, and between

Pl. 15. The domes at the religious-funerary complex of Sultan Barsbāy.

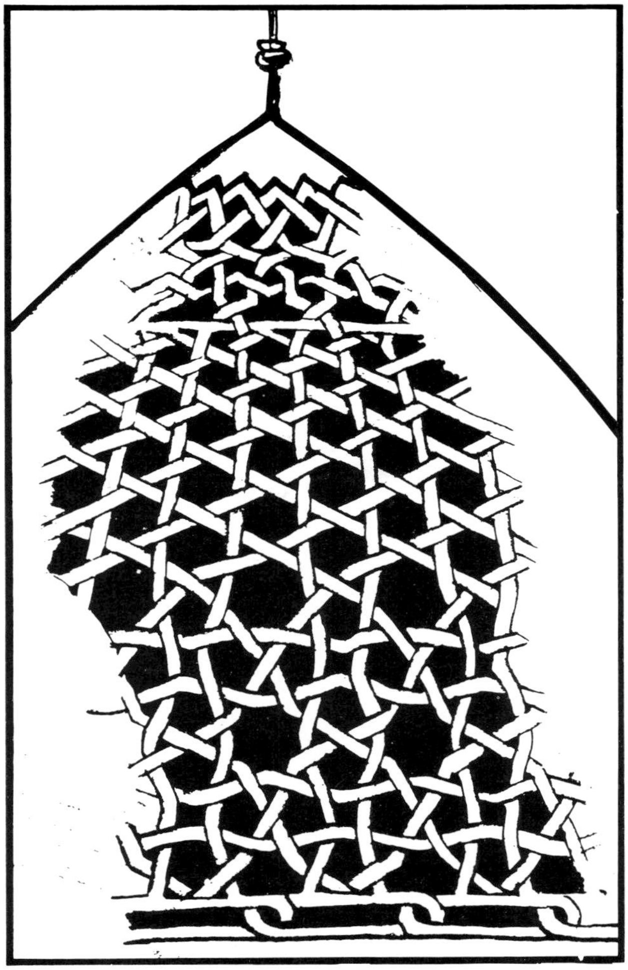

Fig. 2. The star pattern on the mausoleum of Sultan Barsbāy.

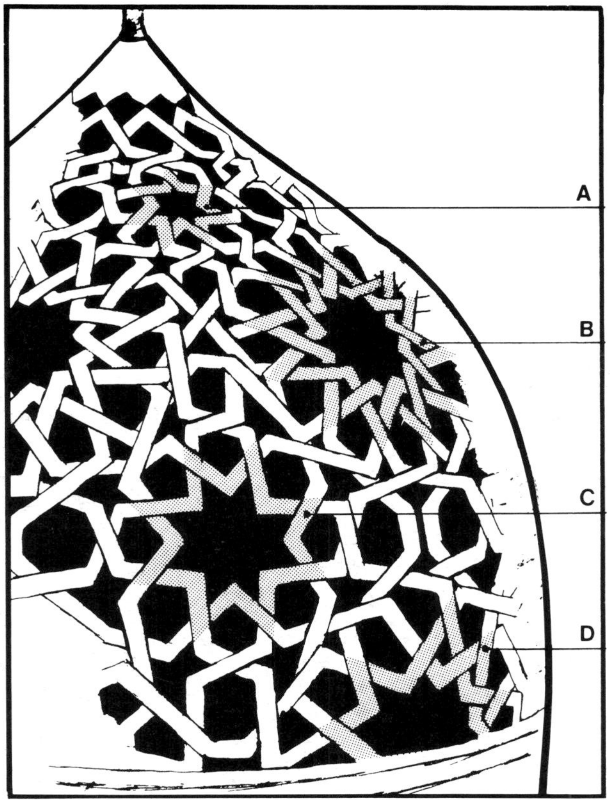

A 7 pointed Star. B 12 pointed Star. C 8 pointed Star. D 12 pointed Star.

Fig. 3. The star pattern on a mausoleum built by Barsbāy.

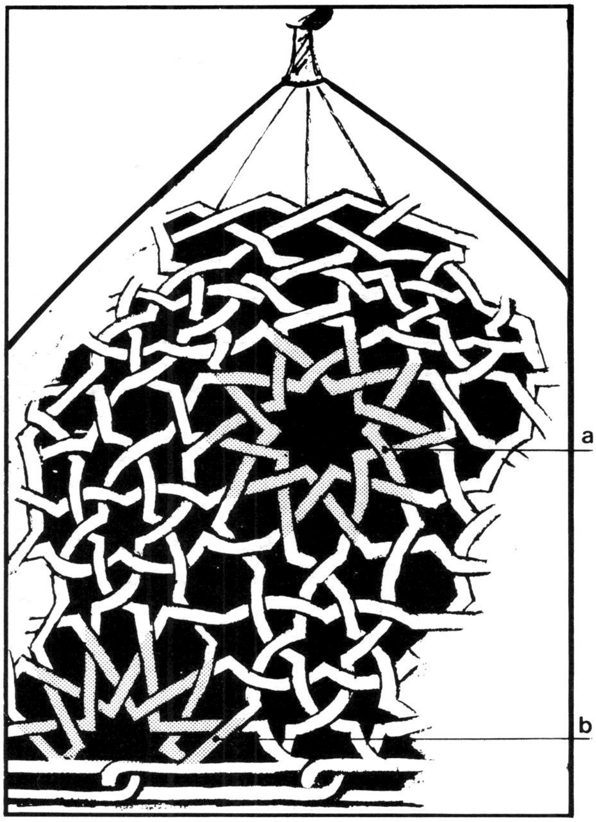

a 10 pointed Star. b 12 pointed Star.

Fig. 4. The star pattern on the mausoleum of Jānibak built by Barsbāy.

them on each side is an eight-pointed star. The whole surface appears homogeneous, if somewhat crowded, because the stars are so tightly connected. Toward the apex of the dome seven-pointed stars lead to the top. In both these cases, there is a consistency in the star pattern that is lacking in the larger, first dome. In all of them, however, the weak point was at the apex, and the next step in the evolution of stone domes dealt with this problem.

The dome of Sultan Qāytbāy

The Qāytbāy period introduced new ideas on the subject of dome construction. The small dome Qāytbāy had built before becoming sultan has a floral star pattern, based as usual on geometric calculations. The lower half has twelve-pointed stars and above them full eight-pointed stars, the whole executed in curves with arabesques.

The dome on the mausoleum attached to Qāytbāy's mosque in the cemetery shows that the designer for the first time reversed these principles. Instead of basing the pattern on the principle of a star applied on a decreasing, or triangular, base to apex surface, the star was designed for a circular surface, the center of which is the apex of the dome. Of course, unlike a flat circular area, the dome surface has irregularities. In this case they met with the star pattern not near the apex, but nearer to the base of the dome, where the lines resulting from the central star at the apex have to be logically continued. Thus, the design of Qāytbāy's dome is made from a bird's eye view: a sixteen-pointed star centered on the apex and covering the upper half of the dome, with the lines continued to form a row of seven-

a 16 pointed Star. b 10 pointed Star.

Fig. 5. The star pattern on the mausoleum of Sultan Q̲āytbāy.

Pl. 16. Detail of a stone dome carved with arabesque, Sultan Q̲āytbāy, before 1474.

pointed irregular stars surrounding it and, at the base of the dome, halves of ten-pointed stars. To conceal the irregularities resulting here at the middle part of the dome, arabesque patterns fill the whole space framed by the angular geometric lines.

This is perhaps the most beautiful carved stone dome in Cairo, and it seems to have discouraged any imitations. Afterwards, masons were content with repetitive geometric or floral patterns, such as those seen on the domes of Q̲ānṣūh Abū Saᶜīd (1499), al-ᶜĀdil Ṭumānbāy (1501), Khāyrbak (1502), and Q̲ānibāy (1503).

As long as brick domes were built, the transitional zone was developed from plain to composite squinches built on several tiers with a pyramidal layout; the result was the formation of stalactites. In the early fourteenth century, triangular pendentives were also used in the transitional zone. They were first built in wood, as at the Citadel mosque of al-Nāṣir Muḥammad, and later

Pl. 17. The mausoleum of Sultan Q̲āytbāy.

Pl. 18. The mosque of Amir Jānim al-Bahlawān, 1478-1510.

also in stone. Early stone domes, such as the anonymous dome added at Sanjar's mausoleum and the dome of Aydumur al-Bahlawān, had stone composite squinches imitating brick architecture. Domes moved toward greater height rather than greater diameter. This was achieved by extending the transitional zone, so that eventually the domes looked almost like small towers.

On the outside, the zone of transition, instead of being stepped at the corners, sometimes had pyramidal structures as on minarets leading from the rectangular to circular part. Both types are used at the funerary complex of Sultan Barsbāy, which also used a new decorative device. Its steps are carved concave-convex to form an undulating profile. At the dome of Qijmas the exterior transitional zone is composed of several superimposed pyramids.

Minarets

The minarets of this period are slender and elegant. They were usually octagonal in the first story and circular in the second, except in the reign of Sultan al-Ghūrī when totally rectangular minarets were used for the first time since Qalāwūn. At their top were double bulbs. There are four bulbs at the funerary complex of Sultan al-Ghūrī. The minarets were richly carved, more so than ever before. The fashion of carved shafts appeared by the end of the fourteenth century to replace stone inlaid ablaq patterns previously used to adorn the middle section. Craftsmen applied their most careful work to the middle sections, creating a different pattern on each minaret.

Portals

In the fourteenth century, the trilobe portal developed from a plain conch on stalactites to more intricate variations on the same theme, with molding and carvings framing the trilobed arch, carvings adorning the conch, pendentives used underneath the stalactites, and use of various types of stalactites in different proportions. In the fifteenth century we see a new type of portal treatment. The portal vault is still trilobed, but its interior is carved with groins in the shape of a half-star. Sometimes the niches formed by the intersecting groins were filled with stalactites, and often the conch was adorned with an ablaq inlaid pattern as in some prayer niches of this period. In the second half of the fifteenth century, both types of portals were used simultaneously.

Groin vaults became fashionable beginning in the late fourteenth century; a fine example is found in the vestibule of the madrasa of Iljāy al-Yūsufī. Other magnificent vaults of this type can be seen in the Khān al-Khalīlī at the portal of Sultan al-Ghūrī. Later, the groin vault will influence the architecture of domes, as in the squinches of the Rifāʿī zāwiya of Barsbāy, probably redone later, and at the two domes of Amir Yashbak.

Decoration

The decoration of domes and minarets in this period consisted primarily of stone carving. It reached its highest quality during the reign of Sultan Qāytbāy and abruptly declined thereafter.

Marble inlay was also used extensively in facade decoration, as at the mosque of Qijmas and the sabīl of Sultan Qāytbāy. Stucco decoration almost disappears, though we see it used extensively at the Qubbat al-Fadāwiyya. There are also remains of stucco wall decoration at the mosque of Sultan Qāytbāy at Rawḍa. The only area where stucco decoration shows continuity, however, is in window grills. Window grills used as decoration evolve continuously from Ibn Ṭūlūn to the Ottoman period. In the fifteenth century they are no longer repetitive geometric or floral patterns; the surface of the grill is divided into fields with inscriptions, horizontal bands, and medallions with various patterns, and filled with colored glass.

Prayer Niches

The use of marble inlay was less frequent in fifteenth-century prayer niches. It was replaced by stone, and the conchs are either plain, decorated with ablaq masonry, or are carved. Marble dadoes were still used to panel the interior walls of mosques, but a new style of marble inlay appeared at the mosque of Abū Bakr Ibn Muzhir. There, the marble is finely carved and filled with red and black paste in a delicate scroll arabesque pattern that contrasts with the fourteenth-century geometric inlay patterns. The new style was used until the early sixteenth century, though its quality declined compared to the examples signed by ʿAbd al-Qādir al-Naqqāsh. An earlier example of such mar-

Pl. 19. The groin-vaulted portal at the religious-funerary complex of Sultan Qāytbāy.

ble inlay is found on an inscription slab on the north wall of the sanctuary of the Maridānī mosque. The marble is carved and filled with a green gypsum paste.

Arches

Until the fourteenth century both round and pointed arches were used, but in the fifteenth century the pointed arch prevails, always framed by a voussoir of ablaq masonry. The īwāns of cruciform mosques, with open or covered courtyards, have pointed arches. Inside, they are no longer vaulted but covered by a flat wooden ceiling, richly decorated. An exception, however, is the madrasa of Amir Qānibāy al-Rammāḥ (Amīr Akhūr), where a cross vault is used at the īwān opposite the prayer niche. The qibla īwān itself is covered by a shallow dome on pendentives carried by round arches.

THE OTTOMAN PERIOD (1517-1914)

The Sixteenth and Seventeenth Centuries

The Ottoman conquest of Egypt in 1517 changed the status of Cairo from an imperial seat to a provincial capital. It became a city without a sultan, governed by a viceroy called a pasha, sent from Istanbul for a limited period. Cairo was simply a stage in the pasha's career. There were a multitude of Ottoman governors between 1517 and 1798 when Napoleon conquered Egypt. Some of them left religious buildings of interest, but others remained only a name in a long list. Buildings, however, were erected not only by the pashas, but by amirs and members of the religious establishment. The Ottoman period has left us nearly one hundred sabīl-kuttābs in various styles.

The Ottoman conquest did not radically disturb the evolution of Cairene architecture. It introduced some

Pl. 20. The minaret of the mosque of Amir ᶜUthmān Katkhudā.

Pl. 21. Detail of a molding typical of the Ottoman period.

new architectural and decorative patterns that resulted in innovations when incorporated into the local repertoire.

The Ottomans built three types of mosque architecture in Cairo: buildings totally Ottoman in style, though not necessarily in decoration, such as the mosques of Sulaymān Pasha and the mosque of Malika Ṣafiyya; buildings of hybrid style, such as the mosque of Sinān Pasha, and a Mamluk style of mosque with an Ottoman style of minaret, such as the mosques of Maḥmūd Pasha and ᶜUthmān Katkhudā. In place of the Mamluk khanqāh, the *takiyya*, an institution where Sufis lived, studied, and worshipped, appears with the Ottomans. A new plan came with the takiyya, a courtyard surrounded by cells that is independent of the mosque. The Takiyya Sulaymāniyya and the takiyya of Sultan Maḥmūd (1750) are both, however, called "madrasa" in their founding inscriptions.

The dome and minaret were the most characteristic features of Mamluk architecture, and they were both affected by the new political situation. The mausoleum dome nearly disappeared from religious architecture. Governors did not stay long enough in Cairo to die there, or at least did not plan to remain until the end of their lives. There are, however, a few funerary domes, that of Amir Sulaymān, built shortly after the conquest (1544), the mausoleum of Maḥmūd Pasha, and the stone dome of the shrine of Athar al-Nabī dedicated to objects attributed to the Prophet, not to a person, built in the seventeenth century (1662). The mosque of Yūsuf al-Ḥīn had a family mausoleum next to it that was pulled down in the nineteenth century. Amir ᶜAbd al-Raḥmān Katkhudā built onto the mosque of al-Azhar, when restoring and enlarging it, a mausoleum for himself. In general, sponsors of religious buildings were buried in a corner of the mosque and not even near the qibla, as were Muḥammad Bey Abū'l-Dhahab and Muḥammad ᶜAlī.

The tradition of domed mausoleums for rulers was revived again in the nineteenth century when Muḥammad ᶜAlī built a funerary complex for his family near the mausoleum of Imām Shāfiᶜī. Later, the mother of the Khedive Ismāᶜīl erected the Rifāᶜī mosque, which includes other royal tombs.

When the funerary dome disappeared, the domed mosque, which had existed in Cairo before the Ottoman period, reappeared. It had been typical of

Ottoman architecture, followed and developed the Byzantine tradition. The mosque of Sinān Pasha followed the pattern of the Fadāwiyya dome, and was later imitated by Muḥammad Abū'l-Dhahab at his mosque near al-Azhar. All these domes were built on squinches without an exterior transitional zone. The profiles of Ottoman domes, unlike those of the Mamluk domes, are round and lack the exterior transitional zone enhancing their height. With the Ottoman conquest, the round arch, used earlier by the Fatimids and Bahri Mamluks, again became common.

An abrupt change is observed in minaret architecture. The Mamluk shaft was replaced by the provincial version of the pencil-shaped minaret, rather squat, with only one balcony, and usually decorated with vertical moldings to enhance the faceted structure of the shaft. Ibn Iyās writes that Ottoman conquerors traditionally took home craftsmen from conquered countries and introduced their own craftsmen, and it must have been in this way that the Ottoman minaret reached Cairo. In the Egyptian hinterland, however, minarets continued to be built in the pre-Ottoman style.

With the loss of domed mausoleum architecture and Mamluk minarets, the art of stalactites declined in Cairo, since the transitional zone of the funerary domes, the balconies of minarets, and portals were the features that best displayed Mamluk stalactite carving. Portals of the Ottoman period were often simple shallow trilobed recesses without a vault. When they were vaulted, the trilobed groin-vaulted type was usually adopted.

Mamluk-style windows continued, as did the Mamluk tradition of paneling interiors with polychrome marble dadoes. The prayer niche of the mosque of ᶜUthmān Katkhudā, built in the early eighteenth century, looks totally Mamluk. Turkish elements were introduced, such as the use of Ottoman tiles with floral patterns, as at the mosque of Aqsunqur restored by Ibrāhīm Aghā, the sabīl-kuttāb of ᶜAbd al-Raḥmān Katkhudā, and the Siḥaymī house. Their quality was usually inferior to the tiles in Istanbul, and their installation showed that local craftsmen did not become familiar with the technique. Blue-green Turkish tiles were often used to decorate the lintels of mosque entrance doors.

An interesting evolution in this period appears in the style of moldings and in their more extensive use. In the Bahri Mamluk period there were two parallel lines connected with circular loops placed in a few spots, usually at the apex of arches, and they often framed portals and

Pl. 22. The sabīl-kuttāb of Amir ᶜAbd al-Raḥmān Katkhudā.

arches. Later moldings show an increase in the number of loops. In Ottoman moldings, the loops are placed at small intervals and are angular instead of circular.

Ottoman floral elements are sometimes used in stone and marble carvings. A prominent example is the portal of the al-Azhar mosque added by ᶜAbd al-Raḥmān Katkhudā, with the typically Ottoman cypress tree.

The cushion voussoir of Byzantine origin, used in the Fatimid and early Mamluk periods, also reappears in the Ottoman period. We find it at the entrance to the madrasa of Qalāwūn, rebuilt by ᶜAbd al-Raḥmān Katkhudā, and at an Ottoman gate of the Citadel. In fact, Ottoman architecture in Cairo shows a revival of several Byzantine and Anatolian patterns including the round arch and spherical pendentive. These patterns,

Pl. 23. The portal of the sabīl-kuttāb of ᶜAbd al-Raḥmān Katkhudā.

abandoned in the late Mamluk period, were reintroduced to Cairo architecture by the Turks, who had preserved them from Byzantine heritage.

The Late Eighteenth Century

ᶜAbd al-Raḥmān Katkhudā (died 1776/7) was an amir who made notable contributions to Cairo's architectural heritage. He restored or rebuilt almost all the important shrines of the city and a number of old mosques, the most prominent one being the al-Azhar. A certain style with several characteristic features developed during these works of building, restoration, and rebuilding. The use of wide round arches, sometimes scalloped, with a row of small round and lobed arches, is seen at Katkhudā's mosque in the Mūskī quarter (1754/55) and at his zāwiya at Mugharbilīn (1729). Round arches also characterize the triple facade of his sabīl on Muᶜizz street (1744).

Bands of stone carved in repetitive arabesques had no local precedent in Cairo. Such bands frame the double arch at the al-Azhar entrance (1753/54), the entrance to the Ṭaybarsiyya madrasa at al-Azhar, the entrance of the zāwiya at Mugharbilīn (1754), and the facade of ᶜAbd al-Raḥmān's mosque in the Muski quarter.

The stalactites decorating the buildings of ᶜAbd al-Raḥmān Katkhudā show considerable improvement in quality compared to those of the previous century. We see this quality at the sabīl-kuttāb in Muᶜizz street, the

Pl. 24. The portal at al-Azhar built by ᶜAbd al-Raḥmān Katkhudā.

Pl. 25. The facade of the mosque of ᶜAbd al-Raḥmān Katkhudā near al-Mūskī.

Pl. 26. The sabīl-kuttāb of Ruqayya Dūdū, 1761.

balcony of the zawiya of Mugharbilīn, and the portal of the mosque he rebuilt near the madrasa of Barsbāy, known as the Jāmiᶜ al-Muṭahhir (1774), whose handsome stalactite portal, rare during this period, is signed by the craftsman in the middle of its fluted conch. The stalactites are carved and pierced. Another innovation of this period is seen in the iron grills of mosque and sabīl windows. Instead of plain rectangles, they are often more elaborate, with geometric or floral patterns. A good example is the window at the Ṭaybarsiyya madrasa at al-Azhar restored by ᶜAbd al-Raḥman Katkhūda, and the sabīls of Ruqayya Dūdū (1761) and Nafīsa al-Bayḍā (1796).

A feature characteristic of late Ottoman architecture are the cartouches with inscriptions in nastaᶜlīq, later also riḥānī, scripts. They usually contain either verses of poetry or the foundation date.

The Ottoman Period Sabīls

Sultan Qāytbāy had built a free-standing sabīl-kuttāb in the city when all others of the period were attached to the corner of a mosque. The Ottoman period left a great number of these structures.

The sabīl-kuttāb of Khusraw Pasha (1535) near the mausoleum of al-Ṣāliḥ Najm al-Dīn and opposite the madrasa of Qalāwūn is an imitation of the sabīl-kuttāb of Sultan al-Ghūrī that protrudes as a rectangular building with three facades on the street, decorated with marble inlay and joggled lintels. The upper structure, which is the kuttāb, is shaped like an arcaded loggia, like all Mamluk sabīl-kuttābs. Not far away is the sabīl-kuttāb of ʿAbd al-Raḥmān Katkhudā occupying the corner of two intersecting streets, a landmark of the medieval city. It also has three facades and a portal on the eastern side. Mamluk-style marble inlay decorates the spandrels of its round arches which also include Ottoman floral patterns carved in marble. An elaborate stalactite cornice separates the upper and lower parts on the exterior. The windows of the sabīl, instead of being rectangular as was usual, are round-arched like the arches including them. Their iron grills are more elaborate than the Mamluk grills. At the corners, flanking the windows, are engaged marble columns carved with flutes half oblique and half vertical. The kuttāb on the upper floor is built entirely of wood. The interior of the sabīl is paneled with Iznik style blue and green tiles. Some are floral, and some form a stylized representation of Mecca. Others carry inscriptions.

In the course of the eighteenth century, the sabīl form developed from three angular facades into a semicircular shape with three facets, each including a window. The round arches on marble columns that give a relief decoration to the facade include round-arched windows with elaborate bronze grills, often framed with dense moldings and loops and sometimes including bits of blue-green Turkish tiles and Turkish flower motifs.

Architecture in the time of Muḥammad ʿAlī

The architecture of the first half of the nineteenth century, corresponding to the reigns of Muḥammad ʿAlī and the Khedive ʿAbbās, is characterized by a style that was totally alien to Cairo architectural traditions.

Fig. 6. The sabīl-kuttāb of Sultan Maḥmūd, 1750 (Coste).

Pl. 27. The sabīl-kuttāb of Ismāᶜīl Pasha, 1828.

Turkish architecture and decoration, already influenced by Europe, was introduced into Cairo.

We no longer see stalactites, arabesques, or geometric designs, nor Mamluk naskhī or thuluth script. Instead, there are vases with acanthus-like leaves and realistic flowers forming oval rings, applied repetitively. Epigraphy is also treated differently, set in cartouches in nastaᶜlīq or riḥānī script; carved or painted poetry passages are sometimes written in Turkish. White marble is often combined with carved, painted and gilded wood.

The round arch predominates and is often curved at the springings. Window grills are made of cast bronze and are often the most attractive feature of facade architecture, with their elaborate, lacy openwork patterns. These grills were also used for funerary enclosures in mosques.

Funerary architecture appears again, bringing with it the onion-shaped dome, decorated with moldings or ribs, as at the mausoleum of the Muḥammad ᶜAlī family at Imām Shāfiᶜī. The domed mausoleum attached to the complex of Ḥasan Pasha Ṭāhir has no prototype in Cairene architecture.

Pl. 28. The sabīl-kuttāb of Ibrāhīm Pasha, late nineteenth century.

CHAPTER THREE

DOMESTIC ARCHITECTURE IN CAIRO

The Palace

There are no remains of Fatimid or earlier palaces, and very few Mamluk palaces have survived, none in its entirety. However, masses of waqf documents from the Mamluk period give us a wealth of written information about the layout of palaces and houses during this period. Some palaces, such as the Īwān al-Kabīr, were built with columns supporting domes. Others were built on the qāʿa plan with two īwāns facing each other and the central space covered by a dome or a lantern. The architecture of princely city residences differed from royal residences in the Citadel.

The principal structure of a Mamluk residence was the qāʿa. The word originally meant courtyard, but the qāʿa was a reception hall, either on the ground floor or a second story. In either case, it was the highest structure in a house and occupied most of its elevation. A central lantern protruded above roof level. The qāʿa also must have occupied the optimal orientation of the house, dictating arrangement of the smaller, private rooms surrounding it on different levels.

The qāʿa arrangement is documented from the Fatimid period. The descriptions indicate that folding doors closed each of the two īwāns and that the central area was not roofed, though it most likely was protected by tents or awnings. The central area, as in Mamluk residences, had doors to the other rooms, to the latrines, and to the exterior, as well as doors leading to the mezzanine loggias overlooking the qāʿa. These are called *maghānī* (Mamluk) or *aghānī* (Ottoman), suggesting that they were intended for musicians entertaining the audience below in the qāʿa. In the Mamluk period, they were decorated with turned-wood screens called *mashrabiyya*.

In houses excavated in Fusṭāṭ, a Mesopotamian plan was identified. A courtyard was surrounded by four unequal īwāns, the principal one having a tripartite arrangement with the central space wider than the lateral rooms. A fountain stood in the middle of the courtyard. Multistoried houses also are described by several visitors to Fusṭāṭ, and these had precedents in pre-Islamic Egypt.

Domestic architecture appears to have undergone a development parallel to that in religious architecture, as courtyards became reduced and roofed and lateral īwāns became mere recesses. There was, however, in very large residences another type of courtyard that was not the center of daily life as was the qāʿa, but which played the role of a vestibule.

The covered qāʿa was high with a protruding lantern or dome, and a marble jet fountain in its center. In Mamluk and Ottoman qāʿas, both the lantern and fountain were octagonal in shape, and the fountain was usually inlaid with multicolored marbles. In some halls, water flowed from an opening in the īwān, down a marble slab called the *salsabīl* to be collected in the basin of the central fountain. This running water cooled the hall in summer, aiding hot air to move upwards and escape from the wooden lantern on the roof, and thus improving ventilation. An air shaft, the *malqaf*, had been used in Egypt since Pharaonic times. This shaft was behind the wall of the main īwān and connected at roof level with a sloping vent oriented to the north. The qāʿas that survive from the Ottoman period are similar in plan to those of the Mamluk period, though their proportions are different.

Fenestration

The windows of great residences are described as having iron grills surmounted by arched windows with stucco and colored glass, as in the mosques. Iron grills were precious and less wealthy people used wood. The palaces of the Citadel were famous for their gilded iron grilled windows overlooking the entire city.

The palace of Bashtāk on Muʿizz Street is described by Maqrīzī as overlooking the street through its iron grills. Speaking of a dilapidated palace, he notes that its marble was replaced by stone and its iron by wooden windows. Often, the iron grills of mosque windows were taken down and melted to provide funds to maintain the rest of the premises, another proof of the value of iron. Like the mosques, residential architecture was extroverted, with windows onto streets wherever possible.

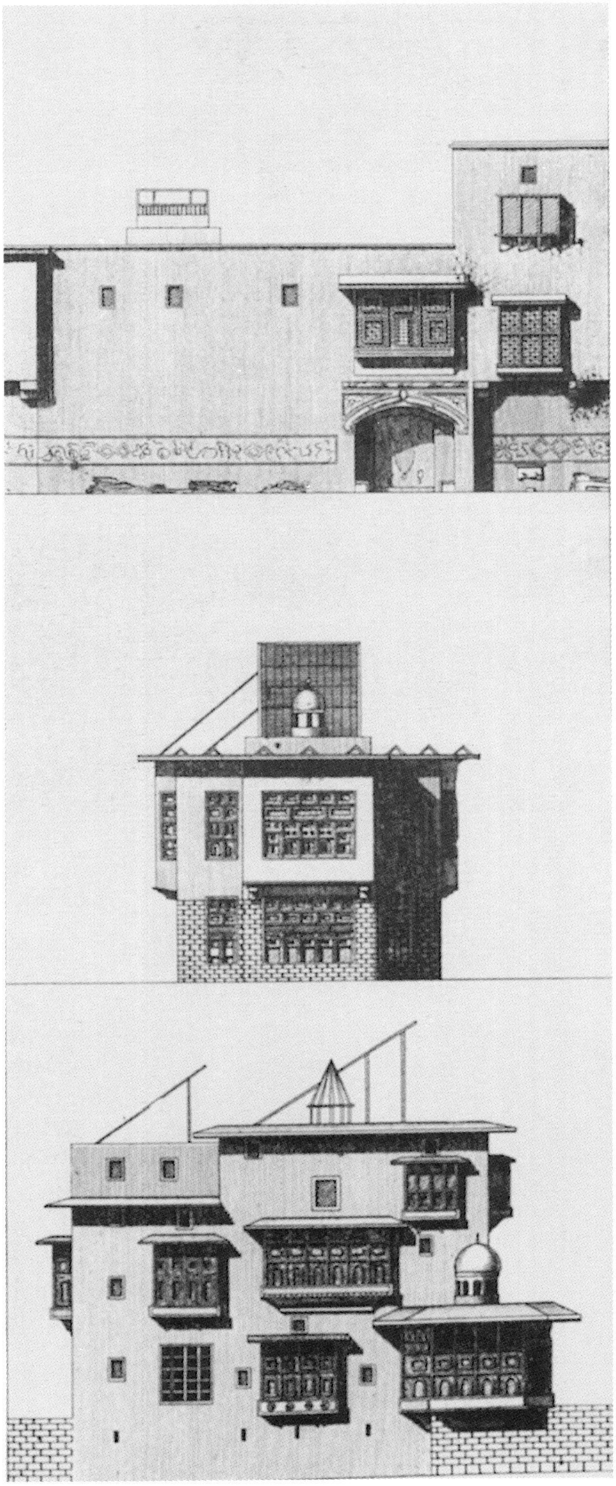

Pl. 29. Houses of Cairo (*Description de l'Egypte*).

The mashrabiyya or latticework panel of turned wood is an art typical of Cairo. The name is derived from the *mashraba*, the niche made of turned wood to hold the porous clay jugs that cool water by evaporation. The advantage of mashrabiyya work is that it filters light while increasing ventilation, and allows one to look outside without being seen. City streets that were very narrow made such devices necessary for ventilation, and nineteenth-century illustrations show these mashrabiyya loggias, supported by corbels, almost touching each other over the narrow street below. The Islamic Museum in Cairo has a multitude of these mashrabiyya patterns on display.

As no Mamluk palace has survived complete, it is difficult to know what their doors, or portals, were like. The palace of Qūṣūn, however, has a stalactite portal that is surpassed in magnificence in Cairo only by the portal of the mosque of Sulṭan Ḥasan. We know that important amirs were entitled to have a loggia or *ṭablakhāna* for a ceremonial orchestra, performing according to the amir's rank. This ṭablakhāna must have resembled the loggia of a kuttāb, and the amir put his carved and painted emblems, with his name and titles, on the exterior of the residence. Some residences were occupied by the amirs during their lifetimes, but not inherited by their families. Rather, they went to the inheritor of the amir's function, as did the royal residences at the Citadel.

Bent entrances were used for residences, as might be expected, leading into a courtyard. This courtyard was not a gathering place or reception area, but a semi-private place for the inhabitants and visitors to dismount. Around the courtyard were storerooms and the entrance to the stable. The courtyard was generally not paved, and might have a well and trees. A residence might have another courtyard for a garden. From the courtyard, several doors led to the qāᶜa and its apartments. Important residences had more than one qāᶜa.

The facade of the courtyard in extant Mamluk and Ottoman houses has a high portal like that of contemporary mosques and its rich decoration is in the style applied on exteriors rather than interiors, confirming the character of the courtyard and the *maqᶜad* as extroverted and connected to the street, rather than as the center of private life.

The semi-public function of the courtyard is complementary to the street pattern of medieval cities, where only a few wide thoroughfares existed. The rest were narrow winding lanes that protected the privacy and security of the inhabitants. The small lanes had doors that were closed at night. The entrance courtyard

Pl. 30. The palace of Amir Bashtāk at Bayn al-Qaṣrayn, 1334-39.

was a source of air and light, and a place where visitors could dismount, a merchant offer his goods, and wares be loaded and unloaded. Women would not be seen in this semi-public area.

The Maq^cad

The maqʿad, or sitting room, common in houses of the late Mamluk and Ottoman periods, is an arcaded loggia overlooking the residence's courtyard from the first floor and facing the prevailing breezes from the north. It had smaller rooms and a latrine attached. This is where the master of the house sat to oversee his stables and storerooms and receive visitors. In houses along the Khalīj or ponds, the maqʿad opened onto the view of water and gardens. In the earlier Mamluk period, the maqʿad is described as a mezzanine loggia built to overlook the stables of the residence. The importance of stables in the Mamluk cavalry society was also seen at the Citadel, where palaces overlooked the royal stables. A houseowner's wealth was also evident in the saddlery kept in the stable area. Later, it appears that the maqʿad developed into a part of the courtyard, facing north and at the same time overlooking the stables.

Domes inlaid with-colored glass over bedrooms are often mentioned in waqf descriptions of Mamluk houses. A fifteenth-century European traveler, Felix Fabri, describes the house of an amir as having a menagerie of wild animals and exotic birds. He stresses the beauty of the stable's horses and the luxurious display of saddlery. He also mentions a prison found within the confines of the palace and a domed tower used as a private apartment.

Pl. 31. Mashrabiyya window at the house of al-Razzāz.

Pl. 32. The portal of the palace of Amir Qūṣūn (palace of Yashbak), 1337.

Decoration

Palaces were decorated in the same style as religious buildings of the same period. Windows, as mentioned before, were treated the same way. Polychrome marble dadoes covered the lower parts of walls; stalactites and inscriptions in painted and gilded wood were used on the upper walls; the ceilings were painted and gilded. Inscriptions of poetry might be found instead of Quranic texts. At the Suḥaymī house, these are presented in cartouches in nastaᶜlīq script, as they are in contemporary religious buildings. The inner portals of Ottoman houses, trilobed and framed with heavy moldings, recall the facade decoration of mosques and sabīls. Turkish style tiles are also found in some

Pl. 33. The maqᶜad at the house of al-Razzāz, fifteenth-eighteenth century.

Pl. 34. Nineteenth century painting showing the interior of a house (Frank Dillon).

Pl. 35. Wakāla and rab^c of Sultan al-Ghūrī at Khān al-Khalīlī, 1511.

Ottoman interiors, including the Suḥaymī house, just as they are in contemporary mosques and sabīls.

Houses were furnished mainly with carpets and wall hangings. Silk was used for summer carpets, wool in the winter. There was no dining room; food was brought on trays that coned be carried away after meals. In the bedrooms, covers were stored in cases during the day. Wooden shelves held china placed as decoration, and the wall cupboards themselves were decorated with inlaid work. Numbers of bronze lamps, with inlay and openwork, and candlesticks inlaid with gold and silver in the Mosul technique that reached Egypt after the Mongol invasion of Baghdad, displayed in the Islamic Museum, give us an idea of how interiors were lit.

The Rab^c

A rab^c is an apartment complex with living units rented by the month. It was composed of a row of apartments reached from a gallery on the first floor. Each apartment was a duplex on two floors, with a private section of roof space. The lower floor had the latrine, a niche for water jugs, and a reception hall; the upper floor included the sleeping area. Usually there was no kitchen. Large houses had private rooms (*ḥarīm*) and other rooms where women were not allowed, but this degree of segregation could not be afforded in small houses or in the units of a rab^c.

A rab^c was usually the structure above a row of shops, though shop people did not necessarily inhabit the rab^c above. A rab^c might also be built above a wakāla, or a khān where there might be up to four such complexes on four sides, corresponding to the rectangular plan of such buildings around a courtyard. In general, the wakāla and khān were commercial centers, while the qaysariyya was industrial. There also, however, those working in the ground floor areas did not necessarily inhabit the rab^c above.

These dwellings were extroverted, meaning that whenever possible windows opened onto the street, otherwise onto the courtyard. There are rab^{c}s above the wakāla of Sultan al-Ghūrī, not far from his religious complex in the city, and at the wakāla of Sultan Qāytbāy near Bāb al-Naṣr. Remains of the khān of Sultan al-Ghūrī at Khān al-Khalīlī suggest that it was multistoried. It is a large complex used today by artisans. The commercial center at Jamāliyya was

Pl. 36. Interior of the wakāla of Sultan al-Ghūrī near al-Azhar, 1504/5.

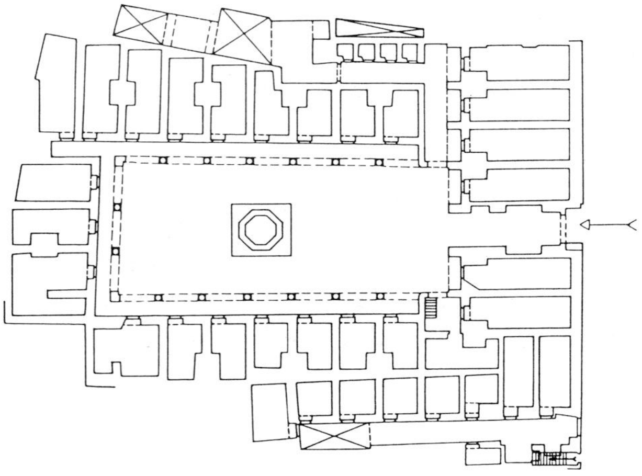

Fig. 7. Ground plan of the wakāla of Sultan al-Ghūrī near al-Azhar (Department of Antiquities).

crowded with such structures, many of them rebuilt in the Ottoman period.

Houses

Between a grand residence and the rab^c apartment unit were other levels of housing, of which very little has survived from the Ottoman period and nearly nothing from the Mamluk. These small, or medium sized, houses are described in their waqf documents as following the same principles of the qā^{c}a complex and the living unit of the rab^c, that is, a reception hall on the ground floor surmounted by smaller rooms on the

Fig. 8. Detail of mashrabiyya.

upper level. In the Bahri Mamluk period, each of the elements, hall and upper rooms, had a separate entrance from the street, and sometimes there was a third entrance to the stable. Later, however, it became common to have one door into a vestibule, from where the other doors led. The vestibule might be open to the sky, forming a small courtyard that in the Ottoman period included a maq^{c}ad. In Ottoman houses, the open courtyard was more common than in Mamluk times, probably because the city had become more densely built and public thoroughfares more limited, so that open courtyards became necessary for light and air. This also explains the extensive use of mashrabiyyas in Ottoman Cairo.

Kitchens

Whereas large residences had their own kitchen, small houses did not. Common people bought their food ready-cooked. It could be that the lack or high expense of fuel, as the traveler von Harff tells us, was the reason common people could not afford to cook at home.

Maqrīzī's descriptions of Cairo streets mention stalls and markets for cooked food, which in modern terms would be regarded as small restaurants. Travelers in

Fig. 9. The wakāla of Dhū'l-Fiqār, 1673 (Coste).

Egypt have always been struck by the number of such stalls, the medieval equivalent of "fast food" outlets. Travelers relate that cooks wandered the streets with their stoves and utensils or settled along the pavements, offering a large variety of foods—chicken and meat grilled or boiled, fish and vegetables. Fried cheese is often mentioned in Arabic accounts as the popular dish of Cairenes. A German fifteenth-century traveler estimated that 12,000 cooks with their portable kitchens, as well as 48,000 bakers, provided food to Cairo's population, and another contemporary traveler estimated their numbers at 24,000 cooks, 48,000 bakers, and 30,000 water carriers, commenting, "Now reckon how many people there must be to eat and drink all this!"

Large Ottoman houses had, apart from the usual kitchen, a kitchen for coffee. Coffee was introduced to Egypt in the first quarter of the sixteenth century, under Ottoman rule, and soon became the popular beverage. Coffee houses, found in all quarters of the city, also became places to smoke tobacco, while entertainment was offered by storytellers, musicians and singers. Coffee houses were a favorite investment for the wealthy, and were often endowed to religious foundations, even though coffee was at first banned by the religious establishment. The coffee houses also became the locale of narcotics smoking, hashish and opium, particularly by Ottoman soldiers.

Baths

While large houses frequently had a kitchen, a bathroom was less common. The fourteenth-century jurist Ibn al-Ḥājj deplores the fact that people who built luxurious houses failed to provide a room for washing. Maqrīzī, who gives the list of Cairo's ḥammāms, describes them as usually located near princely residences, implying that they were not only used by the amir's household, but also by the public, and were built as a commercial investment. These were Roman-style steam baths, common in Egypt in pre-Islamic times. In the Ottoman period, however, waqf documents refer regularly to a ḥammām in large residences and a *mustaḥamm* in smaller dwellings, which seems to have been a small room lacking the sophistication of the larger bath. The private ḥammāms surviving in Cairo are all from the Ottoman period. The Ottoman period thus brought an obvious improvement in domestic architecture.

Provision of private houses with ḥammāms did not, however, diminish the role that public baths had played in Egypt since Roman times and whose functions were far wider than hygiene. Their primary aspect was social, particularly the women's baths, which were comparable to clubs. Women in particular enjoyed the opportunities the ḥammāms offered to gather, away from their houses, and their only opportunity to go out without their husbands. Marriages were often arranged in the ḥammāms where the matchmakers went to look for potential brides. Further, a bride's visit to the ḥammām was an obligatory part of wedding ceremonies and festivities. Ibn al-Ḥājj criticized women's visits to ḥammāms, saying they merely led women to show off their clothes and jewelry, adding that such female gatherings were harmful. On the other hand, in the tale of Abū Sīr and Abū Qīr in the *Arabian Nights*, is the comment, "Your city is not perfect unless it has a ḥammām." Ibn Khaldūn wrote that ḥammāms are a mark of highly civilized cities, since luxury reveals wealth and prosperity.

The ḥammām had not only social and hygienic, but also medical functions, as heat was believed to cure illnesses. Public baths were lucrative businesses and are often mentioned in waqf documents as endowments. They had sections for men and others for women, and were sometimes attached to religious foundations. When establishing a khanqāh in a Fatimid palace, Ṣalāḥ al-Dīn added a bath for the use of Sufis; this suggests that there had been none before. The khanqāh of Amir Shaykhū had a ḥammām nearby, most likely endowed upon the foundation, as was the bath with the complex of Sultan al-Muʾayyad. Religious foundations often provided the Sufis with the fee for their visits to the ḥammām and for soap as well. Because of their

Pl. 37. The ḥammām of Sultan al-Muʾayyad (Pauty).

sophisticated infrastructure, the ḥammāms had local continuity; new ones were always built on the site of previous structures to make use of its infrastructure. This often makes them difficult to date.

A traveler to Fusṭāṭ in the Tulunid period gives us the following account: He arrived at Ḥammām al-Rūm (the Greek Bath), very popular at the time, and found no one to serve him, though there were at least seventy attendants, each with three assistants, to serve customers. He left the bath and went to another, with the same experience. Only at the fourth bath did he find an available attendant. He was astonished to imagine the population of Fusṭāṭ, when told that the city had 1,170 baths! This most likely was an exaggeration, though it is also reported that Fusṭāṭ's atmosphere was highly polluted primarily from the smoke from the multitudinous bath ovens. Until the last century, Cairo's ḥammāms flourished and often impressed travelers, scholars and orientalists. There are still a few traditional baths operating, though they have quite lost their glamor.

The thirteenth-century physician ʿAbd al-Laṭīf writes that the ḥammāms of Egypt were the best in the Orient. He mentions their decoration, the marbles, columns, vaults, painted ceilings, and vivid colors. The remains of stucco stalactites, once in a Fusṭāṭ ḥammām, showing a dancer and a man seated with a cup in hand, is displayed at the Islamic Museum in Cairo.

Architecture of the Ḥammām

According to Pauty, ḥammāms are difficult to date as they bear no inscriptions and have been throughout their long history often restored and remodeled. The Egyptian ḥammām is based upon Roman bath tradition, with some modifications. In general, the traditional ḥammām was entered through a narrow door like that of a shop, having no facade except for the entrance; the rest of the building was usually behind a row of shops. Next to the entrance was a small room for a doorman, and the entrance was bent. The first hall, the *maslakh*, for undressing, was paved with marble and had a central fountain.

This hall was surrounded by recesses with benches spread with carpets and mattresses. Marble columns flanked the recesses, and latrines were nearby. The hall was similar to a residential reception hall. The next hall, *bayt awwal* (first room), was rectangular and vaulted, with openings in the vault filled with glass to introduce light. The hall was slightly warmed, and included mattresses for guests to relax upon. A narrow door led to the next room, the center of the ḥammām, the *bayt al-ḥarāra* (hot room). Its center was enhanced by a dome and marble inlaid floor. Here the customer got his massage. From the hot room, corresponding to the

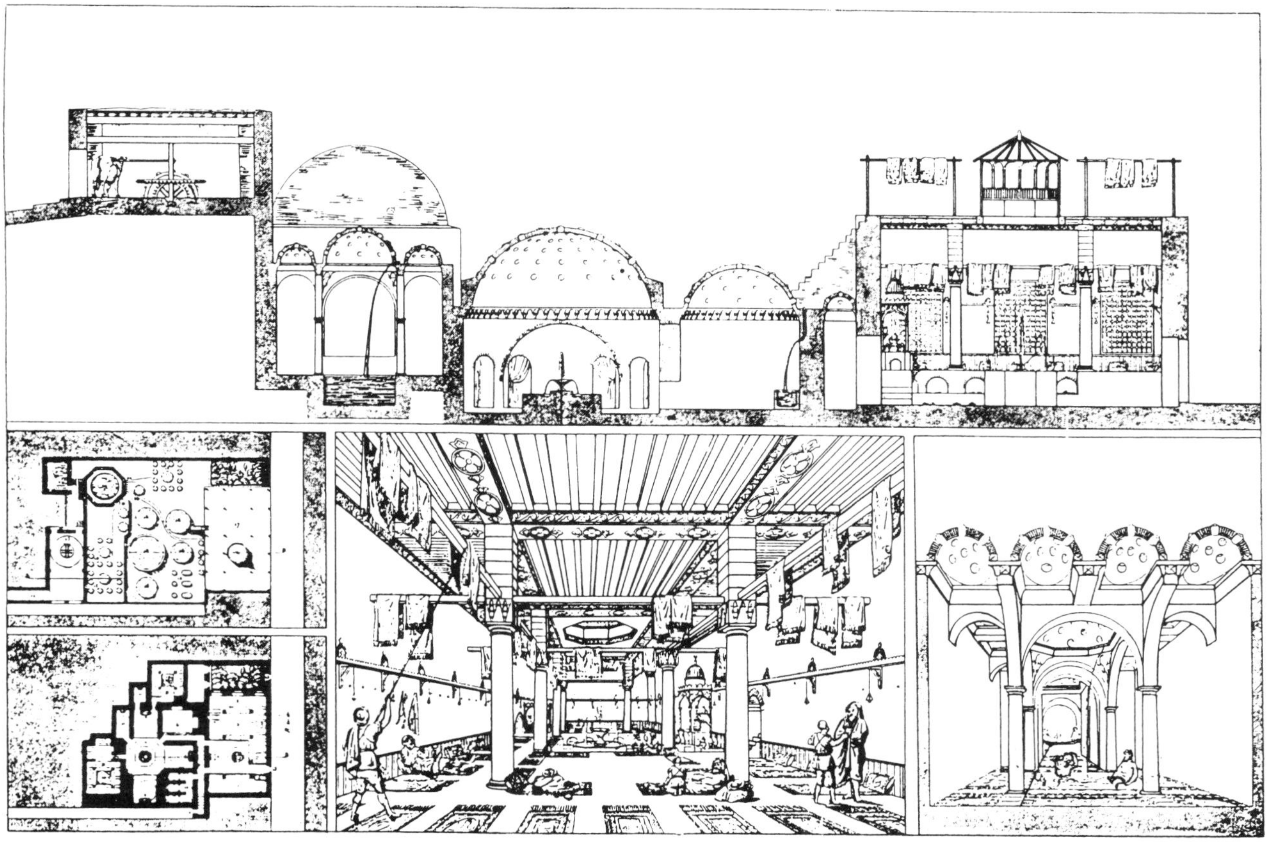

Fig. 10. Ḥammām al-Ṭanbalī (Coste).

caldarium of Roman baths, one passed to the *maghṭas* (Roman laconicum) equipped with water taps in recesses and basins for bathing. The maghṭas had warm-water basins set into the floor, usually with two different temperatures, and this was the most highly decorated part of the ḥammām. Near the maghṭas was the heating-equipment room, the *bayt al-nār*. Its huge water containers were heated by fires fed by garbage collected in the neighborhood.

The plans of Cairo's ḥammāms studied by Pauty show great variations in layout, size, number of rooms, and decorations. The ḥammām that Sultan al-Muʾayyad built near his religious complex has a magnificent dome on stalactites, surrounded by four unequal īwāns facing the domed area through pointed arches, similar to a madrasa plan. While the *maslakh* or vestiary was treated with great lavishness, the rest was more modest and reduced.

PART II

THE MONUMENTS

CHAPTER FOUR

EARLY ISLAMIC ARCHITECTURE IN CAIRO

THE MOSQUE OF ᶜAMR IBN AL-ᶜĀṢ AT AL-FUSṬĀṬ (641/2)

The mosque of ᶜAmr, the first mosque to be built in Egypt, was founded by the commander-in-chief of the conquering Arab troops, ᶜAmr Ibn al-ᶜĀṣ. Arab medieval historians call it Tāj al-Jawāmiᶜ, or the Crown of the Mosques.

The mosque of ᶜAmr in its present form is of no particular interest for the art historian, for its configuration is the result of a series of enlargements, restorations and reconstructions that include only one wall from the medieval period, and even that is not original but a ninth-century addition. For the historian in general and the urban historian in particular, the mosque's importance today is that it indicates where ᶜAmr's house, built near the original mosque, once stood.

Although medieval historians are usually silent on the subject of architecture and its development, they always mention religious foundations of special historic or religious importance. Thus, the history of the first mosque of Egypt is fairly well documented in their accounts.

The First Mosque

The mosque was founded in 641-42 as a place of prayer for the Arab troops in their garrison city, al-Fusṭāṭ. The original building, much smaller than the present one, measured no more than fifty by thirty cubits, or about twenty-nine by seventeen meters. On its northeastern side, separated from it by a lane, was the house of ᶜAmr and nearby, that of his son.

The original mosque was unpretentious, without a courtyard, plaster, or decoration. Its floor was not paved, it lacked a minaret, and the qibla or Mecca orientation was not, as in all later mosques, indicated by a concave niche. Creswell assumes that it must have been built of mud brick and palm trunks, like the Prophet's mosque attached to his house at Medina. This predecessor of all mosques established only minimal requirements for those to follow. Not even the minaret was essential, for Bilāl, the Prophet's muezzin (*muᶜadhdhin*), had called the faithful to prayer from a rooftop. Indeed, the only indispensable feature of a mosque was its orientation toward Mecca, dictated by Muslim prayer ritual. However, the fourteenth-century historian Ibn Muyassar says that a convert to Islam, the nephew of the Patriarch of Egypt, al-Muqawqis, contributed to the design of ᶜAmr's mosque. This implies that as far as architectural design was concerned, the mosque could not have been an entirely primitive building, as it was planned by a local craftsman familiar with sophisticated architecture.

It appears that the idea of enhancing the Mecca orientation by a concave prayer niche was not adopted immediately by the first mosque designers. Qalqashandī, the fifteenth-century Egyptian historian, writes that in the original mosque of ᶜAmr, four columns were inserted on the qibla wall to point out the Mecca orientation. The presence of four columns suggests that a flat niche might have existed, composed of two pairs of columns with an arch drawn between them. Each of the three other walls of the mosque included two entrances.

Additions

Only thirty-two years after the mosque's foundation, the growing Muslim community found it too small. It was pulled down and replaced by a larger one that had mats on its floors and plastered walls. Creswell's reconstruction shows the enlargements the mosque underwent throughout its history.

During the expansion works in 673, the Umayyad Caliph of Damascus, Muᶜāwiya, ordered minarets to be added to each of the four corners of the mosque. They were reached by an outer staircase, indicating that the mosque had no interior staircase leading to the roof. Creswell interprets this addition as being inspired by the prototype of the Great Mosque at Damascus. There, where the mosque was built on the temenos or enclosure of a Roman temple, preexisting towers at the four corners became the minarets. The arrangement was quite practical, allowing the *adhān*, or call to

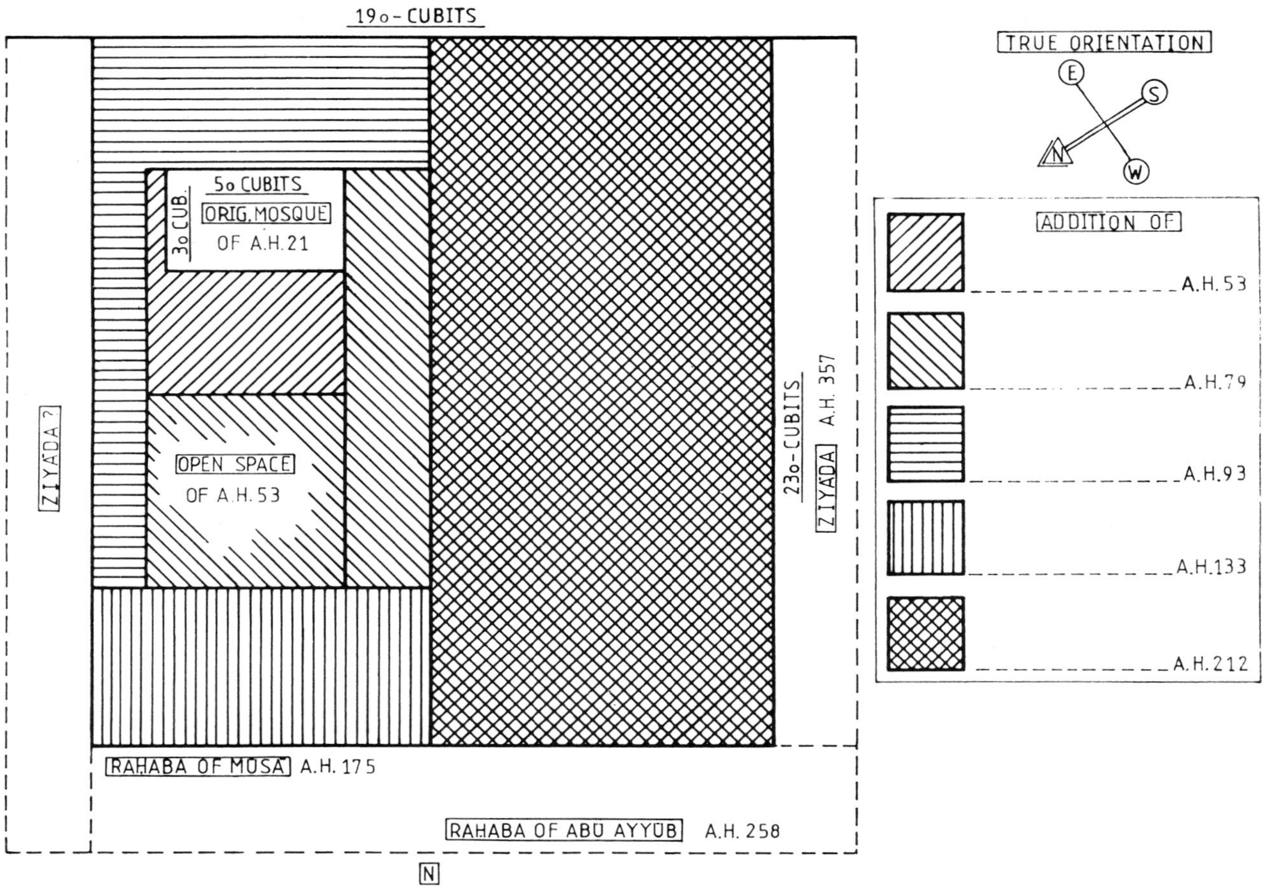

Fig. 11. Plan showing the consecutive enlargements at the mosque of ᶜAmr (Creswell).

prayer, from the mosque of ᶜAmr to be heard on all sides and taken up by the other mosques of the city. The name of the governor of Egypt who carried out the works, Maslama Ibn Mukhallad, was written on the minarets. Minarets were then added to all other mosques at al-Fusṭāṭ, which had formerly announced prayer times with a *nāqūs*, a kind of bell used by the Copts.

The southern wall of the present mosque is attributed by Creswell to the reconstruction by ᶜAbd Allāh Ibn Ṭāhir (827) that enlarged the mosque to its present size. It shows the remains of windows, now walled up, alternating with niches whose conches are carved in a hooded shell motif. All windows and niches are flanked with colonnettes and have round arches. The windows have colonnettes on the outside wall as well as on the inside. Inside the mosque, this south wall shows the remains of the springing of arches that once ran parallel to the qibla wall. They are joined to columns by wooden beams carved in a late Hellenistic pattern that is unique in Cairene medieval architecture and recalls the cornice on the piers of the Dome of the Rock in Jerusalem. Because of the orientation of these arch springings, Creswell concludes that the original arcades of the mosque were all parallel to the main wall. This side of the mosque today has perpendicular arcades, attributed to a nineteenth-century reconstruction of the mosque.

Thanks for shopping with us.
Kindest Regards, Customer Care

RETURNING GOODS

Please re-pack, in the original packaging if possible, and send back to us at the address below. **Caution!** Don't cover up the barcode (on original packaging) as it helps us to process your return.

We will email you when we have processed your return.

---✂---

PLEASE complete and include this section with your goods.

Your Name: ______________________________

Your Order Number ______________________________

Reason for return ______________________________

Would you prefer: Refund ☐ or Replacement ☐?

(Please note, if we are unable to replace the item it will be refunded.)

Return to:

---✂---

PBS RETURNS
801 Penhorn Avenue
Unit 5
Secaucus
NJ 07094

The Prayer Niche

Several additions and restorations were made at the mosque of ᶜAmr, apart from the enlargements. The original flat prayer niche was replaced by a concave prayer niche, a device that predominated in all religious architecture from then on. Medieval historians give different dates for this innovation. Some attribute it to the governor Maslama Ibn Mukhallad (667-81) or to the governor ᶜAbd al-ᶜAzīz (684-703); others, including Creswell, to work done in 711. In the last case, it would be the second concave prayer niche in Islamic architecture, coming after the one added to the mosque of Medina by ᶜUmar Ibn ᶜAbd al-ᶜAzīz during the reign of the Caliph al-Walīd (707-709). The origin of the concave prayer niche was of considerable interest to medieval Arab historians, one of whom, al-Suyūṭī, states that it was at first avoided because it was used in churches. Coptic craftsmen from Egypt were employed in the works at Medina at the time the first concave prayer niche was introduced. By the fifteenth century, the mosque of ᶜAmr had three prayer niches.

The Pulpit

ᶜAmr Ibn al-ᶜĀṣ used a pulpit for the Friday sermon. In this matter, also, the historians give different accounts. One says that this pulpit was taken from a church, while another says it was a gift to ᶜAmr from a Nubian Christian king, a wooden structure made by a carpenter named Buqṭur. The Caliph ᶜUmar Ibn al-Khaṭṭāb at Medina, hearing that ᶜAmr was preaching from a pulpit, disliked the idea of the leader standing above the believers, and prohibited ᶜAmr from using it. It is reported, however, that he continued to use it after the Caliph's death.

The pulpit, or minbar, in time became an integral part of the furniture of all mosques, though its use was restricted to the jāmiᶜ, or mosque where the Friday sermon was held. In the early period of the Islamic empire, each city had only one congregational, or Friday, mosque where the Friday sermon, or *khuṭba* could be preached. Subsequently, Friday mosques increased in number until each quarter and even each street had one. In 777, the Abbasid Caliph al-Mahdī gave orders to lower the height of pulpits in all mosques in the empire, and to abolish use of the *maqṣūra*, an enclosure near the prayer niche in which the ruler prayed in private. The maqṣūra seems to have originated as a safety precaution, as more than one leader had been murdered during prayer, and the Caliph's decree was not honored for long. The mosque of ᶜAmr acquired a maqṣūra in the first century after its foundation. In 1050, a wooden maqṣūra and wooden prayer niche were built for summer use, indicating that the structures must have been portable and used outside the sanctuary.

Other Structures

During the reign of Ibn Ṭūlūn, in 870, a structure composed of wooden columns with horizontal sticks for awnings was added to the mosque when people complained about the heat inside. This feature was removed by the Caliph al-Ḥākim, after the structure had been painted with red and green paint that failed to stick.

The traveler Muqaddasī, visiting the mosque of ᶜAmr in the tenth century, reported that the walls of the mosque were decorated with glass mosaics. Along with the four minarets, this would have been another feature in common with the Great Mosque of Damascus, many of whose exquisite glass mosaics can still be seen. In 997, by order of the Caliph al-Ḥākim, some of the mosaics of ᶜAmr's mosque were removed and the walls were plastered. The caliph also donated a gigantic bronze chandelier.

Among the various structures in the mosque of ᶜAmr that were common to many early mosques was the *bayt al-māl*, or treasure for the needs of the community. It was a domed structure on columns. In 989, a decorative fountain was installed under the columns. A similar *bayt al-māl* structure can be seen today at the Great Mosque of Damascus.

Gold and silver were used to embellish the mosque, though this was condemned by orthodox interpreters of Islamic tradition. In 1046-47 the Fatimid Caliph al-Mustanṣir added a silver belt to the prayer niche and silver to its columns. Under the Ikhshidids in 937 the capitals of the mosque's columns were gilded, and in 989-90, the Caliph al-ᶜAzīz ordered a gilded pulpit.

During the Fatimid period (969-1171) the mosque of ᶜAmr had five minarets, four at the corners and one at the axial entrance. Each had a name: al-Ghurfa (or ᶜArafa), al-Kabīra (the big one), al-Jadīda (the new one), al-Mustajadda (the newly made), and al-Saᶜīda (literally, the happy one, but this could refer to a sponsor's name, al-Saᶜīd). All these have disappeared and the two present minarets, one near the main entrance and another on the southwest corner, were built by

Murād Bey who rebuilt almost entirely the mosque in 1800.

In the early history of the mosque, the roof is reported to have been crowded with various rooms, some for the muezzin and some for the equipment for calculating the time for the call to prayer. The roof was also used as an ambulatory, as ritual walks around a sacred place were believed to bring blessings. Later, these structures were removed. Waterwheels were used to lift water to the roof for the mosque's drinking water, ablution fountains, latrines, and cleaning.

One of the most prominent restorers of the mosque of ᶜAmr was Ṣalāḥ al-Dīn al-Ayyūbī (1171-93), who restored it after the fire set in al-Fusṭāṭ to repel the Crusaders. He built a belvedere underneath one of the minarets and removed the silver belt from the prayer niche. The Mamluk sultans al-Ẓāhir Baybars and al-Manṣūr Qalāwūn contributed to the upkeep of Egypt's first mosque, and after the earthquake of 1303, Amir Salār restored the building and sponsored a stucco prayer niche on the outer wall which disappeared only a few years ago.

Between the restorations carried out by Sultan Qāytbāy in the late fifteenth century and those of Murād Bey in 1800, no interest in the mosque is reported, and its neighborhood must have been all but abandoned during this period. Murād Bey's restorations were damaged shortly afterward by Napoleon's troops.

The mosque of ᶜAmr, like all medieval mosques, was a place not only for prayer but for important civil gatherings as well, particularly in the early days when the community leader's functions were both religious and political. Tribunals for religious and civil cases were held in the *ziyāda*, the enclosure between the mosque and the street. Above all, it was a center for teaching theology, law, and all other subjects of interest to medieval society. At one time, more than a hundred different classes were held, and in the Fatimid period there were also classes for women. Imām Shāfiᶜī, founder of one of the four rites of Islamic Sunni law, taught there in the eighth century. Recent excavations in the prayer hall have brought to light some of the structures referred to by Maqrīzī as *zāwiya*s, or chapels built within the mosque for teaching, each with its own latrine.

At this cultural and religious center, the whole population of the city met, especially on Fridays for prayer. It is thus not surprising that the most prestigious markets were also concentrated around the mosque, making it also the commercial center of al-Fusṭāṭ.

Bibliography

ᶜAbd al-Wahhāb, Ḥasan. *Tārīkh al-masājid al-athariyya*. Cairo, 1946, pp. 23 ff.

Ahmad, Muhammad. *The Mosque of ᶜAmr Ibn al-ᶜAs at Fustat*. Cairo, 1939.

Aḥmad, Yūsuf. *Jāmiᶜ Sayyidna ᶜAmr Ibn al-ᶜĀṣ*. Cairo, 1917.

Creswell, K. A. C. *Early Muslim Architecture* (*E.M.A.*). Oxford University Press, 1932-40, II, pp. 171 ff.

Ibn Duqmāq. *Kitāb al-intiṣār li wāsiṭat ᶜiqd al-amṣār*. Būlāq, 1314 H., IV, pp. 59 ff.

Maqrīzī. *Kitāb al-mawāᵓiẓ wa 'l-iᵓtibār fī dhikr al-khiṭaṭ wa 'l-athār*. Būlāq, 1306 H., II, pp. 246 ff.

Mubārak, ᶜAlī. *al-Khiṭaṭ al-jadīda al-tawfīqiyya*. Būlāq, 1306 H., IV, pp. 3 ff.

al-Qalqashandī, Abū al-ᶜAbbās Aḥmad Ibn ᶜAlī. *Subḥ al-Aᶜshā fī Sināᶜat al-Inshā*. Cairo, 1963, III, pp. 337 ff.

Whelan, Estelle. "The Origins of the *miḥrāb mujawwaf*: A Reinterpretation." *International Journal of Middle East Studies*, 18 (1986), pp. 205 ff.

THE NILOMETER AT RAWḌA (861)

The Nilometer (in Arabic *miqyās*, or measurer) at Rawḍa is the oldest structure in Egypt built after the Arab conquest that survives in its original form. Its all-important function was to measure the annual Nile flood in August-September, to regulate distribution of

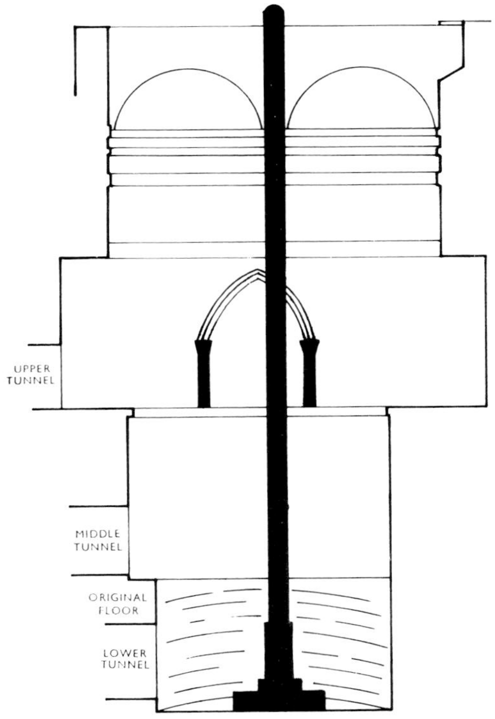

Fig. 12. The Nilometer (Creswell).

water and the levy of taxes paid as tribute by Egypt to the Caliph.

The Umayyads had built a Nilometer of the simple type used earlier in Egypt, a graduated wall in the Nile. The Nilometer we see today was built in 861 by order of the Abbasid Caliph al-Mutawakkil (847-61). It is a rather sophisticated instrument, based on the principle of communicating vessels.

The Nilometer consists of a pit on the southern tip of Rawḍa Island, facing al-Fusṭāṭ to the east, communicating with the Nile through tunnels dug on three levels on its eastern side. The pit itself is circular at the bottom and rectangular at the top and is lined with stone. On its walls are four recesses with pointed arches, flanked by colonnettes showing two types of voussoir decoration. Creswell points out that these arches are the same type as those used in Gothic architecture, but they preceded the Gothic arch by four hundred years. In the middle of the pit is a marble column squeezed between a millstone at the bottom of the pit and a wooden beam spanning the Nilometer at the top. The column, which has a Corinthian capital, is graded and divided into 19 cubits (a cubit is slightly more than half a meter).

The walls of the Nilometer have carved inscriptions in plain Kufic, the earliest surviving example of architectural epigraphy in Egypt. They are Quranic texts referring to water, vegetation and prosperity (Sūra XIV:37) and thus have a talismanic meaning. A historic inscription referring to the founding of the Nilometer by al-Mutawakkil has been removed. According to Creswell, this was done by Ibn Ṭūlūn who restored the Nilometer in 872-73, removing the name as part of his campaign to assert his independence from the Caliphate. The inscriptions were originally on a background of blue; they were themselves left in the natural stone color. The wooden painted conical dome covering the Nilometer is part of a modern restoration.

What the Nilometer announced was vital to rulers as well as to the whole population of Egypt. An ideal flood filled the Nilometer up to the sixteenth mark; nineteen cubits meant flood catastrophe; and less than sixteen cubits spelt drought and famine.

Throughout the medieval period and until the end of the nineteenth century, the Rawḍa Nilometer was the departure point of the greatest of Cairo's celebrations, *Fatḥ al-Khalīj*, the Festival of the Opening of the Canal. The Khalīj, starting opposite Rawḍa Island, bordered the medieval city to the west and irrigated its outlying gardens and fields. The Nile summer flood filled the Khalīj and many ponds, whose beds in winter were green with vegetation. During the hot summer months, the Khalīj and the ponds were filled with pleasure boats and its shores were lined with entertainments. The Khalīj was blocked with an earth dam and cleaned before the flood, then opened when the Nile flood reached the sixteen-cubit level. The caliph, and later sultans and pashas, came out to open the Khalij and, in celebrations lasting several days, decorated boats crowded the waters, the most splendid of them being the caliph's, or sultan's, boat. Today, the Nile sailing houseboat called a *dhahabiyya*, or golden one, recalls the splendor of the ruler's boat. This festival, which ceased in 1899 when the Khalīj was filled in, was described by all who witnessed it as Cairo's most spectacular event. Near the Nilometer was a mosque for prayers accompanying the flood celebrations and a palace for banquets held by the rulers. In the days spent waiting for the flood, the columns of the Nilometer were annointed with saffron and musk to induce a good water level. If the Nile flood waters failed to reach the sixteen cubits mark, celebrations were canceled and prayers and fasting were held instead to ward off the coming drought and famine. After one delayed flood, Sultan al-Muʾayyad (1412-21) himself took a dip in the Nilometer as a token of gratitude.

Bibliography

Creswell. *E.M.A.*, II, pp. 200 ff.

Behrens-Abouseif, Doris, "Fêtes populaires dans le Caire du Moyen-Age". *Quaderni dell' Istituto Italiano di Cultura per la R.A.E.* Cairo, 1982.

Ghaleb Bey, K. O. *Le Miqyas ou Nilomètre de l'Île de Rodah*. Cairo, 1951.

Popper, William. *The Nilometer: Studies in Ibn Taghrībirdī's Chronicles of Egypt* (Part 1). Berkeley, 1951.

THE MOSQUE OF IBN ṬŪLŪN (876-79)

Ibn Ṭūlūn was sent from Samarra, the Abbasid capital, as governor of Egypt, where he soon founded his own capital, al-Qaṭāʾiʿ. The new city was situated in the area known today as Ṣalība street and the area between the Citadel and Sayyida Zaynab. Nothing but the mosque and an aqueduct has survived from Ibn Ṭūlūn's city.

Al-Fusṭāṭ and al-ʿAskar no longer had room for Ibn Ṭūlūn's large garrisons, and the mosque of ʿAmr was too small for the whole Muslim population of the growing capital. Ibn Ṭūlūn built a very large mosque on a

Pl. 38. The mosque of Ibn Ṭūlūn.

hill called Jabal Yashkur; today it is the oldest mosque in Egypt in its original form.

An original inscription slab on one of the piers in the sanctuary bears the foundation text of the mosque and the completion date 265 (879) written in plain script, and another is now at the Islamic Museum. Maqrīzī further indicates that the mosque was started three years earlier in 876. The Mamluk Sultan Lājīn ordered important restorations at the mosque that were carried out in 1296/97.

General Description

Architecture in the Egyptian province of the Abbasid Caliphate followed the royal style of the Muslim empire's capital, and the architecture of Ibn Ṭūlūn's mosque and most of its decorations follow the Samarran style of the period.

The mosque of Ibn Ṭūlūn is built around a courtyard with four arcaded halls (*riwāq*), the largest being the sanctuary on the qibla side. It is built of brick except for the stone minaret, and as a novelty, its arcades are supported by piers instead of columns. These piers are rectangular, decorated with four masonry engaged columns at the corners. Their capitals have the same bell shape as the bases, and both are plastered and carved. The arches of the arcades are pointed. Because piers were used instead of columns, a feature alien to local tradition, it has been said that the architect, a Christian, wanted to avoid having columns taken from churches as spoils to build the mosque. The true interpretation, however, is easily found at Samarra, where this device was used because brick was the natural building material in Mesopotamia. There are two Byzantine-style pairs of marble columns flanking the prayer niche, the only spoils used in Ibn Ṭūlūn's mosque.

Pl. 39. The mosque of Ibn Ṭūlūn, view of the interior.

Pl. 40. Side arcade at the mosque of Ibn Ṭūlūn.

Pl. 41. Stucco window grill at the mosque of Ibn Ṭūlūn.

The sanctuary, or qibla riwāq, of the mosque has five aisles parallel to the prayer niche; the other three sides have three aisles each. On the three minor sides, the mosque is surrounded by an enclosed space (*ziyāda*) separating and protecting the mosque from the noise and bustle of the streets. Outside the mosque on the qibla side, there used to be a palace, the *dār al-ᶜimāra*, from which Ibn Ṭūlūn could enter the sanctuary directly through a door near the prayer niche.

Both the walls of the mosque and the ziyāda are crowned with a most peculiar and intricate type of crenellation made of open brickwork, which upon closer inspection turns out to be a repetition of the Samarra stucco motifs decorating the walls of the mosque.

Doors and Windows

The mosque has nineteen doors on three sides, each door corresponding to another door in the ziyāda. There are three more doors on the qibla side.

The upper part of the mosque wall is pierced with pointed-arch windows flanked with colonnettes. The windows alternate on the outside wall with blind niches with a shell conch, an arrangement already seen on a wall of the mosque of ᶜAmr and attributed to a ninth-century addition. Creswell attributes only four of the windows' stucco grills to the Tulunid period, those with a plain geometric design; the rest, displaying a large variety of more complicated geometric patterns, date from the Fatimid and Mamluk periods. There are altogether 128 windows and their arrangement on the walls is independent from the arcades so that not every arch has a centered window. The arched windows of the arcades fill the double function of providing light and reducing the weight carried by the arches.

The Fountain

The ablution fountain covered by a dome in the center of the courtyard was added to the mosque in the late thirteenth century by Sultan Lājīn. Originally, there was a *fawwāra* in the center, a decorative fountain with a dome on ten columns surrounded by sixteen other columns, all made of marble and gilded. This fountain structure had a sundial used by the muezzin for the second call to prayer (*iqāma*), the prayer performed inside the mosque. The *fawwāra* was destroyed by fire in 986. The present ablution fountain's inscription band carries the Quranic text on the duty of ablution. The domed rectangular room, open on four sides, was built by Sultan Lājīn when he restored the mosque. The profile of its dome resembles that of al-Ṣāliḥ Najm al-Dīn Ayyūb built in 1243, with the curve beginning at its lower part. Ablution fountains originally were not within the mosque at all, but outside in the ziyāda, where latrines and even a clinic for treating the sick were located.

Prayer Niches

The mosque of Ibn Ṭūlūn has six prayer niches dating from various periods. The main one, in the middle of the qibla wall, is also the tallest. Its stucco molding and two stucco bosses on each side of the arch are original. The inner decoration of the niche was redone by Sultan Lājīn; it consists of an upper decoration of painted wood, a band of glass mosaics with the text of the shahāda, and a lower part made of marble panels. This prayer niche is the only concave one; the other five are flat. There is a small prayer niche on the qibla wall to the left whose stalactite cresting and naskhī script assign it to the early Mamluk period, so that it is possible that it also was sponsored by Sultan Lājīn.

On one of the piers leading from the courtyard to the main prayer niche is to the right a prayer niche of which only the upper Samarran style stucco decoration has survived. A chain from which a medallion with a star is hanging; it is the only decoration of its kind in Cairo.

The style of the Kufic script of the shahāda text is similar to that of the prayer niche on the opposite side of the aisle, with which it must be contemporary. The latter is also decorated with Samarran stucco motifs and, like the first, carries the text of the shahāda without the Shīᶜa reference to ᶜAlī. It can thus be assigned to the pre-Fatimid period, either Tulunid or Ikhshidid (935-69). A very similar niche was found in a Tulunid house in excavations at Fusṭāṭ and is now in the Islamic Museum. The curved Kufic script differs, however, from the original inscriptions at Ibn Ṭūlūn, resembling more the inscriptions of the Ikhshidid period. On the prayer niche to the right, the reference to ᶜAlī is carved in small characters, like graffiti, as a later, obviously Fatimid, addition.

The most remarkable prayer niche at the mosque of Ibn Ṭūlūn is that of al-Afḍal Shāhinshāh, a vizier of the Fatimid Caliph al-Mustanṣir (s. Pl. 6). It is lavishly decorated in stucco and carries an inscription in ornate Kufic script with a historic reference to the Caliph who sponsored it. Creswell attributes the style of this prayer niche, with its arrangement of one frame inside another, to Persian influence. The prayer niche is a replica; the original is in the Islamic Museum of Cairo.

On the left side of the aisle, opposite al-Afḍal's prayer niche, is another, less well preserved one that is a copy of al-Afḍal's, the only difference being that the text refers to Sultan Lājīn. The shahāda also lacks the Shīᶜa reference to ᶜAlī. This prayer niche is a copy of much older one, a rare occurrence in Cairo's medieval architecture.

The Dikka

In the sanctuary near the courtyard there is a wooden bench on marble columns. It is called *dikkat al-muballigh* and is used for Quranic recitations, chants and calls to prayer inside the mosque (*iqāma*). Nearly all later mosques have this feature.

The Minaret

The minaret of Ibn Ṭūlūn stands on the north side of the ziyāda, slightly off the axis of the main prayer niche. It is an unusual stone structure with an outer staircase and a Mamluk top of the type named *mabkhara* by Creswell. This minaret is the subject of controversy among Cairo's architectural historians; it is attributed by some, most prominently by Creswell, to Sultan Lājīn and by others to Ibn Ṭūlūn. The sources do not yield enough information to determine its date.

We know that Ibn Ṭūlūn built a minaret with an outer staircase, a feature found in Samarran minaret architecture. The shape of the minaret is connected with a legend: Ibn Ṭūlūn was sitting with his officials and absentmindedly winding a piece of parchment around his finger. When asked by someone what the gesture meant, he answered out of embarrassment that he was planning the shape of his minaret. At Samarra, surviving minarets do have the exterior staircase, but are built of brick and are totally circular. The Ibn Ṭūlūn minaret begins as a rectangle and then becomes circular, and is built entirely of stone.

We know also that Sultan Lājīn restored the mosque of Ibn Ṭūlūn, which at the time was abandoned but had provided him shelter from some enemies. The top of the minaret and the ablution fountain are in a style unmistakably of this period (1296).

There are several arguments for attributing the whole structure to Lājīn. Apart from the minaret's being built in stone while the rest of the mosque is of brick, the manner in which the bridge of the minaret abuts on the mosque is quite awkward, blocking one of its windows, an aesthetic mistake that would not have been made by the Tulunid architect. The style of the bridge, with its Andalusian horseshoe arch and corbels, and the style of the double arches on the minaret itself refer it to the late thirteenth century, as does the top with its ribbed helmet. Moreover, analysis of the masonry reveals only one type of stonework technique.

To these arguments, it can be answered that the traveler al-Muqaddasī in the tenth century reported that the minaret of Ibn Ṭūlūn was built in stone. The style of the bridge and the arches on the minaret are in fact late, of an Andalusian style that occurs in early Mamluk architecture. The bridge is not original and the arches on the minaret, which have no structural function, are also not original. They must have been part of a restoration that included a new stone facing, together with the bridge and the top of the minaret, in other words with Sultan Lājīn's restoration.

The fact that the minaret was built in stone does not preclude its being original. Egyptian, unlike Mesopotamian, craftsmen had been building in stone since the dawn of history, so it is not surprising that they preferred to build the minaret in stone. Moreover, being a solid stone structure, without an inner staircase, it is unlikely that it could have been so shortlived. Had it been demolished, historians certainly would have mentioned it, as they did the destruction of the original fountain. Furthermore Lājīn would have at least left an inscription commemorating his construction, or his biographers would have referred to it. Medieval architects repeatedly restored and added to buildings, incorporating the style of their particular period. Had Lājīn rebuilt the minaret totally, it would have been a Mamluk minaret. The fact that the outer staircase was left is an argument in favor of the survival of Ibn Ṭūlūn's original structure which was then restored by Lājīn.

The whole structure lacks the harmonious proportions of a Mamluk building. The shape of the top, quite alien to the rest of the structure, suggests that the minaret as we now see it was not built at one time.

It is recorded that the architect made a drawing to show Ibn Ṭūlūn the plan and appearance of the mosque, so we know that drawings were made by architects, though none from the medieval period have survived. Such drawings must have been particularly necessary when local craftsmen were confronted with having to execute a design or architectural device alien to their experience.

Restorations

An inscription slab above the entrance of the mosque refers to restorations done by the Fatimid vizier Badr al-Jamālī in 1177. His son, al-Afḍal, sponsored the prayer niche described above. In the Fatimid period, the mosque of Ibn Ṭūlūn was one of the four mosques in which the caliph led Friday prayers, the others being the al-Azhar, al-Ḥākim, and ᶜAmr mosques.

The restoration works of Sultan Lājīn thus included the minaret, the new ablution fountain in the courtyard, and the wooden dome above the main prayer niche. He also introduced teaching of the four rites of Islamic law at the mosque, and even the teaching of medicine. A primary school for boys, or kuttāb, for teaching writing and reading of the Quran, was attached to the mosque. Lājīn also sponsored a sabīl, or public fountain. Of these additional structures, however, only the ablution fountain and the prayer niche dome survive.

In the thirteenth century, when the neighborhood had fallen into decay, the mosque of Ibn Ṭūlūn was used as a caravanserai for North African pilgrims on their way to Mecca. In the nineteenth century the mosque was used as a factory, and later as a lunatic asylum. During the fourteenth century, a *qāḍī* (Islamic judge) attached to the mosque added two minarets at the corners of the main prayer hall. One of these was removed some years ago as it was unstable.

Pl. 42. Stucco carved soffit at the mosque of Ibn Ṭūlūn.

Decoration

The decorations of Ibn Ṭūlūn's mosque show both the remaining influence of Byzantine rule and the Samarran political hegemony of the time. The window grills identified as originals by Creswell are similar to Umayyad window grills in the great mosque of Damascus, and are based on geometric compass work typical of the late classical Byzantine tradition. The large variety of designs in the soffits of the arches around the courtyard, though having Samarran floral fillings, no doubt also belong to Byzantine tradition. Creswell notes a design here that is found as a window grill in the mosque of Damascus.

In addition to the stucco soffits and voussoirs of the arcades, there are rosettes decorating the outer and inner facades. A wooden frieze with Quranic inscriptions runs around the entire mosque just under the ceiling, in the same plain Kufic script in which the foundation slab was carved. The stucco band framing the arches and the wood carvings on the doors are obvious adaptations of a mixture of the Samarran decorative styles known as Samarra B and C.

Samarra Style

The Abbasid Caliph al-Muᶜtaṣim first resided in the palace of his predecessor, al-Maᵓmūn, at Baghdad, the capital of the Caliphate. When his soldiers, Turks recruited from Central Asia, began molesting the city's population, he decided to move his residence and founded the new city of Samarra, 110 kilometers north of Baghdad on the eastern bank of the Tigris. Beginning his gigantic scheme in 836, al-Muᶜtaṣim gathered a multitude of craftsmen from all parts of his empire, including many from Egypt, to erect and decorate the great buildings that suited his aspirations as emperor. Samarra was soon abandoned, in 863, and because it was no longer inhabited, its ruins have preserved a great deal of the stucco carved and painted decorations which could not be moved or plundered. They have thus come down to us as an invaluable document of the origins of Islamic decoration.

Just as Byzantium dominated the arts of the Umayyads at Damascus, so Sassanian culture inspired the works of the Abbasids. Both influences were the result of the geographic location of each capital. In all periods, however, Islam, which rejected animate representations in religious art, contributed to the evolution of abstract and floral decorative patterns. The use of script, particularly in Quranic texts suited to the meaning or dedication of an architectural structure, whether religious or secular, was also peculiar to its building.

The building of Samarra, a huge undertaking completed within a short period of time, involved intensive work in a new, homogeneous style adapted to the immediate needs of the Caliph. This style is characterised by its abstract, symmetrical and repetitive form based on floral and geometric elements. Its origins were various including Central Asian influences introduced by Turks. Samarra decorative styles are termed A, B, and C.

Style A, the earliest, includes geometric figures filled with floral patterns, primarily vine leaves, grapes, palmettes and stalks. The floral patterns contrast with the background by having their surfaces carved in small geometric patterns of various types—zigzags, chevrons, roundels, and triangles.

In style B, the rosette shape dominates, and there are no stems or stalks. This is the predominant style at the mosque of Ibn Ṭūlūn. The floral representations are not naturalistic, and are thus the origin of arabesque—that is, geometrically arranged representations of plants. Both styles A and B are derived from Sassanian art.

Style C differs from the others in its regular use of molds. The strong contrast effect of styles A and B is thus lacking in this style, where hand carving is minimized. The varied and primarily abstract motifs of style C are attributed by Creswell to influences introduced by the Abbasid Caliphate's contacts with Central Asia, where they recruited soldiers for their armies.

Fig. 13. Carved stucco bands in the Samarra style on the arches of the Ibn Ṭūlūn mosque.

The method of using molds, in style C, to which only small touches needed to be made by hand, was time and labor saving and thus quite appropriate for the construction and decoration of the new city. The stuccos were painted in vivid colors.

The Samarran style, like any other Islamic style of architectural decoration, was not confined to religious architecture but was adopted in secular architecture as well. Many excavated houses of the Tulunid period have Samarra-style stucco panels.

Bibliography

ᶜAbd al-Wahhāb. *Masājid*, pp. 32 ff.

Creswell. *E.M.A.*, II, pp. 348 ff.

Hautecoeur, Louis, and Wiet, Gaston. *Les Mosquées du Caire*. Paris, 1932, pp. 208 ff.

Maqrīzī. *Khiṭaṭ*, II, pp. 265 ff.

Yūsuf, Aḥmad. *Jāmiᶜ Ibn Ṭūlūn*. Cairo, 1917.

CHAPTER FIVE

ARCHITECTURE OF THE FATIMID PERIOD

THE AL-AZHAR MOSQUE (970)

Al-Azhar is today the most celebrated of all Cairo's medieval mosques, more because of its historic and religious importance than its aesthetic value. It was the first mosque built in Fatimid Cairo and the first theological college, and has played a continuous role in the history of the city from its foundation to the present day. The mosque of ᶜAmr, though important as Islam's first mosque in Egypt, did not retain its role though the centuries.

Like the mosque of ᶜAmr, al-Azhar was established as the central mosque of a new urban foundation. It does not carry the name of its founder, the Fatimid Caliph al-Muᶜizz. Al-Azhar is an epithet meaning "The Flourishing". Some medieval sources call it simply the Great Mosque (*jāmiᶜ*) of Cairo.

Caliph al-Muᶜizz li-Dīn Allāh, after conquering Egypt and founding al-Qāhira, assigned his general and vizier Jawhar al-Ṣiqillī the task of building al-Azhar. The first prayers were held in the mosque in 972, and in 989 it acquired the status of a college with the appointment of thirty-five scholars to teach the Ismāᶜīlī Shīᶜa theology to which the Fatimids adhered. A hostel was built for them near the mosque.

Following the mosques of ᶜAmr, al-ᶜAskar, and Ibn Ṭūlūn, al-Azhar was the fourth congregational mosque in Egypt. After the Ottoman conquest, when the Mamluk colleges (madrasa) were in decline, al-Azhar became the center of Islamic scholarship in Egypt and one of the principal theological universities of the Muslim world.

Because of its importance, the mosque of al-Azhar, like the mosque of ᶜAmr, has undergone a series of enlargements and restorations throughout its history. Today, all styles and all periods of Cairo's history are represented in its architecture.

The original mosque of al-Azhar was much smaller than the present building, and it was not at the exact center of the capital. Al-Qāhira itself did not occupy much more than one square kilometer. The great Fatimid palace complex dominated the entire city. Al-Azhar is at a short distance from what was the main avenue, Bayn al-Qaṣrayn (lit., "between the two palaces").

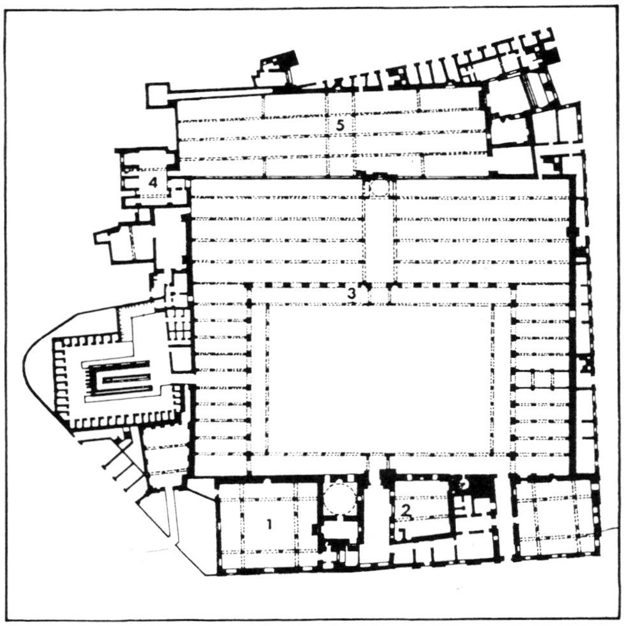

The al-Azhar mosque and its dependencies

Fig. 14. Plan of the al-Azhar mosque (Creswell).

The Orginal Mosque

As reconstructed by Creswell, the mosque originally had only three arcades around the courtyard; today it has four. This plan was common in North African and Andalusian architecture. The arcades are all carried on pre-Islamic columns with Corinthian capitals. Its original arches are round. The sanctuary had five aisles parallel to the qibla and a transept with an aisle wider and higher than the rest that runs perpendicular to the main wall, thus enhancing the prayer niche to which it leads from the courtyard to the prayer niche.

Pl. 43. The al-Azhar mosque.

There were three domes, one over the prayer niche and the two others at the corners of the qibla wall, but none has survived. This feature of three domes in the sanctuary was also found in North African architecture and must have been introduced to Egypt by Fatimid craftsmen. The two other arcades had only three aisles each. The mosque is said to have had a ziyāda.

The original minaret was a small construction standing above the main entrance and built of brick.

Of the original mosque the arcades, part of the stucco decoration, including the conch of the prayer niche and a few window grills have been preserved.

Fatimid Additions

In 1009 the Caliph al-Ḥākim restored the mosque, donating a new wooden door which is now in the Cairo Islamic Museum. In 1125, the Caliph al-Āmir donated a wooden prayer niche, now also at the museum. The most important Fatimid works, however, were carried out during the rule of the Caliph al-Ḥāfiẓ li-Dīn Allāh (1129-49), who added an arcade around the courtyard to give the mosque four arcades, the fourth composed of only one aisle on the northwestern side. The arches of this new courtyard facade differ from the original arches. They are called keel arches, as their profile resembles a ship's keel pointing upwards. Al-Ḥāfiẓ also added a dome in front of the transept. It is hidden to the viewer from the courtyard by a screen wall (*pīshṭāq*)—a portion of the facade wall taller than the rest which is meant to enhance the entrance to the sanctuary through the transept. This dome is richly decorated in carved stucco.

Fatimid Decoration

Original decorations include the conch of the prayer niche and the stucco inscriptions and arabesques on the

Pl. 44. The original prayer niche of al-Azhar with Mamluk stucco carving in the spandrels.

arcades. The conch of the prayer niche is decorated in a style very similar to that of the two unidentified prayer niches at the mosque of Ibn Ṭūlūn, which could be either Tulunid or Ikhshidid. This decoration is not in pure Samarra style, but is combined with the scrolls of palmettes typical of Byzantine decoration. Slightly ornate curved Kufic script frames the various arches of the prayer niche, windows, arcades and panels.

It appears that different periods of Fatimid decoration are represented in the stuccos of al-Azhar, but scholars have not yet sorted them out. On the wall facing the prayer niche, a naturalistic representation of a palm tree is repeated. Windows with geometric grills framed with bands of Kufic inscriptions appear to date from the foundation of the mosque. The stucco decorations added by al-Ḥāfiẓ adorning the walls and the dome are quite different from the original style, which is not surprising, as they were done more than a century later. The dome in front of the transept is decorated with a ring composed of lobed arches pointing toward the center. These arches carry ornate inscription bands. Interestingly, one of the stucco grills of the transitional zone of the dome of al-Ḥāfiẓ includes bits of green and yellow glass, the earliest known example of such a window decoration. This late-period Fatimid decoration shows a more ornate type of Kufic script and more composition in surface designs, involving less repetition of patterns.

Ayyubid and Mamluk Restorations

Ṣalāḥ al-Dīn, who followed the Shāfiʿī rite in which only one congregational or Friday mosque within an urban agglomeration is allowed, cancelled Friday prayers at al-Azhar and permitted them only at the mosque of al-Ḥākim, which he no doubt preferred because of its larger size. He also removed the Fatimid silver belt from the prayer niche. The mosque of ʿAmr continued to serve as al-Fusṭāṭ's congregational mosque during Ṣalāḥ al-Dīn's reign.

Under the Mamluks, the Ḥanafī rite had priority, and Sultan al-Ẓāhir Baybars reestablished the Friday sermon at al-Azhar in 1266. He also replaced the minaret at the entrance with a higher one, and carried out other restorations.

The 1303 earthquake, significant in Cairo's architectural history because of the restorations of monuments that followed, also damaged al-Azhar. Amir Salar restored the prayer niche and redecorated its spandrels. It was he who also added a beautiful prayer niche on the exterior wall of the mosque of ʿAmr, which we now know only from early photographs. Both of Salār's prayer niches are decorated in the same style, with a row of niches filled with stucco geometrical ornaments and surmounted by delicate arabesques, a device we see also at the smaller Lājīn prayer niche at Ibn Ṭūlūn.

Sultan Barqūq found al-Azhar's minaret too short, and in 1397 replaced it with a taller one in stone. Its structure, however, was defective, and it had to be destroyed a few years later. Sultan al-Muʾayyad built another minaret in the same place in 1424, but it also leaned and had to be removed. Sultan Qāytbāy, whose architects were more skillful, ordered several restorations at al-Azhar, in 1468, 1476, and 1495. Among these were the main portal and the minaret above it,

Pl. 45. Stucco panels on the western wall of the sanctuary at al-Azhar.

both fine examples of the golden age of stone carving that characterizes Qāytbāy's architecture. Sultan al-Ghūrī built a huge minaret in 1510, also near the main entrance. It has a double bulb and its shaft is decorated with pieces of blue faience.

In addition to restorations of individual structures, new buildings were added regularly to al-Azhar, for example the three madrasas of the Mamluk period. The madrasa of Ṭaybars on the right side of the main entrance has not survived in its original architectural form, but it has a magnificent prayer niche with carved and inlaid marble, one of the finest in Cairo, with representations of trees in mosaics in the spandrels.

The madrasa of Amir Aqbughā, built in 1340 on the left side of the entrance, has its original portal, a minaret, and qibla wall decoration, including glass mosaics in the prayer niche and window recesses, where a vase and stylized plant motif is repeated. Both these madrasas are on the site of a former ziyāda of the mosque.

The madrasa of Jawhar al-Qanqabāʾī, built in 1440 on the northern side of the sanctuary, is fully preserved in its original architectural form, along with its decorations and a carved stone dome covering the mausoleum of the founder.

Ottoman Restorations

In the Ottoman period, a long series of restorations and enlargements were made at al-Azhar. The most important of these was Amir ʿAbd al-Raḥmān Katkhudā's enlargement in 1753, when the area of the mosque behind the original prayer niche was widened. He added a new facade, the one we see today, with its double round arches and the typical Ottoman cypress

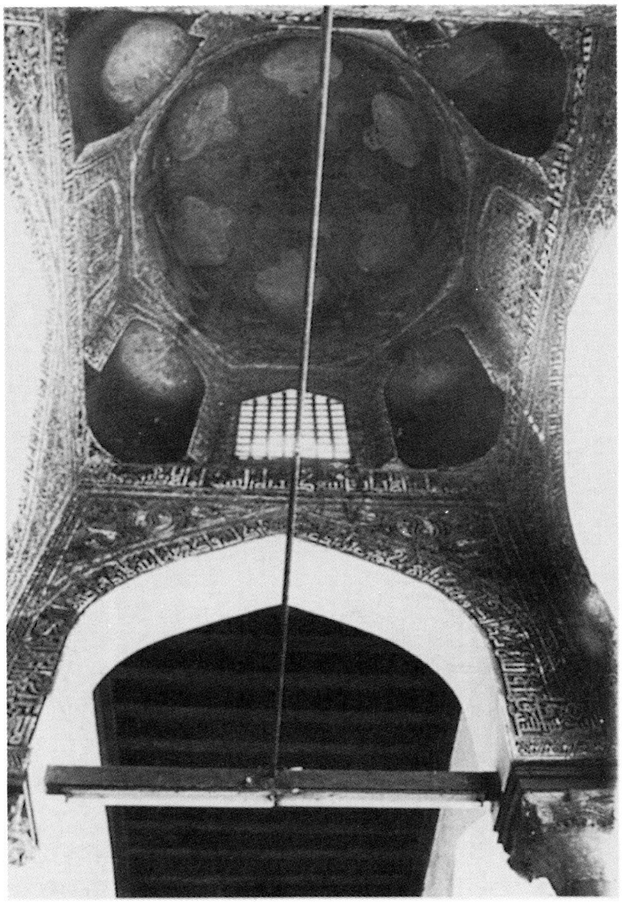

Pl. 46. The dome of the Caliph al-Ḥāfiẓ li-Dīn Allāh at al-Azhar.

tree carved above them. He also had three minarets built, two of which have survived on the southern and eastern walls. On the southern facade, he added a portal similar to the Gothic portal of al-Nāṣir Muḥammad's madrasa at the Naḥḥāsīn mosque. He rebuilt the facade of the Ṭaybarsiyya and erected for himself a mausoleum dome on the southeastern corner of the enlarged mosque. Still more additions and restorations were carried out in the nineteenth and twentieth centuries.

Minor Structures

Over the centuries, al-Azhar acquired several maqṣūras, one of them built by the founder Jawhar, and more than one prayer niche. There was a talisman to prevent birds from nesting in the mosque. Waterwheels served the fountains and latrines with water stored in cisterns.

There was a kitchen attached to the mosques where meals were prepared that were provided by charitable donations. At one time a large number of poor people were attached to the mosque and lived there on an almost regular basis. In 1415 a count was made of 750 such people, representing all the provinces of Egypt, along with foreigners. Orders were given to expel them from the mosque along with all their furniture and effects, as it was reported that forbidden things were going on in the mosque. Later, however, al-Azhar was surrounded by living quarters for a multitude of students and poor visitors.

Like the mosque of ᶜAmr at al-Fusṭāṭ, al-Azhar at al-Qāhira led the calls to prayer to be followed by the other mosques. It therefore had a number of sundials and a number of astronomers serving the mosque for the calculation of prayer times.

Instruction

Al-Azhar has been famous above all as a teaching center for Muslim theology. This tradition was begun soon after its foundation, with the teaching of Shīᶜa theology. Ṣalāḥ al-Dīn's overthrow of the Fatimids led to the abolition of Shīᶜa teaching in Egypt, and Sultan al-Ẓāhir Baybars introduced Shāfiᶜī teaching when he restored the mosque. Later, Sultan Ḥasan added the Ḥanafī rite, and eventually, all four rites were represented at al-Azhar.

During the Mamluk period, many madrasas in Cairo taught law and theology, but their decline after the Ottoman conquest raised the status of al-Azhar to its role of primary seat of Muslim learning in Egypt. Under the Ottomans (1517-1914), who, like the Mamluks before them, adhered to the Ḥanafī rite, the head of al-Azhar nonetheless remained a Shāfiᶜī scholar, in common with the majority of the Egyptian population. In the Ottoman period, students came from all parts of the Ottoman Empire and the rest of the Muslim world to study at al-Azhar. The rulers and members of the ruling establishment were generous in endowing al-Azhar. Several kuttābs, primary schools for boys, were also attached to the mosque.

Today, Cairo's al-Azhar University is a modern university where all topics are taught. It is housed in buildings in the vicinity of the mosque.

Bibliography

^{c}Abd al-Wahhāb. *Masājid*, pp. 47 ff.

Creswell. *The Muslim Architecture of Egypt* (*M.A.E.*). Oxford University Press, 1952-60. I, pp. 36 ff.

Flury, Samuel. *Die Ornamente der Hakim und Ashar Moschee; Materialen zur Geschichte der aelteren Kunst des Islam*. Heidelberg, 1912.

Maqrīzī. *Khiṭaṭ*, II, pp. 273 ff.

Mubārak. *Khiṭaṭ*, IV, pp. 17 ff.

THE MOSQUE OF CALIPH AL-ḤĀKIM BI AMR ALLĀH (990-1003)

The circumstances in which the mosque of Caliph al-Ḥākim was built are rather unusual. It was founded in 990 by the Caliph al-^{c}Azīz, al-Ḥākim's father, and a year later the first prayer was celebrated there, although the building was still incomplete. There is nothing unusual about this. The direction of Mecca dictates the orientation of every mosque, so the sanctuary is generally built first, followed by the rest of the structure. However, it was not until twelve years later, in 1002-3, that the Caliph al-Ḥākim is reported to have ordered completion of the mosque. The inscription on the southern minaret carries his name and the date 393/1003. In 1010 important alterations were made to the minarets, and in 1013 the furniture of the mosque was added and prayers again inaugurated.

Originally, the mosque stood outside the city walls of Jawhar. When Badr al-Jamālī later rebuilt the walls in stone, he enlarged them slightly so as to include the mosque of al-Ḥākim within the confines of the city, and the northern wall of the mosque was incorporated in the city's wall. Like al-Azhar, this mosque has a epithet, al-Anwar, "the Illuminated".

The mosque of al-Ḥākim suffered much throughout its history, in the 1303 earthquake and later. Nineteenth-century artists show it in an advanced state of ruin. It was recently restored.

General Description

The mosque is an irregular rectangle with four arcades surrounding a courtyard, and its architecture combines features of both the Ibn Ṭūlūn and al-Azhar mosques. Like Ibn Ṭūlūn's mosque it has pointed arches supported by rectangular brick piers, but the arcades are higher and the mosque is smaller than Ibn Ṭūlūn's, giving the whole a more vertical appearance. Like al-Azhar, it has a transept crossing the prayer hall perpendicularly and three domes at the qibla wall, one over the prayer niche and two at the corners. The new features are the building of two minarets protruding at the facade corners of the mosque, and the monumental portal. The whole facade configuration is inspired by that of the mosque in Mahdiyya (Tunisia), the Fatimid capital in North Africa. The facade and the minarets are built in stone; the rest is of brick.

The Minarets

Maqrīzī, the fifteenth-century historian, writes that in 1010, alterations were made to the minarets of al-Ḥākim, adding to them two *arkān* (sing. *rukn*, "corner"), 100 cubits (about 60 meters) high. These are the

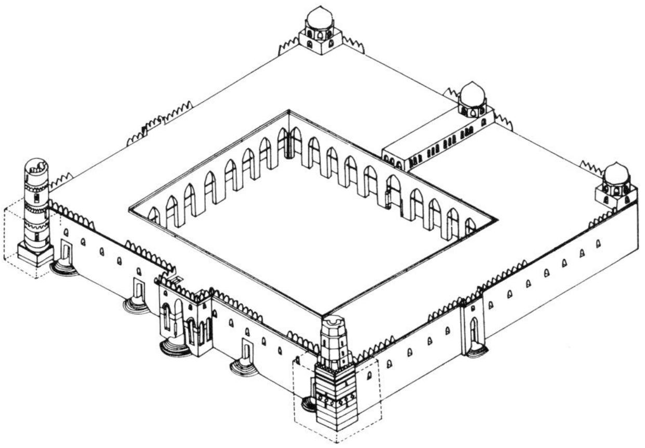

Fig. 15. Reconstruction of the mosque of al-Ḥākim (Creswell).

Pl. 47. The mosque of al-Ḥākim.

two minaret structures we see today; they resemble propylons of an ancient Egyptian temple, wrapping the original minarets.

Creswell misinterprets the 100 cubits indicated by Maqrīzī as referring to the circumference of the cubes. But the word *ṭūlan* means "in height" as opposed to *ʿarḍan* "in width," even if Maqrīzī's 100 cubits is an exaggeration. The cubes originally must have totally hidden the original minarets except perhaps the very tops.

Al-Ḥākim is presented by medieval historians as the most eccentric and whimsical man who ever ruled Egypt. He is popularly known for having forbidden the preparation of *mulūkhiyya*, the favorite meal of the Egyptians. In architectural matters, he was certainly not always pragmatic. He demolished a belvedere built by his father and ordered it to be plundered. He also more than once tore down and rebuilt the mosque of Rāshida at Fusṭāṭ. The possibility cannot be excluded that he disliked the minarets built by his father and therefore decided to hide them behind the cubes. The mosque was in use long before al-Ḥākim carried out his alterations. The fact that the original minarets were only hidden, not pulled down, may have been the architect's device to preserve these two masterpieces of stonework, which are unparalleled in Cairo's minaret architecture.

Pl. 48. Crenellation on the outer southwestern minaret of al-Ḥākim.

The Outer Minarets

The two square minarets of al-Ḥākim are not identical. The southern minaret has a lower band of foliated Kufic inscriptions carved in stone. At roof level, it is adorned with crenellations very similar to those at Ibn Ṭūlūn's mosque, the only surviving imitation of this remarkable and intricate type of cresting. It is possible that the mosque, so largely inspired by that of Ibn Ṭūlūn, had more of these crenellations, destroyed in the 1303 earthquake, which severely damaged the mosque. The upper story is adorned at its top with a band of interlaced geometrics in stucco similar to those that crown Fatimid prayer niches.

The northern cube's lower part was incorporated into the masonry of Badr al-Jamālī's wall adjoining the mosque. The upper story's eastern side has a band of Mamluk naskhī script of Quranic text which must be attributed to Amir Baybars al-Jashankīr, who restored the mosque after the earthquake. Both mabkhara style minaret tops are also attributed to Baybars al-Jashankīr, and do not quite fit with the rest of the structure. They are similar, but not identical, and are of light brick construction replacing the originals toppled by the earthquake.

The Original Minarets

Inside the cubes, the original minarets of al-Ḥākim's mosque were found well preserved in their wrappings when discovered in modern times. As the space between the inner and outer structures is rather small, the best way to admire these original minarets is to look at Creswell's photographs and drawings.

Pl. 49. Detail of the inner southwestern minaret of the mosque of al-Ḥākim (Creswell).

The two towers are differ from each other in shape and decoration. The southern shaft begins as a rectangle that turns octagonal above the roof level, while the northern tower is a tapering cylinder which Creswell compares to a stethoscope, standing on a rectangular base. The northern minaret is decorated with horizontal carved bands and with lozenges, and its windows are decorated with carved frames. Its decoration is similar to that of the minaret of Sfax in Tunisia.

The southern minaret's decoration resembles that of the entrance, with a large band of Kufic inscriptions carrying al-Ḥākim's name and the date. It also has a band of alternating rectangles, one protruding and the next receding, the first example of a pattern that appears later at the mosque of al-Ṣāliḥ Ṭalāʾiʿ and the mausoleum of al-Ṣāliḥ Najm al-Dīn. At the level of the roof there is a small room inside this minaret with carved niches, a carved ceiling, and carved entrance. It is possible that the roof of the mosque was used for some religious purpose. So was the roof of the mosque of ʿAmr, as it once had a small brick prayer niche. It was photographed by Creswell before it disappeared.

Decoration

As in al-Azhar, but unlike the mosque of Ibn Ṭūlūn, the windows of the al-Ḥākim mosque are set in such a way that they correspond to the position of the arcades, so that there is a window on the axis of each arch.

Only a few of the original window grills have survived. Among these is a window with a stucco grill made of elongated Kufic letters forming the word "Allāh," repeated symmetrically from right to left and left to right, as if reflected in a mirror. This style, which is North African but of later date, may have been done in a later Ayyubid or early Mamluk restoration.

The inscriptions of Ibn Ṭūlūn are on a wooden frieze running along the arcades, hardly visible beneath the ceiling, but al-Ḥākim's mosque, like al-Azhar, has a stucco band running along the arches of the mosque with ornate Kufic inscriptions of Quranic texts. In the transept stucco panels show a stylized tree motif of mixed Byzantine and Samarran style. The wooden beams between the arches are carved with Samarran patterns. The original decoration of the prayer niche has not survived.

The mosque of al-Ḥākim had a ziyāda added later. It was begun by the Caliph al-Ẓāhir (1021-36) and completed by Sultan al-Ṣāliḥ Najm al-Dīn at the end of the Ayyubid period (1240-49), and by Sultan al-Muʿizz Aybak (1250-57) at the beginning of the Mamluk period. This ziyāda, on the southern side of the mosque, has an entrance which Creswell assigns to the late eleventh century.

Later Additions

At the time of the restorations carried out by Amir Baybars al-Jashankir in 1303, teaching of the four rites of Islamic law was introduced at al-Ḥākim, along with a kuttāb for boys.

The mosque was restored in 1360 by Sultan Ḥasan, and in the fifteenth century a merchant added a minaret to the sanctuary which is no longer extant. In the nineteenth century it was restored by Shaykh ʿUmar Makram, who added a prayer niche inlaid with marble. The first Islamic Museum was housed in the mosque at the end of the nineteenth century.

Descriptions of the Caliph's Friday sermons at al-Ḥākim have survived. The Caliph arrived riding under a golden umbrella, wearing white silk and holding a scepter. Five thousand guards and an orchestra accompanied the procession. The Caliph entered the mosque from an entrance near the pulpit, his ministers carrying carpets and curtains to spread before him. In front of the miḥrāb were carpets, and curtains with Quranic inscriptions hung on both sides of the prayer niche. The Chief Qāḍī perfumed the pulpit with incense as the Caliph arrived accompanied by drums and horns and greeted his officials gathered around the maqṣūra in order of protocol. He rose to the pulpit and his vizier kissed his hands and feet while standing on a lower step, and closed the curtains, hiding the Caliph's face, at the top of the pulpit, which resembled a litter topped by a dome. The Chief Qāḍī stood at the foot of the pulpit while the Caliph read a short sermon prepared by the office of protocol. The Caliph recounted his ancestors descending from the Prophet's daughter Fāṭima, one by one. The vizier then opened the curtains and backed down the steps, and the Caliph stood on the silk rugs of the prayer niche to lead the prayer, his officials arranged behind him in proper order. Some stood round the maqṣūra with their backs to the qibla, as security guards. Trumpets and drums accompanied the procession back to the palace.

Bibliography

Bloom, Jonathan M. "The Mosque of al-Ḥākim in Cairo". *Muqarnas*, 1 (1983), pp. 15 ff.
Creswell. *M.A.E.*, I, pp. 68 ff.
Flury, S. *Ornamente*.
Maqrīzī. *Khiṭaṭ*, II, pp. 285 ff.

Pl. 50. The mashhad of al-Juyūshī.

THE MASHHAD OF AL-JUYŪSHĪ (1085)

On top of the Muqaṭṭam hill, overlooking the cemetery of the city, the city itself, and its environs, stands a small mosque. It is known as the mosque of al-Juyūshī, after the title of its sponsor, Amīr al-Juyūsh (Chief of the Armies), the Armenian vizier of the Fatimid Caliph al-Mustanṣir (1036-1094), Badr al-Jamālī. The mosque has a foundation inscription above its entrance identifying it as a mashhad, or shrine. In whose memory was it founded? Neither the inscriptions of the mashhad nor the historians tell us.

While Farīd Shāfiᶜī interprets the mashhad al-Juyūshī as a watchtower disguised as a mosque, Grabar sees it as a memorial to the victories of Badr al-Jamālī over the rebellions and disorders that had long plagued the Fatimid Empire. A small domed chamber projecting on the northern side of the sanctuary could have been intended as a mausoleum, but the mashhad is not the tomb of Badr al-Jamālī, who according to Maqrīzī was buried outside Bāb al-Naṣr. There is indeed a Fatimid mausoleum there, marked on the map of the *Description de l'Egypte* as the "chapel of Shaykh Badr," which would have been the popular version of al-Jamālī's name. A street in the same area is called Shaykh Najm, and Abū'l-Najm was one of the honorific titles of Badr al-Jamālī.

The building is the most complete mashhad that has survived from the Fatimid period, probably because it was not dedicated to a person of religious importance, and therefore was not the center of a cult, which would have subjected it to restorations and embellishments by the cult's followers. In the Ottoman period, the mosque of al-Juyūshī was used by dervishes as a monastery.

General Description

The small structure is built around a courtyard. One enters it from a plain door without a portal, underneath the minaret situated on the axis of the prayer hall. On the lateral sides and on both sides of the minaret are rooms. The facade of the courtyard is composed of a

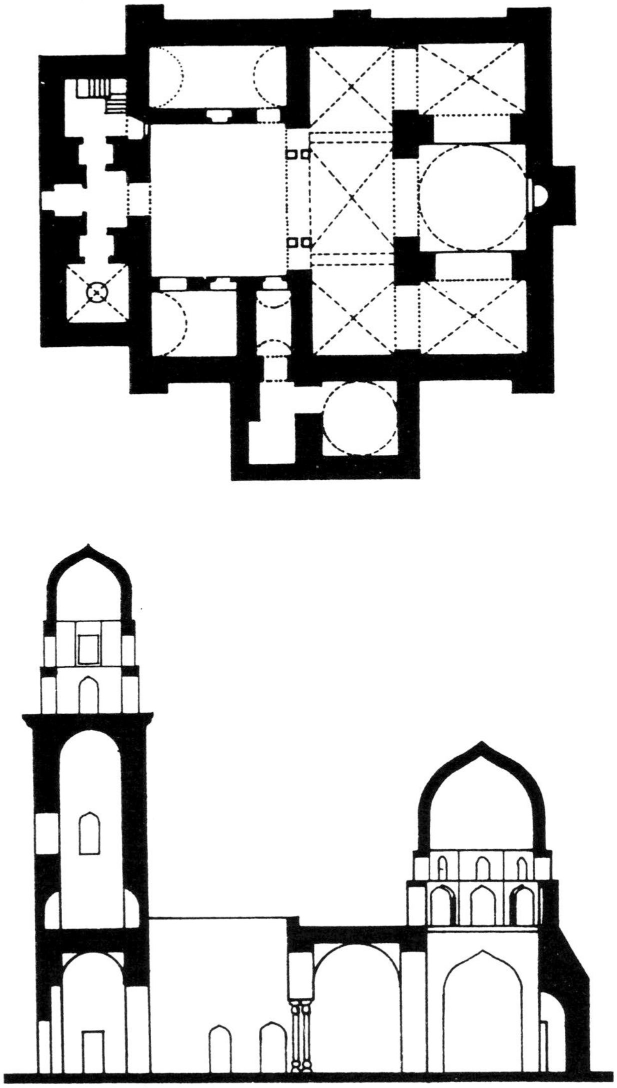

Fig. 16. The mashhad of al-Juyūshī, plan and elevation (Creswell).

large keel arch supported by two pairs of columns and flanked by two smaller arches, giving the facade the tripartite composition frequently found in Fatimid architecture. The prayer hall itself is roofed with cross-vaults except for the bay above the prayer niche, which is crowned by a dome on plain squinches. A small domed room on the northeastern side of the sanctuary, projecting outside, was thought by Creswell to be a later addition, but Farīd Shāfiᶜī's investigation of the masonry showed that it is part of the original construction.

The prayer niche of this mashhad is lavishly decorated with stucco carving in the spandrels of the niche arch. The conch itself has eighteenth-century Ottoman painting that covers other parts of the sanctuary as well. The decoration of the Juyūshī prayer niche was compared by Creswell to Persian stuccoes. The prayer niche at the mosque of Ibn Ṭūlūn added by al-Afḍal Shāhinshāh, son of Badr al-Jamālī, also resembles Persian prayer niches in composition and decoration.

The dome's interior is decorated with stucco carving and at the summit is a medallion with the names of Muḥammad and ᶜAlī; on the square part of the dome an inscription band carries a Quranic text.

The Minaret

The minaret is a rectangular shaft with a second, receding story topped by a dome similar to the one above the prayer niche. The shape of the minaret is reminiscent of the minaret at the great mosque of Qayrawān in Tunisia, erected in the ninth century. A very special feature of this minaret is the stalactite cornice on the upper edge of the rectangular shaft. It is the earliest surviving example of stalactites on a building in Egypt.

Stalactites or *muqarnas* are honeycomb-like carvings in stone or stucco in which a multitude of small embedded niches are repeated in an intricate geometric arrangement. Muqarnas are characteristic of Islamic architecture; they are found almost everywhere in the medieval Islamic world, and nowhere outside the realm of Islam. When and were muqarnas was invented has not yet been determined by art historians or archaeologists, though east Iran seems to be the most likely place.

Another interesting feature of the al-Juyūshī mosque is the presence of two small domed structures on the roof, like small kiosks, less than one meter in width, with prayer niches carved on their southeastern sides. These kiosks, and the presence of a minaret in such a remote place, prompted Farīd Shāfiᶜī to intepret the Juyūshī mosque as a watchtower disguised in the shape of a mosque; the small domed structures were for guards. Badr al-Jamālī was commander of the armies, and a successful one, who built the fortifications of Cairo whose surviving three gates and parts of the city walls are testimony to the power of their sponsors. A watchtower on the Muqattam hill, according to Shāfiᶜī, would have served to give early warning of any suspect movements from outside the country or from within, such as the rebellion from the south that al-Jamālī had to suppress. However, one may question why a watchtower should be disguised. The presence of the prayer niches in the domed structures on the roof suggests that these small rooms were intended for the meditation and seclusion the location of the mosque obviously provided. Grabar's interpretation, supported by Rāġib, is that it commemorates Badr al-Jamālī's military achievements. Rāġib sees the building as part of the group of shrines built by the Fatimids in the cemetery.

During the vizirate of al-Afḍal, son of Badr al-Jamālī, the observatory which used to be at another place on the Muqaṭṭam further to the south was transferred to the neighborhood of the Juyūshī mosque, because it was thought to be more appropriate for astronomic observations.

Bibliography

Creswell. *M.A.E.*, I, pp. 155 ff.
Grabar, Oleg. "The Earliest Islamic Commemorative Structures," *Ars Orientalis*, 6 (1966), pp. 27 ff.
Rāġib, Yūsuf. "Un Oratoire Fatimide au Sommet du Muqaṭṭam." *Studia Islamica* LXV (1987), p. 51 ff.
Shāfiᶜī, Farīd. "The Mashhad al-Juyushi: Archeological Notes and Studies." *Studies in Islamic Art and Architecture in Honor of Professor K. A. C. Creswell.* Cairo, 1965, pp. 237 ff.

THE WALLS AND GATES OF BADR AL-JAMĀLĪ (1087-92)

When it was founded by al-Muᶜizz and his general Jawhar al-Ṣiqillī, the city of al-Qāhira was surrounded by brick walls with several gates on each side of the rectangle. Later, Badr al-Jamālī, vizier of the Caliph al-Mustanṣir and Amīr al-Juyūsh (commander of the armies), replaced these walls with walls of stone. The new enclosure was only slightly larger than the first, and most of the new gates carried the names of those they replaced.

Substantial portions of these walls on the northern side of the city and the gates, Bāb al-Futūḥ and Bāb al-Naṣr, have survived. On the south side are remains of the walls and the gate called Bāb Zuwayla. None of the several other city gates has survived, but Maqrīzī's accounts show us that they were Badr al-Jamālī's outstanding achievements. The gates and walls of Badr al-Jamālī are considered masterpieces of stone architecture. Many pharaonic temples were destroyed to construct them, and we can see large blocks of stone bearing pharaonic inscriptions and motifs. Marble, cut stone, and wood were always expensive materials in Egypt; quarrying old monuments for building materials is as old as the Old Kingdom, and still goes on today.

Badr al-Jamālī's walls are built on three levels. The street level, including the vestibules or entrance halls of the gates, was originally higher than the street, and the gates were reached by ramps. Between the stone blocks, horizontally set columns were used to consolidate the masonry in the lower part of the walls. The second level consists of galleries connected with vaulted rooms and halls with arrow slits on the outside and larger openings on the city side. These run along the entirety of the walls except at the junctures of the gates. The gates are solid up to the level of two-thirds of their height, and thus block the passage from one section to the other, for the sake of better defense.

Towers are interspersed along the walls with halls and rooms. They protrude, with slits on three sides, to allow the guards a full view of the exterior. The third level forms a terrace, protected by the upper part of the walls and their round topped rectangular crenellations. During the Fatimid period there was an observatory on the terrace above Bāb al-Naṣr.

The outstanding features of Badr al-Jamālī's fortifications are the quality of the stone treatment, unparalleled in Cairo, and the variety of vaults used in the walls and gates: shallow domes, barrel vaults, cross vaults, and also a spiral vault in a staircase at Bāb al-Naṣr. Only round arches are used in the architecture of the whole wall complex.

Bāb al-Naṣr (Gate of Victory)

Bāb al-Naṣr is composed of two rectangular towers, which are solid stone up to the second level. The entrance vestibule is cross vaulted and a pair of shallow domes on spherical pendentives cover the upper level of the towers. At Bāb al-Futūḥ, the arrangement is the opposite, with the entrance vestibule having a shallow dome and the towers each with a cross vault with a carved medallion at the intersection. Above the entrance arch an inscription slab in Kufic carries the shahada with the Shīʿa reference to ʿAlī.

A very significant feature of decoration at Bāb al-Naṣr are the shields and swords that Creswell identifies as Byzantine in shape. Some point downward and some are circular; they are no doubt symbolic of the walls as being the shields of the city, protecting it against invaders. The name, "Gate of Victory," like Bāb al-Futūḥ, "Gate of Conquest," should also be understood as talismanic. Interestingly, these fine walls were never challenged by invaders, and by the late medieval period were so encroached upon by other buildings that travelers often reported that Cairo had no fortifications at all.

During the reign of the Caliph al-Āmir, his vizier, al-Maʾmūn al-Baṭāʾiḥī who built the al-Aqmar mosque, transferred the observatory from the Muqaṭṭam hill and established it at Bāb al-Naṣr. The transportation of the heavy metal observatory was an extremely difficult task that needed scaffolds and wheels, a large team of workers, and an architectural structure to support it. Al-Maʾmūn, however, fell in disgrace before the observatory could be used, and the angry Caliph ordered it to be dismounted because it had been named *al-raṣad al-maʾmūnī*, which attributed it to the vizier instead of the Caliph.

Bonaparte's troops (1798-1801) used Badr al-Jamālī's fortifications to protect themselves from the rebellious Cairo population. The Ḥusayniyya quarter, famous for its untamed character, was not easy to subdue. After a French officer of Polish origin, Schulkowsky, was killed by a Ḥusayniyya resident, the French troops bombarded Ḥusayniyya from the walls and entirely demolished the quarter. French officers' names can still be seen carved near the upper level of the gates. The French blocked up the crenellations at the top and enlarged the arrow slits for canon holes. Creswell also attributes the *machicoulis* at Bāb al-Naṣr, a protruding structure used to spill burning liquids on attackers, to the French. It was not until the twentieth century that the walls were cleared and made visible again.

Between Bāb al-Naṣr and Bāb al-Futūḥ, a handsome Kufic inscription of Quranic texts carved in stone runs along the wall. The northern wall of the mosque of al-Ḥākim is incorporated in this part of the fortifications.

Pl. 51. Bāb al-Naṣr.

Bāb al-Futūḥ (Gate of Conquest)

Bāb al-Futūḥ's towers are semicircular; its decoration is both different and more extensive than that at Bāb al-Naṣr. The towers each have a carved round arch and above each arch is a carved rectangle with three arrow slits, lighting the upper rooms. A carved molding running along the facade of the towers, two parallel lines with loops between them, is the earliest example of such decoration in Cairo but it later became typical in Mamluk architecture.

The inner flanks of the towers on both sides of the entrance have round arches with cushion voussoirs (s. Pls. 68 & 72), and the entrance itself is decorated with a row of carved lozenges filled with crosses and rosettes. Atop the entrance arch are carved brackets, two of them with a ram's head. The ram is the sign of the zodiac related to the planet Mars, or al-Qāhir, the sign in ascendancy when the city was officially founded. Following an ancient oriental tradition, particularly in Egypt, the rams' heads obviously had talismanic meaning. The only Islamic motifs on the walls apart from the Quranic inscriptions are the carved rectangles with an eight-pointed star found between the carved brackets.

The vestibule is covered with a shallow dome and the transition between the rectangular room and the spherical dome and the transition between the rectangular room and the spherical dome are formed by pendentives rather than squinches. Squinches are more typical of eastern—Persian and Mesopotamian—architecture; pendentives were used in Byzantine dome architecture.

Bāb Zuwayla

Bāb Zuwayla is on the southern wall of the city, and is dated 1091-92. The Fatimid armies included mem-

Pl. 52. Bāb al-Futūḥ.

Pl. 53. Bāb Zuwayla.

bers of the Zuwayla, a North African tribe. Like Bāb al-Futūḥ, it has a pair of semicircular towers, solid stone for two-thirds of their height. The inner flanks of the towers near the entrance are decorated with lobed arches (s. Pl. 4). These arches had been used earlier in North African architecture and must have been introduced by craftsmen accompanying the Fatimids' conquest of Egypt. This type of arch is often seen in later Fatimid and Mamluk architecture. Inside the vestibule to the right, coming from the south, there is a half-domed recess with two exquisitely carved arches at the corners. They have a trilobed curve and the upper part is treated like a shell. The left-hand side was modified when Sultan al-Muʾayyad built his mosque near the gate and had his minarets placed on the towers. Between the two towers and facing the southern outskirts of the city is a loggia that Creswell identifies as the place for the ceremonial orchestra announcing royal processions to the accompaniment of music. The presence of an orchestra at the city gates was an old oriental tradition.

Looking at Bāb Zuwayla from within the city, we see a gabled roof between the two towers that clearly show the Byzantine origins of the gate architecture. In fact, as noted above, most features of the walls and gates are entirely foreign to Islamic art, apart from some Quranic inscriptions. Maqrīzī comments that Bāb al-Futūḥ, Bāb al-Naṣr and Bāb Zuwayla, the only gates that did survive, were built by three Christian monks from Edessa (eastern Turkey) who came to Egypt fleeing from the Saljūq conquest of eastern Anatolia.

Unfortunately, nothing similar in that area, or in Armenia, the homeland of Badr al-Jamālī, where Creswell believes prototypes of the Cairo gates should be found, has survived. The only analogous architecture is in Hadrian's tower in the Coptic quarter of Old Cairo.

As the Byzantine Empire covered a large area of Anatolia and the eastern Mediterranean, including northern Mesopotamia where Edessa is situated, there is little reason to question Maqrīzī's account of the origins of Badr al-Jamālī's fortifications. Round arches with spherical pendentives, Byzantine-style shields, lozenges filled with rosettes, and cushion voussoirs all belong to Byzantine architectural tradition.

Bibliography

Creswell. *M.A.E.*, I, pp. 161 ff.
Hautecoeur and Wiet. *Mosquées*, pp. 232 ff.
Maqrīzī. *Khiṭaṭ*, I, pp. 127; II, pp. 380 ff.

THE AL-AQMAR MOSQUE (1125)

In the heart of the Fatimid city, north of the site once occupied by the great Fatimid palace, stands a small mosque known as al-Aqmar. This again is not the name of its founder, but an epithet that can be translated as "The Moonlit." It was founded by the vizier of the Caliph al-Āmir, Maʾmūn al-Baṭāʾiḥī.

The Exterior

This building is of major importance for Cairo's architecture, for several reasons. One is the lavish decoration of its facade. Though the mosque has its own unique features, it also inspired the decoration of many buildings of subsequent periods. Another reason can be seen in the architectural plan of the mosque. The facade is aligned with the street, while the interior of the mosque is properly oriented toward Mecca and has an otherwise regular layout. The adjustment is made in the facade wall, which is thicker on one end than the other. Small rooms are inserted in the thicker part of the wall. This device is typical of later urban

Pl. 54. The al-Aqmar mosque.

religious architecture and expresses the great care architects took to avoid disturbing the street alignment with mosque facades set askew.

The facade of al-Aqmar mosque is brick faced with stone and has a highly sophisticated decoration scheme. Originally, the portal must have been in the center of the facade. A later building hid the right side, but it is assumed that the right side was decorated like the left. The middle of the tripartite composition is dominated by a protruding portal decorated with a large keel arch niche carved with fluting radiating from a central medallion, like a sunrise or shell motif. The medallion has the name Muḥammad repeated in a circular interlacing pattern forming a circle, with the name ᶜAlī at the center.

On both sides of the main niche, smaller niches, also with fluted hoods, are surmounted with recesses crowned with stalactites, the earliest extant stalactites on a facade decoration.

To the left of the portal another shallow niche repeats the sunrise or shell motif with a medallion in the center. Above it, a circular clean cut in the stone reveals the brick wall, indicating that a medallion once existed there. Two lozenges, one with geometric carving and the other with a vase and plant motif, are surmounted on both sides of the missing medallion by two strange, carved panels. The one to the right represents a closed door, similar to the door of al-Ḥākim (in the Islamic Museum), and the one to the left shows a niche with a geometric grill resembling a window, from whose apex hangs a lamp.

The al-Aqmar mosque no doubt has a highly symbolic meaning within the Shīᶜa context. Caroline Williams has interpreted the two plants standing in the vase as symbolic of Ḥasan and Ḥusayn, sons of the Caliph ᶜAlī by his wife Fāṭima. This pattern is frequent in Coptic art, with many examples in the Coptic Museum in Old Cairo. The niches with the hanging lamp and closed door placed symmetrically on each side of the missing medallion might be more than mere decoration.

Two inscription bands run along the facade. The one at the top has a historic text referring to the Caliph al-Mustanṣir in whose reign the mosque was built, and the lower band underneath the hooded portal niche has a Quranic text. Another special feature of this facade is a chamfered corner carved with the names of Muḥammad and ᶜAlī.

The original minaret did not survive. Today we see on the left door jamb of the portal the circular base of the minaret built in the late fourteenth century by Amir Yalbughā al-Sālimī. It is a brick construction covered with stucco chevron carving and a molding with openwork bosses and a stalactite cornice. The structure above the balcony is of more recent date.

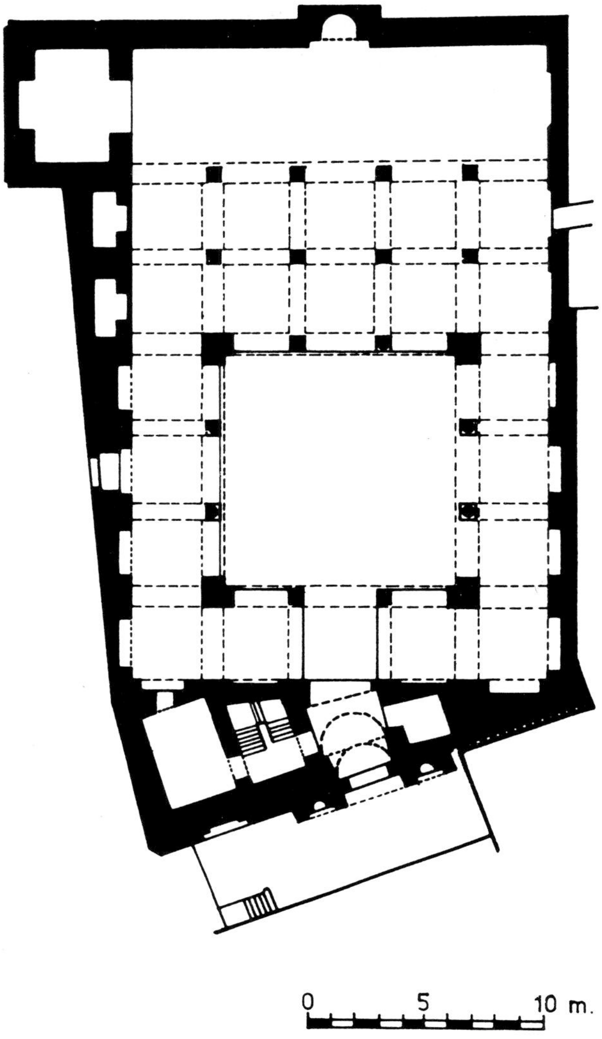

Fig. 17. The al-Aqmar mosque (Creswell).

The Interior

The interior of the mosque has not retained much of its original form. The small sanctuary has three aisles and faces the courtyard with only a triple arcade; the three other arcades have only one aisle each.

A special feature of the interior architecture is that each bay's ceiling is covered by a shallow brick dome, instead of being flat, except for the aisle parallel to the qibla wall, which is wider than the rest and is covered with a flat wooden ceiling. As the mosque was in ruins when the Mamluk Amir Yalbughā al-Sālimī restored it in 1397, Creswell assumes that he also restored the ceiling, which originally could have been flat. This type of roofing is not known from the Fatimid period, but is used in the early fifteenth century at the mosque of Faraj Ibn Barqūq.

Except for some wood carving on the beams and doors and a stucco inscription band along some of the arches, nothing of the original interior decoration remains.

The mosque was again restored in the nineteenth century during the reign of Muḥammad ᶜAlī by Amir Sulaymān Aghā al-Silāḥdār, who also built the mosque across the street from al-Aqmar.

The Shops

The mosque of al-Aqmar was not at street level, as it is today, but much higher than the street level of the time, standing above a row of shops. The rising level has buried the shops; at the mosque of al-Ṣāliḥ Ṭalāʾiᶜ, the shops have been excavated.

The shops had an important functional purpose. The income of their rents were waqf, endowments for the benefit of a pious institution to maintain the institution and pay its personnel long after the founder's death. The founding of a religious institution was always accompanied by an endowment of land or commercial structures in the city such as apartment buildings, public baths (*ḥammām*), shops, or factories. The founder himself also thereby secured tax-free income from the rents collected.

Bibliography

ᶜAbd al-Wahhāb. *Masājid*, pp. 69 ff.
Creswell. *M.A.E.*, I, pp. 241 ff.
Maqrīzī. *Khiṭāṭ*, II, p. 290.
Williams, Caroline. "The Cult of ᶜAlid Saints in the Fatimid Monuments of Cairo. Part I: The Mosque of al-Aqmar." *Muqarnas*, I (1983), pp. 37 ff.

THE MASHHAD OF SAYYIDA RUQAYYA (1133)

The shrine, or mashhad, of al-Juyūshī most likely commemorates a secular person or idea, but the mashhad of Sayyida Ruqayya built in the Fusṭāṭ cemetery is a religious building. Sayyida Ruqayya, a descendent of the Caliph ᶜAlī, son-in-law of the Prophet, never came to Egypt, so this shrine is not a mausoleum, but what is called a *mashhad ruʾya*, a visual memorial.

Pl. 55. The dome of the mashhad of Sayyida Ruqayya.

The architecture of the shrine recalls that of al-Juyūshī, except that this building appears truncated: the facade through which we enter today must originally have overlooked a courtyard or enclosure, but is now open to the cemetery.

A dome above the prayer niche forms the center of a hall wider than it is deep, and the side rooms are not vaulted as they are at al-Juyūshī, but have a flat wooden ceiling. The two side rooms flanking the domed area each have a prayer niche; the third, the central one, is the main prayer niche. Two more prayer niches are carved on either side of the entrance, outside the sanctuary. The dome is larger than any previous dome and is also fluted, inside and out, with the profile of a curved keel arch.

Instead of a plain squinch as in previous domes, the octagonal transitional zone of this dome is more complex. It is higher, and has four two-tiered squinches at the corners subdivided into keel-arch niches, thus forming large stalactites. The windows set between the squinches repeat the outline of the squinches themselves, a device used earlier in plain domes where the squinch arch alternates with a similar blind arch.

Above the transitional zone is an octagonal drum, the space just underneath the spherical part of the dome. This drum is unique in Fatimid architecture. Each side of the octagon is pierced by a pair of lobed

Pl. 56. The prayer niche at the mashhad of Sayyida Ruqayya (drawing, "The Mosques of Egypt").

windows with stucco geometric grills, a feature occurring in Cairo architecture only at the mosque of Sinān Pasha (1571). Similar lobed arches are found at Bāb Zuwayla, where they are carved in stone on each side of the entrance, and inside the dome added at al-Azhar by the Caliph al-Ḥāfiz, where they also appear as decorations carved in stucco. This type of window is found in earlier North African architecture.

The glory of Sayyida Ruqayya's shrine, as Creswell calls it, is its main prayer niche, one of the great masterpieces of stucco in Egypt, carved in a manner totally different from that of the mosque of al-Juyūshī. Here, the conch is filled with flutes radiating from a central medallion in the lower part of the conch like a sunrise motif, whose origin is the shell of classical niches. The flutes, or ribs of the niche, form along the arch's edges a large stalactite frame. This was no doubt inspired by the niches decorating the facade of the al-Aqmar mosque. Fluted niches can be seen at the ninth-century outer wall at the mosque of ʿAmr and at the mosque of Ibn Ṭūlūn. Fluted domes were built at the mosque of Qayrawān in the ninth century. The two secondary prayer niches are minor in size and decoration, but follow the same pattern. The fluted dome seems to have been inspired by the use of fluted niches, which themselves are half domes. An interesting feature is the complicated interlaced band of geometrical decoration that crowns the whole decorative field of the miḥrāb, a feature also found on the southern minaret of the mosque of al-Ḥākim, and in many Fatimid prayer niches. A concave band of Kufic inscription curves forward to allow easier reading of the inscription set above the prayer niche. This feature, also of North African origin, is used in the inscription band of the mosque of al-Ḥākim and the prayer niche of the mashhad of al-Juyūshī.

In the Islamic Museum is a wooden portable prayer niche that was found at the shrine of Sayyida Ruqayya. Its style is Fatimid, with geometric work, and it shows traces of green paint. It is also decorated on the back, suggesting that it was to be freestanding, perhaps in a courtyard for special congregational occasions.

Bibliography

Creswell. *M.A.E.*, I, pp. 247 ff.

MAUSOLEUM OF YAḤYĀ AL-SHABĪH
(c. 1150)

In the southern part of the cemetery, not far from the dome of Imām Shāfiʿī, is the mausoleum of Yaḥyā al-Shabīh. At first glance, its dome, which dominates the whole structure, looks much like that of Sayyida Ruqayya. It is also ribbed and has a similar profile, but it lacks the octagonal drum with lobed windows of Sayyida Ruqayya's dome. The plan of the building is also different. The dome stands above a chamber that is open on four sides and thus connected to a corridor or ambulatory surrounding it on three sides. On the southeast side of this ambulatory are three prayer niches, the central and larger one of which is on the axis of the domed chamber and crowned by a small plain dome.

The prayer niches are decorated in the style of Sayyida Ruqayya, but are plainer and inferior in quality. According to Creswell's reconstruction of this building, an adjacent space on the northeastern side could have included a courtyard with rooms on the qibla side. This type of plan was applied in other shrines, such as those of Qāsim Abū Ṭayyib and Umm Kulthūm.

The domed chamber of Yaḥyā al-Shabīh includes several wooden cenotaphs (*tābūt*) with plain Kufic inscriptions that belong to tombs of earlier date, above which this mausoleum was erected. Yahya, a descendant of the Prophet, was called al-Shabīh, "The Similar One," on account of his supposed resemblance to the Prophet.

Bibliography

Creswell. *M.A.E.*, I, pp. 264 ff.

Ragib, Y. "Les sanctuaires des Gens de la Famille dans la Cité des Morts au Caire." *Rivista Degli Studi Orientali*. Vol. LI, Fasc. I-IV (1977), pp. 47 ff.

THE MOSQUE OF VIZIER AL-ṢĀLIḤ ṬALĀʾIʿ (1160)

Like al-Aqmar, the mosque of al-Ṣāliḥ Ṭalāʾiʿ was built by a vizier. Originally it was intended as a shrine for the head of al-Ḥusayn brought from Askalon to Cairo by al-Ṣāliḥ. The Caliph, however, decided that such a sacred relic should not be placed anywhere but in the Caliph's palace itself. The relic is still on the same site, today in the mosque of Sayyidnā al-Ḥusayn; the palace itself disappeared long ago.

The mosque of al-Ṣāliḥ was built outside Bāb Zuwayla, facing it from the south. When it was built it was not a Friday mosque. It became so only in 1252, when the mosque was first renovated.

Again like al-Aqmar, the mosque of al-Ṣāliḥ Ṭalāʾiʿ was built above a row of shops. The shops have been excavated and are now more than two meters beneath the street level. They are again being used. A few steps lead to the mosque itself.

The Exterior

The mosque has several noteworthy features. Like al-Azhar, it was originally built with only three arcades around the courtyard. Instead of a fourth arcade on the northwest, the mosque had an arcade outside, forming part of the facade, a feature unique in Cairo mosques. The arcade, used here as a portico, is composed of four columns carrying five keel arches flanked on each corner by a small room. The ceiling of this arcade has its original decoration and is the only Fatimid ceiling still extant.

The mosque was damaged by the 1303 earthquake, and restored in the late fifteenth century. When it was restored at the beginning of this century by the Committee for the Preservation of Islamic Monuments, a northwest arcade was added inside the mosque, a misreading of the original plan. The mosque, which at that time was very dilapidated, had to be almost totally rebuilt. Only the original qibla wall remained, but old stones with original decorations were reused when possible. The original minaret must have been at the main entrance. The mosque also has two other side entrances.

A carved molding runs along the arches of the stone facades on all four sides of the mosque, as well as the similar arches of the recesses, and the four walls were originally free standing. Each of the four arched recesses had a large iron grilled window, now walled up, placed near the floor level of the mosque. Cairo architects adopted this facade treatment in nearly all later mosques.

As in Badr al-Jamālī's city walls, horizontally placed columns have been used to strengthen the masonry. Remains of a stepped and stucco-carved crenellation can still be seen on the northern facade. The northwest corner of the building is chamfered, a device already used at al-Aqmar, though here the treatment is different.

Other facade decorations include a band with alternating rectangles, one receding, one protruding, as on the southern minaret of al-Ḥākim. There are two more bands with inscriptions, the upper one at the top of the facade.

The northern facade is prolonged beyond the qibla wall, suggesting that another structure was once enclosed here, perhaps the shrine for al-Ḥusayn.

The magnificent carved and lathed wooden screen, a modern copy of an older one, was not originally outside the mosque, but inside, to screen the prayer hall from the courtyard, as in many medieval mosques.

The Interior

While the outer walls are of stone, the inner arcades are of brick, also with keel arches. These were originally framed with a carved band bearing stucco Kufic Quranic inscriptions. The Kufic script here is of the ornate, late Fatimid type, with curved letters on a background decorated with scrolls representing stylized stalks with floral motifs.

The prayer niche, not original, was redecorated with painted wood in the Mamluk period. Some of the

Pl. 57. The mosque of al-Ṣāliḥ Ṭalā᾽iᶜ.

original window grills have survived. A very interesting one is that near the prayer niche showing the earliest extant use of naskhī script in architectural decoration in Cairo. From then on, both Kufic and naskhi scripts were used, but naskhi predominated in the Mamluk period. Next to the prayer niche is a rectangular opening framed with stucco decoration. This opening is not a window, but a *malqaf* or windcatcher connected to a shaft in the qibla wall that goes to the roof. It was once topped by an enclosure with a sloping lid that opened to the north to catch fresh breezes.

Decoration

In addition to the stucco band framing the arches and the Corinthian capitals, which were once gilded, the mosque is decorated with rosettes carved on the arcaded walls. They are fluted, and the rosette's center is below the true geometric center, compensating for distortion when seen from below, a device used in classical art. Rectangular openings above the arches are decorated with beautifully carved stucco grills, and the tie beams between the arches are carved in a repetitive floral pattern.

The door of the mosque, a replica, is wooden, carved on the inner side and covered on the outside with sheet bronze that has an applied geometric star pattern. The original door is at the Islamic Museum.

The wooden pulpit in the mosque of al-Ṣāliḥ Ṭalā᾽iᶜ is the second earliest Mamluk pulpit in Cairo, dated 1299 and commissioned by Amir Baktīmūr al-Juqandār. The oldest is that commissioned by Sultan Lājīn at the mosque of Ibn Ṭūlūn.

Bibliography

ᶜAbd al-Wahhāb. *Masājid*, pp. 97 ff.
Creswell. *M.A.E.*, I, pp. 283 ff.
Maqrīzī. *Khiṭaṭ*, II, p. 293.

CHAPTER SIX

ARCHITECTURE OF THE AYYUBID PERIOD

THE CITADEL (1183-84)

Ṣalāḥ al-Dīn (1171-93), an Orthodox Sunni Muslim from Syria sent to rescue the Fatimids from the Crusaders, contributed to the development of Cairo on several levels. After repulsing the Crusaders and seizing power from the Fatimid ruler, he expanded the capital city to include all elements of the native and ruling population (al-Fusṭāṭ and al-Qāhira), and dealt also with subversive Shīᶜa movements. Ṣalāḥ al-Dīn is a hero in the Muslim world because of his victories against the Crusaders and the liberation of Jerusalem.

In Egypt, he unified the two capitals into one large complex that was to be encompassed by an enormous set of walls, thus abolishing the exclusive nature of Fatimid al-Qāhira. To meet the Crusader threat, he added to the city's fortifications, founding the Citadel on the Muqaṭṭam hill to serve both as a fortress and residence of rulers and their garrisons.

The foundation of the Citadel, like all major architectural works, is associated with a popular story. Ṣalāḥ al-Dīn, having ordered that several pieces of meat be hung in various places in the Egyptian capital, found that the meat hung on the Muqaṭṭam hill remained fresh much longer than the rest, and this prompted him to choose this site as having the healthiest air. This is, of course, an anecdote, and later interpretation. The Citadel was built on top of a hill because Ṣalāḥ al-Dīn came via Syria, and it was traditional in Syria at the time to build hill fortifications. The Muqaṭṭam hill was also Cairo's only natural site for the fortifications required in medieval warfare.

Ṣalāḥ al-Dīn assigned his vizier Badr al-Dīn Qarāqūsh to begin the works in 1183-84, according to an inscription slab over the main entrance, Bāb al-Mudarraj, but he did not live long enough to occupy the residence. A successor, al-Malik al-Kāmil, was the first to use the Citadel as a royal residence, in 1207-8, and from then until the nineteenth century, the Citadel was the residence of the rulers of Egypt.

The main function of the Citadel was of course to connect and fortify the city's walls, which Ṣalāḥ al-Dīn had ordered built to encompass all parts of the capital. Situated between al-Qāhira and al-Fusṭāṭ, the Citadel formed a sort of joint between the northern and southern part of the walls. The Citadel was never besieged. It did, however, fulfill its residential role by housing the royal palace and its dependencies, just as the Fatimid's walled al-Qāhira was exclusively the residence of the Caliph and his entourage.

The Citadel of Cairo is a gigantic complex of walls and towers to which all periods of Cairo's history have contributed. Its present configuration is in two parts, the earlier northern enclosure, and the southern part constructed primarily by the Mamluks.

The Northern Enclosure

The northern part, an independent enclosure, was begun by Ṣalāḥ al-Dīn and completed by his Ayyubid successors, though later periods of history have also left their traces on its walls. This enclosure is an irregular polygon, whose walls and towers measure some 1,700 meters. Some towers are circular, built of dressed stone; others are rectangular and built of embossed stone. The differences of shape and type of stone cutting are Creswell's argument for attributing the round towers to Salah al-Din and the rectangular ones to his successor, al-Malik al-ᶜĀdil. To build the Citadel, several small pyramids at Giza were demolished, and Crusader prisoners put to work on the construction.

Like the walls of Badr al-Jamālī, the walls and towers are built on three levels. The lower parts are buried today, and excavations are currently underway to expose them. Each tower is composed of several impressive halls large enough for several hundred soldiers. The function of each rectangular tower was to allow for the separate defense of each section of the fortress.

Originally, the northern enclosure had two main entrances. The one facing the city, Bāb al-Mudarraj, is today incorporated in the walls and gates of Muḥammad ᶜAlī and is accessible only from within the enclosure, though the original ramp, cut in rock, still

Pl. 58a. The Citadel of Cairo, Ayyubid walls.

Pl. 58b. The Citadel of Cairo, Ayyubid walls.

leads up to the gate. The gate has its original foundation inscription naming Ṣalāḥ al-Dīn and his vizier Qarāqūsh. The vestibule of this gate has a painted blazon added later by Sultan al-Nāṣir Muḥammad which is the earliest surviving painted blazon. Other late Mamluk inscriptions can also be seen there, commemorating later restoration works. The second gate, Bāb al-Jabal, also called Bāb al-Qarāfa because it overlooks the cemetery, is located on the same axis as Bāb al-Mudarraj, on the southeast side of the enclosure.

The architects of the Citadel produced some innovations. Unlike the earlier Fatimid walls of Badr al-Jamālī, the Citadel had bent entrances for better defense, and the arrow slits reached to the floor, giving archers more flexibility. There are also machicoulis, projecting structures in the walls above the entrance from which hot liquids could be poured on invaders. Military improvements in the architecture were the result of long campaigns against the Crusaders.

The Double Headed Eagle

On top of one of the walls of the Citadel facing west barely visible from below is an eagle carved in stone, which is popularly attributed to Ṣalāḥ al-Dīn. This now headless bird, reported by travelers to have once had a double head, must originally have been located elsewhere, for its present location is atop a wall that was rebuilt several times. Casanova, the primary historian of the Citadel, notes that al-Malik al-Kāmil had a coin struck in his name with a double-headed eagle on one side, which might have been the sultan's emblem, though Creswell believed, without indicating his reasons, that the eagle was of later date. The double-headed eagle is a common motif in Islamic art.

Al-Malik al-Kāmil was the first to dwell in the Citadel, and its first residential structures are therefore attributed to him, but very little is known of them and nothing has survived. He is reported to have built the royal stables, which of course were an important and integral part of the Citadel complex, due to the importance of cavalry in both Ayyubid and Mamluk armies. He also most likely introduced the homing pigeon post, in the tower called Burj al-Maṭār.

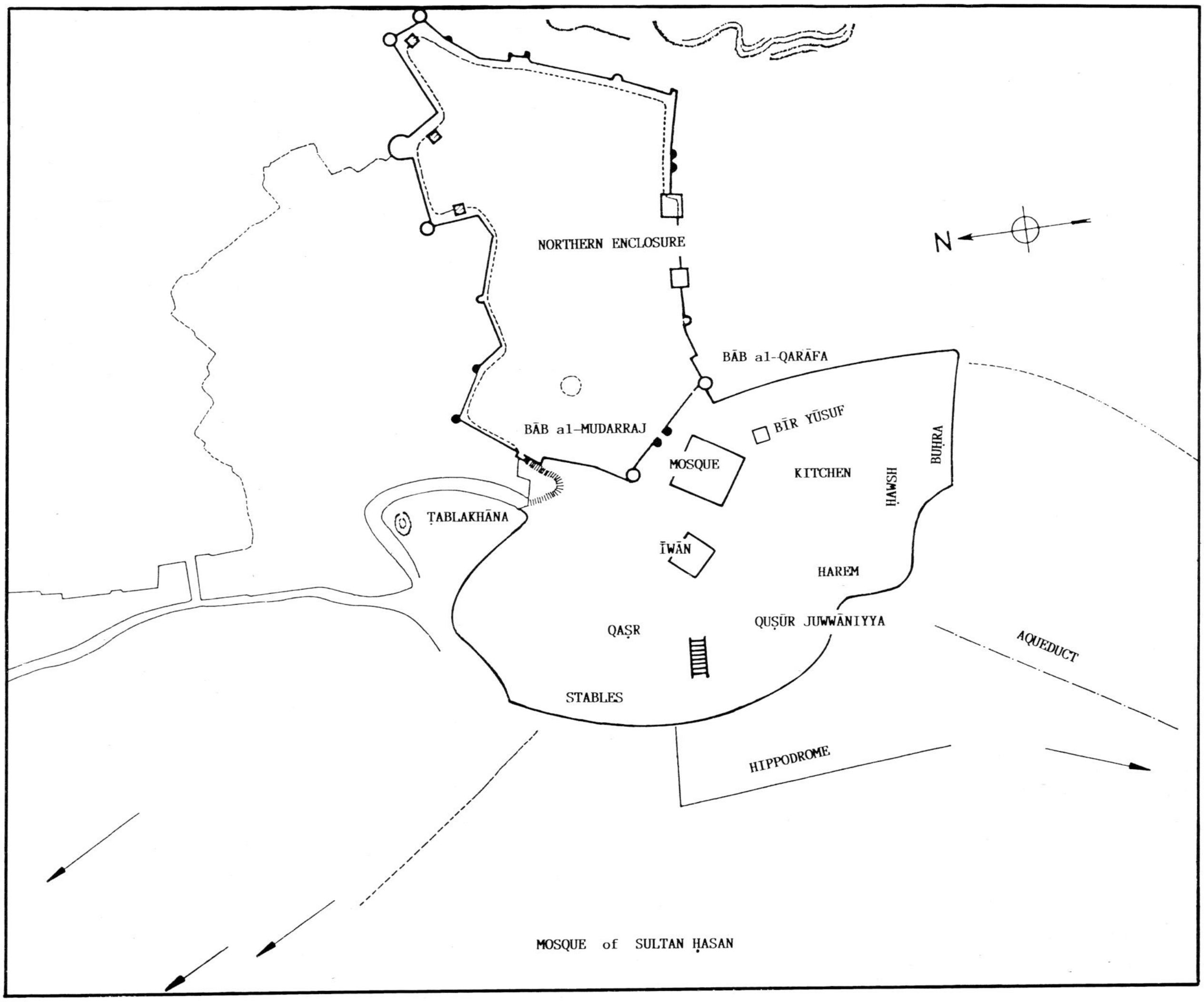

Fig. 18. The Citadel in the Mamluk period (after Casanova).

Water Supply

Elevated and remote from the Nile, the Citadel required special arrangements for the provision of water. Ṣalāḥ al-Dīn built an aqueduct to raise water with the help of waterwheels from the Nile to the hill. The one we see today was built later and further north by Sultan al-Nāṣir Muḥammad and restored by Sultan al-Ghūrī. The large hexagonal building on the Nile corniche at Fum al-Khalīj once had on its top the waterwheels operated by oxen. The water went by slightly sloping channels to the next set of waterwheels and finally to the numerous cisterns of the Citadel, a total waterlift of more than one hundred meters. Ṣalāḥ al-Dīn also carved the famous ninety-meter deep well called Biʾr Yūsuf (his full name was Ṣalāḥ al-Dīn Yūsuf), an impressive achievement that always has astonished visitors. It was built in two levels, with waterwheels and a cistern midway and more waterwheels at the top. Baby oxen were taken down to work the waterwheels, remaining there until they died. The Citadel had a number of such wells, but this surviving one is most famous. There are remains of two other waterwheel complexes attached to the Citadel, one on the northeast side and the other on the southeast side with the name of al-Nāṣir Muḥammad carved on it.

The Southern Enclosure

The northern enclosure, built into solid rock, was the military section of the Citadel, where troops were garrisoned. The southern enclosure was partly erected upon landfills to give the royal inhabitants of the palace complex a view over the whole capital and beyond to the surrounding villages. Its architecture is usually described as extroverted, luxurious buildings overlooking the city, in contrast to the introverted nature of the military fortress.

The two enclosures were connected by a gate called Bāb al-Qulla, or Gate of the Tower, built by Sultan al-Ẓāhir Baybars. The site of this gate is the same as that where Muḥammad ʿAlī rebuilt it in the nineteenth century. Coming from the northern enclosure through this gate, we face the mosque of Sultan al-Nāṣir Muḥammad, probably erected on the site of an older mosque. One can assume that the Citadel had a mosque dating to its earliest foundations. The mosque stands on an esplanade, to the south of which is now the mosque of Muḥammad ʿAlī, itself erected on the site of the former Great Hall, or al-Iwān al-Kabīr.

Pl. 59. Sculptures representing lions on a tower of Sultan al-Ẓāhir Baybars at the Citadel.

The Mamluk palaces within the Citadel did not survive, but we know they were located on the south and west sides, overlooking the horse market. This, along with the royal hippodrome for equestrian sports, parades and ceremonies such as prayers on feast days performed by the Sultan and his court, were all strategically located beneath the Citadel from its earliest days. No spoils from ancient pyramids were used in the southern buildings; stone was cut on the site and the depression that resulted had to be filled in with earth and was then turned into a green park, al-Ḥawsh, for royal entertainments. The Mamluk sultans contributed regularly to the buildings, embellishing and refining the palatial complex of the Citadel.

Shajarat al-Durr (1250)

Shajarat al-Durr, the widow of the last Ayyubid sultan, al-Ṣāliḥ Najm al-Dīn Ayyūb, was the first sultan of the Bahri Mamluk dynasty. Her first husband, al-Ṣāliḥ, did not stay long at the Citadel, but constructed a new citadel for himself and his troops on the Nile island of Rawḍa. The Nile was popularly called *al-baḥr*; hence the name Bahri Mamluks. He did, however, add a hall at the Citadel which before it burned in 1285 was used as the sultan's residence. Shajarat al-Durr built a hall at the Citadel called the "Hall of the Columns," in the residential compound near the privat apartments. It was the harem's main hall and remained for several centuries.

The sultana, a quite remarkable if briefly reigning queen, introduced a new musical ceremony at the Citadel: flute players and drummers were conducted by an amir in ceremonial garb, holding a golden rod and performing acrobatic movements by torchlight to the rhythm of the music. Shajarat al-Durr was fond of ceremonies. The historic funerary procession carrying al-Ṣāliḥ's body from his residence at Rawḍa to the mausoleum she built for him has been carefully recorded by historians.

Sultan al-Ẓāhir Baybars (1260-77)

Al-Ẓāhir Baybars reconstructed some of the walls of the Citadel and added new towers, among others the one at Bāb al-Qulla. He also erected a new palace overlooking the horse market, further evidence of the importance of the cavalry in Mamluk armies. A Palace of Justice, Dār al-ᶜAdl, was built outside the Citadel on its northwest side, where he held audience and performed his judicial functions. A tower with carved lions, Baybars' emblem, has recently been excavated at the Citadel.

Sultan Qalāwūn (1279-90)

Qalāwūn restored the Great Hall (al-Īwān al-Kabīr), whose founder is not identified, though it might have been al-Malik al-Ṣāliḥ, in the southern enclosure. He also enlarged its functions to include those of al-Ẓāhir's Palace of Justice outside the walls, which was then abandoned. He is credited with the building of a large dome standing on columns of marble with gilded capitals. On the walls was a figurative map of the Mamluk empire with the names of its cities, forts, rivers, seas, and mountains. A dome at Bāb al-Qulla replaced the tower of al-Ẓāhir Baybars between the two enclosures. Qalāwūn also added various palaces and living quarters for his officers and mamluks.

Al-Ashraf Khalīl (1299-93)

Al-Ashraf, son of Qalāwūn, built an elevated pavilion with a view of the city, Gīza and the pyramids. Curiously, this pavilion had wall paintings of various amirs and their private guards, and a richly decorated dome on columns.

Al-Nāṣir Muḥammad (1293-1294; 1298-1308; 1309-1341)

Al-Nāṣir Muḥammad was the most prolific builder (also a great rebuilder) in Cairo's history, and his contributions to the residential architecture of the Citadel were by far the most important. He was not only fond of architectural projects, but ruled long enough to realize many of his ambitions, practically rebuilding the entire southern enclosure.

He built a new royal mosque near the Iwān al-Kabīr, the ceremonial center of the residential complex. Al-Nāṣir often destroyed buildings and built his own on their sites, thus glorifying his own name and eclipsing those of his predecessors. His new palace survived until the beginning of the nineteenth century and was depicted by the French Expedition in the *Description de l'Egypte*. Although by that time abandoned and decayed, its remains still were evidence of its unparalleled grandeur. For the construction of the palace huge pharaonic granite columns were brought from Upper Egypt to support the dome—over forty red granite columns, according to the French consul in 1696. His mosque at the Citadel has such columns. A scholar of the *Description* found al-Nāṣir's palace more impressive than both the mosques of Ibn Ṭūlūn and Sultan Ḥasan.

An explanade, where the senior amirs sat before going on duty, separated the Great Hall from the other great palace nearby on the south, the Qaṣr al-Ablaq, named for its striped light-and-dark stone courses.

This palace was less ceremonial, and composed of two halls facing each other, the qāᶜa plan that was used

Pl. 60. The Great Īwān of Sultan al-Nāṣir at the Citadel (Robert Hay).

in Mamluk and Ottoman residential palaces of Cairo. Between a huge dome covered with green tiles and supported by a number of columns, the larger northern īwān was oriented to the northwest breezes, facing the smaller southern īwān. Both had large windows with iron grills, overlooking the cemetery to the south and the whole city and its environs to the west and north. This palace has been recently excavated, together with some of the famous granite columns.

Al-Qaṣr al-Ablaq communicated with three other palaces, two built higher than the rest and reached by stairs. The palaces all had facades of striped yellow and black stone, and interior communications between the private apartments of the sultan and the harem. Inside, the palaces had marble dadoes of various colors while the floor was paved with imported white marble. Glass mosaics with mother of pearl and painting decorated the upper walls, as well as large gilded inscriptions. Some remains of these can be seen in the excavated parts. The gilded iron window grills were surmounted by other windows decorated with colored Cypriot glass. Foreign travelers mentioned wall paintings representing houses and trees, and private apartments roofed by domes. Today, a close look at the remains of lavish decoration at Sultan Qalāwūn's mausoleum gives us a taste of this vanished architectural fantasy.

All that has survived of the Mamluk palaces are a series of vast vaulted halls built on piers, in proportions recalling the pharaohs. The enormous projecting corbels facing the Citadel's square make us wonder what great structures they supported.

The park in the private part of the complex called al-Ḥawsh was green with grass and trees. Horses, sheep, cattle, ducks and chickens were kept for the use the harem. Each of the official wives of the sultan had her own apartment. A staircase led from the private apartments to the stables, and the sultan also had a passage from al-Qaṣr al-Ablaq, where he held audiences twice a week, to the Great Īwān.

Al-Nāṣir Muḥammad died before the completion of the palace called Duhaysha overlooking the park. It was completed by his son, al-Ṣāliḥ Ismāᶜīl.

Sultan Ḥasan (1347-51; 1354-61)

Sultan Ḥasan, son of al-Nāṣir Muḥammad, built the gigantic mosque facing the Citadel, to flatter royal eyes with its imposing dome and double minarets. He also built a domed palace called Bayṣariyya, attached to the private apartments. Its walls were gilded and its height was eighty-eight cubits, or over fifty meters. It had a tower with a private apartment for the sultan, decorated with ivory and ebony, and its windows opened onto a garden.

As nothing of these residential structures has survived, an important, if not major, part of the Mamluks' architectural achievements is difficult for us to imagine. Two interesting points come from these accounts: paintings and portraits decorated the walls, and private apartments had domes. Nothing similar in Cairo architecture has survived.

During the Mamluk period, the northern enclosure continued its important function, as the officers' and armies' quarters, and important officials and amirs had their residences in the Citadel. A prison set up in a cave was later abandoned because of the bad smells, and because al-Nāṣir Muḥammad preferred to keep the prisoners in the towers.

Beneath the Citadel, on the site of Baybars' palace of Justice, al-Nāṣir established the *ṭablakhāna*, a place where the royal ceremonial orchestra performed at intervals throughout the day.

The Citadel is often described as a city in itself, lodging tens of thousands of people, with quarters and streets. It even had a Tatar quarter with a church until 1321. Several mosques and madrasas were located in the northern and southern enclosures, and there was also a great library. It burned in 1296. Remains of the original mint where coins were struck are still visible in the southern enclosure.

Sultan Qāytbāy (1468-96)

Sultan Qāytbāy, was as fond of construction as al-Nāṣir Muḥammad. He enjoyed a fairly long reign, during which he restored the Great Palace and other structures at the Ḥawsh. Van Ghistele, visitor to the court of Sultan Qāytbāy in 1482/3, describes what he found at the Citadel:

> Arriving at the palace, they were led through nine or ten galleries and halls, until they reached a lovely summer residence, built with beautifully cut stone and decorated with paintings in gold and blue and other rich colors. The residence looked from two sides through handsome grilled and gilded windows upon courtyards, gardens and orchards with all kinds of plants and fragrant fruit trees. There were many fountains, not natural ones, but artificial ones to water all the gardens. Finally, in the residence, they found the most sumptuous thing that can be imagined. The walls, like the floors, were covered with polished stones such as black, white and pink marble,

> serpentine, porphyry, and other precious stones. The walls and hallways were decorated with moldings, knots, geometric shapes, and arabesques, as well as with mosaics and other things difficult to explain. In the middle of the residence is a rectangular basin knee-deep and three or four steps wide with fresh water and small fishes. The sultan can cool his hands and feet there whenever he likes! The floors of this place were covered with rich carpets and cushions, some covered with linen, others with silks and velvets, and others with golden draperies, or Indian leather of nice color and good smell. The sultan sat in this place on a cushion, his legs folded like a tailor, playing chess with one of his courtiers.

Another visitor, von Harff, described Sultan Q̲āytbāy in the same year:

> There sits the Sultan at a man's height from the ground beneath a tent with exquisite hangings, on fine carpets, his feet tucked under him as tailors in our country sit working at their table.

Sultan al-Ghūrī (1501-16)

Q̲āytbāy was not the last Mamluk sultan to embellish the Citadel. Al-Ghūrī loved luxury, jewelry, rich clothes and good food. He ordered the renovation of the Royal Kitchen, the Harem, the Q̲aṣr and the Hippodrome in the last of which where he spent the major part of his time. There, belvederes and loggias surrounded a pool forty cubits long, which on occasions such as receptions of embassies or the Prophet's Birthday was filled with roses. The pool received its water from an aqueduct repaired by the sultan, and its water flowed down to irrigate the hippodrome gardens. Trees with fragrant fruits, carrying cages of exotic singing birds as well as kiosks and sumptuous tents pitched within the gardens, provided shade. There was also a Hall of Justice which al-Ghūrī did not much use. A tower connected al-Ghūrī's plaisance quarters with the Citadel through an elevated passage. The sultan would give banquets, with food served on Chinese porcelain, enjoying his last days, while Sultan Selim marched toward Syria and Egypt. The next sultan Ṭūmānbāy, threatened by the advancing Ottomans, fortified the walls of the Citadel — in vain!

The Ottoman Period (1517-1805)

Sultan Selim, despite the great receptions that honored his ambassadors at the Hippodrome of al-Ghūrī, conquered Egypt in 1517. From that date until modern times, Egypt was reduced to the status of a province paying tribute to the Ottoman Empire. It was no longer ruled by sultans, but by governors who changed every two years or so, sometimes more frequently. The Citadel of course lost its imperial splendor. Sultan Selim, conqueror of Egypt, took most of the Citadel's marble to Istanbul, and adopted the whole system of ceremonies, including the running of the kitchens, to those of the Ottoman court, on the scale of a governorate.

The governors, or pashas, appointed from Istanbul did not use the Great Īwān of the Mamluks, and it was abandoned. They stayed in the private quarters of the palace and established the offices of notables and officers there. Al-Q̲aṣr al-Ablaq was used as a factory for weaving the cloth to cover the Kaᶜba in Mecca. The northern enclosure was used by the Janissary corps, and the western dependencies by the ᶜAzab corps. Sulaymān Pasha built an elegant mosque, totally Turkish in style, in the northern part in 1528, and Amir Aḥmad Katkhudā built a mosque for the ᶜAzab corps in 1697 on the site of a Mamluk mosque. A double circular gate, Bāb al-ᶜAzab, facing the mosque of Sultan Ḥasan and imitating the architecture of Bāb al-Futūḥ, was built in 1754.

In the northern enclosure, the arsenal and ammunition stores were kept as well as workshops of carriage makers and other shops. There was also a large bath.

The large circular tower near the mosque of al-Nāṣir Muḥammad was built by Ibrāhīm Pasha in 1520. He also built other towers and restored the city walls near the Citadel. The towers he built were crowned with domes covered with lead. During the Ottoman period, some additions were made in the southern enclosure, where the pashas resided. A Turkish visitor to Egypt, Evliyā Čelebī, who worked at the Citadel for several years, writes that from the towers the pasha could be kept under control in case he made any attempt to declare his independence.

Muḥammad ᶜAlī (1805-1848)

Muḥammad ᶜAlī rebuilt major parts of the western walls of the Citadel, including the gates on the city side. The original gate of Ṣalāḥ al-Dīn was incorporated in a new gate and in the process became invisible from the outside. Several structures were added in both enclosures, including the Jawhara Palace, a Palace of Justice, and a new mint which can still be seen today. In fact, most of the secular buildings inside the Citadel today are the works of Muḥammad ᶜAlī. Muḥammad ᶜAlī himself did not reside at the Citadel, having built other palaces in the city, but the Citadel continued under his rule to be a center of government.

To many Egyptians, and visitors, the Qalᶜa, or Citadel is associated with the imposing building with large domes flanked by a pair of very slender minarets, the mosque of Muḥammad ᶜAlī. This purely Turkish building became a landmark of Cairo after Muḥammad ᶜAlī pulled down the remains of the Great Iwān. That act and his massacre of the Mamluks inside the Citadel ended an important phase of Egyptian history and culture. Muḥammad ᶜAlī's mosque and other structures all belong to an alien style, inspired from Turkey and Europe. The art and architecture of the Mamluks that had prevailed until his reign began in 1805 had become a thing of the past.

Bibliography

Casanova, Paul. *Histoire de la Citadelle du Caire*. Paris, 1894-97 (Arabic transl. Darraj, Ahmad. *Tārīkh wa waṣf qalᶜat al-qāhira*, Cairo, 1974.

Čelebi, Evliya. *Seyahatnamesi X, Mısır, Sudan, Habeş*. Istanbul, 1938, pp. 63 ff.

Creswell. *M.A.E.*, II, pp. 1 ff.

Description de l'Egypte. Etat Moderne, II (2), M. Jomard, "Kaire," pp. 347 ff.

Garcin, J. C., Maury, B. R., Revault, F., Zakarya, M. *Palais et Maisons du Caire I: Epoque Mamelouke, XIIIe-XVIe Siècle*. Paris, 1982, pp. 35 f., 95 f.

von Harff. *Pilgrimage*, pp. 107 ff.

Ibn Iyās, *Badāʾiᶜ al-zuhūr fī waqāʾiᶜ al-duhūr*. Ed. M. Muṣṭafā. Cairo/Wiesbaden, 1961-83.

Maqrīzī. *Khiṭaṭ*, II, pp. 201 ff.

Meinecke, Michael. "Zur mamlukischen Heraldik". *Mitteilungen des Deutschen Archäologischen Instituts Abteilung Kairo*. 28 (1972), pp. 213 ff.

al-ᶜUmarī, Ibn Faḍl Allāh. *Masālik al-abṣār fī mamālik al-amṣār*. Cairo, 1985, pp. 79 ff.

Van Ghistele, de Joos. *Le Voyage en Egypte, 1482-83*. Cairo 1976, pp. 23 ff.

Wiet, Gaston. *Cairo*, pp. 138 ff.

THE MAUSOLEUM OF IMĀM SHĀFIᶜĪ (1211)

We have noted before that the Fatimids erected a number of memorial buildings to celebrate saints of the Prophet's family from whom the Fatimid Caliphs claimed descent. The Ayyubid rulers, who worked systematically to abolish all traces of Shiᶜism in Egypt, destroyed the palaces of the Fatimid Caliphs, but they could not destroy the shrines, for they were sacred to all Muslims. They used the madrasas to consolidate Sunnism, and built in turn their shrine for Imām Shāfiᶜī, founder of one of the four rites of Islamic law. This mausoleum was larger than any earlier shrines, and it can be considered as symbolic of the reinstatement of Sunni Islam in Egypt.

Ṣalāḥ al-Dīn built a madrasa for the Shāfiᶜī rite in the cemetery near the tomb of Imām Shāfiᶜī, and also sponsored a magnificent wooden cenotaph, one of the great masterpieces of medieval Cairo woodwork. Al-Malik al-Kāmil, a later Ayyubid ruler, erected the dome over the grave of Imām Shāfiᶜī in 1211, at the southern extremity of the cemetery of al-Fusṭāṭ.

The Exterior

The mausoleum of Imām Shāfiᶜī has a square base whose inner width measures about fifteen meters. Though the base consists of massive stone walls, it supports only a wooden dome covered with a shell of lead. The exterior of the structure has retained much of its original appearance, though the shrine has been embellished and restored several times.

In addition to its great size, the building differs from Fatimid shrines in the profile of its dome, which curves immediately above the transitional zone. Fatimid domes begin with parallel walls and start to curve nearer the top. The transitional zone, instead of being octagonal and visible between the rectangular base and the dome, is hidden behind a second rectangular, receding story with cut-off corners. Thus from the outside, the building looks as if it were built on two levels; inside there is no such division. The upper level is decorated with keel-arched niches with fluted hoods, and includes elements of Andalusian-style stucco decoration in the treatment of the carved colonnettes and of the spaces between the niches. The upper part of the lower story is decorated with a band of interlaced geometric patterns similar to those used above Fatimid prayer niches, and to the one on the southwest minaret of the mosque of al-Ḥākim.

Atop the dome of Imām Shāfiᶜī is a copper boat which is said to have been filled in the past with grain for birds. The minaret of Ibn Ṭūlūn had a similar finial that has not survived. There is an Egyptian tradition of putting small models of boats in shrines, the most prominent example being the boat at the shrine of Abū'l-Ḥajjāj in Luxor which is taken in the annual procession on the saint's birthday. This is obviously a pre-Islamic tradition that survived in Egyptian Islamic

Pl. 61. The mausoleum of Imām Shāfiʿī.

culture. The shrine of Sīdī Sāryā at the Citadel had a small boat until the mosque in which it is located was recently restored.

The Interior

The interior is more complex than the exterior, with various styles represented. The lower part of the walls with colored marble panels and the prayer niche at the corner correcting the improper orientation of the three original prayer niches must be attributed to Sultan Qāytbāy's late-fifteenth-century restorations. The painting of the dome and its transitional zone was accomplished under Amir ᶜAlī Bey al-Kabīr in the second half of the eighteenth century. Original decoration survives in the wooden frieze running along the walls, as well as the wooden beams from which the lamps once hung.

The transitional zone of the dome reveals the restorations made, as the arrangement of windows alternating with squinches of similar profile has been disturbed by the addition on each side of a large window with a pointed-arch profile. This also must be part of Qāytbāy's restorations. Creswell attributes the whole transitional zone to Qāytbāy because of the sophisticated form of its multiple-tiered squinches. For the period of Qāytbāy, however, this type of transition was already archaic and no longer in use. Moreover, the profile of the dome resembles that of al-Ṣāliḥ, also Ayyubid, and has no parallel in the late Mamluk period. For the Ayyubid period, this squinch style, although it may look more elaborate than was common at that time, might well be justified by the extraordinary size of the dome that made a new transitional device necessary. In the Fatimid period, with increasing dome height, the squinches had already developed from a plain to a composite shape.

Sultan al-Ghūrī is mentioned in an inscription as having restored the dome; he may have covered it with the green tiles found by Creswell under a lead sheet. This sultan's own mausoleum dome was once covered with green tiles (in 1503/4), and tiles of the same type found at Imām Shāfiᶜī were used at the mosque of Sulaymān Pasha at the Citadel (1528), the minaret of Shāhīn al-Khalwatī (1538), and the zāwiya of Shaykh Saᶜūd (1539), all built in the first half of the sixteenth century.

The arrangement of the three prayer niches had been adopted in earlier Fatimid architecture, in the mausoleums of Akhawāt Yūsuf, Sayyida Ruqayya, and Yaḥyā al-Shabīh. The present entrance, according to Creswell, is not the original one. It must have been on the axis of the prayer niches, where a recess used today as a window shows the earliest existing example in Cairo of a wooden coffered ceiling.

The cenotaph sponsored by Ṣalāḥ al-Dīn is one of the great masterpieces of medieval woodwork in Cairo. It has geometric designs with bands of inscriptions in both Kufic and naskhi script. The cenotaph carries the signature of the carpenter-artist who made it, ᶜUbayd al-Najjār Ibn Maᶜālī, and is dated 574 Hijra (1178/9). The marble column with Imām Shafiᶜī's name and date of death, topped with a turban-like structure, is original. When the mausoleum was built, the text carved on it was copied in naskhī on the back.

A second wooden cenotaph for the mother of Sultan al-Kāmil, builder of the mausoleum, is less well preserved. Ṣalāḥ al-Dīn's wife and son are buried in the mausoleum though the exact location is not marked by a cenotaph. He himself is buried in a mausoleum in Damascus.

Bibliography

ᶜAbd al-Wahhāb. *Masājid*, pp. 106 ff.
Creswell. *M.A.E.*, II, pp. 64 ff.
Wiet, Gaston. "Les inscriptions du mausolée de Shāfiᶜi." *Bulletin de l'Institut d'Egypte*, 15 (1933), pp. 167 ff.

THE MADRASA OF SULTAN AL-ṢĀLIḤ NAJM AL-DĪN AYYŪB (1243)

During the Ayyubid period several madrasas were erected in al-Qāhira and al-Fusṭāṭ, many of them within the premises of houses and palaces. The only one of these surviving in a condition allowing us reliably to describe its design is that of al-Ṣaliḥ Najm al-Dīn Ayyūb, the last Ayyubid sultan.

Other madrasas built during this period were dedicated either to the Mālikī or Shāfiᶜī rite, but al-Ṣāliḥ's madrasa taught all four rites of Islamic law, Shāfiᶜī, Ḥanafī, Mālikī and Ḥanbalī, the first madrasa to do so in Egypt. In this it followed the example of the Madrasa Mustanṣiriyya in Baghdad (1233). In 1330, under the Mamluks, the Friday sermon was introduced to the madrasa of al-Ṣāliḥ.

The Exterior

The madrasa of al-Ṣāliḥ was built on part of the site once occupied by the Great Fatimid Palace, that is,

Pl. 62. The madrasa and mausoleum of Sultan al-Ṣāliḥ Najm al-Dīn Ayyūb.

within the heart of the Fatimid city. To the passerby today, only a minaret standing above a passage with an exquisitely decorated entrance is visible; the rest of the facade beneath the minaret is behind a row of shops.

The minaret is the only minaret of the Ayyubid period to have survived intact. It is a brick construction of the mabkhara style. It is supported by the roof of the passage and has a rectangular shaft and a second, receding story of octagonal section. It is topped by a ribbed helmet resting on stalactites.

We have seen that the minaret of the Abū 'l-Ghadanfar in the late Fatimid period marks the beginning of this mabkhara shape in minaret architecture.

The decoration of the rectangular shaft has disappeared on the street side, though on the back it appears as keel-arched panels with fluted hoods of carved stucco. On the upper level, the octagonal section is decorated with lobed openings and stalactites. This is the earliest example of stalactites on the helmet of a minaret, a feature that later forms an integral part of mabkhara minaret decoration.

The minaret stands above a public passage separating the two wings of the complex. A few wooden beams indicate that the passage was originally covered. The entrance is crowned with a handsome keel-arched niche of carved stone with a foundation inscription in naskhī script in its center. From this center radiate flutes to form a large frame of stalactites on the borders of the niche. The niche is flanked with smaller carved niches on both sides, also with fluted hoods, underneath rectangular recesses with stalactite cresting. Though not an exact copy, the facade treatment follows the pattern established at the nearby Aqmar mosque.

The facade of the madrasa now hidden by shops is paneled over its entire width, with keel-arched central panels at the entrance and rectangular panels over the rest. Each panel is recessed and includes a window, a device that appeared for the first time at the mosque of

Pl. 63. Niche above the entrance at the madrasa of al-Ṣāliḥ Najm al-Dīn Ayyūb.

al-Ṣāliḥ Ṭalā'iʿ. The lintels of the windows are carved in stone.

The Interior

The plan of the madrasa was reconstructed by Creswell, who found that it duplicated the plan he identified of the earlier madrasa which is today in ruins, of al-Malik al-Kāmil on the opposite side of the street. The madrasa of al-Kāmil had only one courtyard with two īwāns. The madrasa of al-Ṣāliḥ had two wings separated by a public passage, each wing composed of a courtyard with two vaulted īwāns facing each other across the courtyard, one of them with its back to the street, the other and larger one Mecca-oriented. The lateral sides were occupied by two stories of living units for the students. Today only the northwestern īwān, has survived; the rest of the madrasa has nearly disappeared.

Bibliography

Creswell, *M.A.E.*, II, pp. 94 ff.
Maqrīzī, *Khiṭaṭ*, II, p. 374.

THE MAUSOLEUM OF SULTAN AL-ṢĀLIḤ NAJM AL-DĪN BUILT BY SHAJARAT AL-DURR (1250)

Al-Ṣāliḥ died while his troops were engaged in a battle against Louis XI and his French Crusaders, who had invaded the city of Mansura. His widow Shajarat al-Durr was clever enough to keep the sultan's death secret until the campaign ended with a Mamluk triumph and the capture of the French king, and thereby to prevent the troops' morale from flagging. In the meantime al-Ṣāliḥ's body was kept at his citadel and residence on the island of Rawḍa. Since Al-Ṣāliḥ had left no heir, his mamluks decided to nominate his

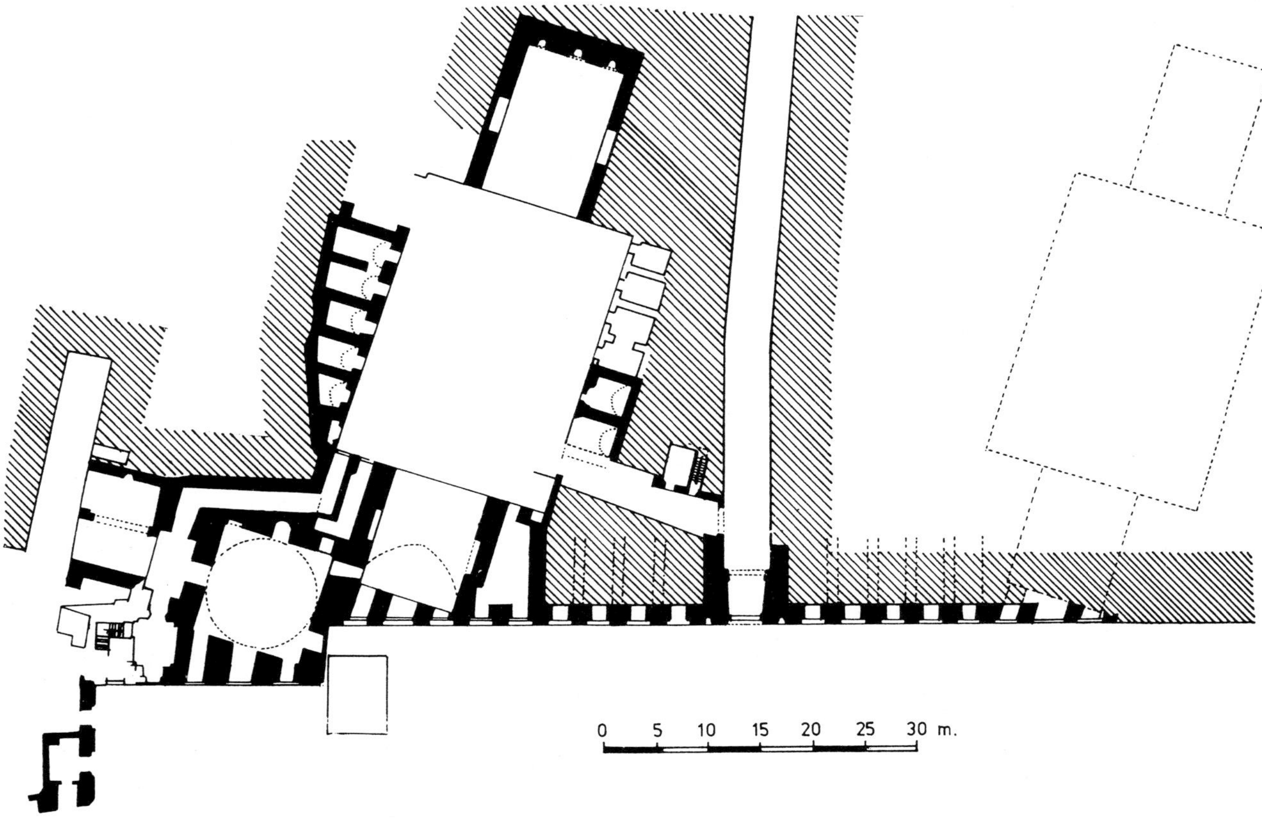

Fig. 19. Plan of the madrasa of al-Ṣāliḥ Najm al-Dīn Ayyūb (Creswell).

Turkish widow and former slave Shajarat al-Durr as his successor to the throne. She was the only woman in Muslim history ever to acquire the rank of a sultan, though only for a few months. Then she married al-Muᶜizz Aybak, the first Mamluk sultan. She managed for a while to hold a powerful position, being the de facto ruler until she was killed.

Between al-Ṣāliḥ's death and his official burial, while Mamluk troops were occupied in fighting the Crusaders, Shajarat al-Durr built the mausoleum for her husband, which was to be attached to his madrasa. Once the building was completed, the body was transferred with great pomp and ceremony from Rawḍa to the tomb. By that time Shajarat al-Durr had abdicated in favor of Aybak, who consequently led the procession. He was followed by the amirs and dignitaries, all dressed in white, their hair cut in sign of mourning. They carried the banners, clothes and weapons of the dead sultan and deposited them in his tomb.

Until Sultan Qalāwūn built his own madrasa-mausoleum, the mausoleum of al-Ṣāliḥ was the place where the ceremony following the nomination of a new amir for Syria was celebrated.

In the history of Cairo's architecture Shajarat al-Durr played an important role because she was the first to introduce the tradition of attaching funerary structures for the rulers to their religious foundations. She also built a mausoleum for herself near her own madrasa. Throughout the Mamluk period sultans and amirs followed this practice.

The Exterior

The mausoleum dome protrudes from the southern facade of the madrasa of Sultan al-Ṣāliḥ Najm al-Dīn. Like the madrasa, its facade is paneled with keel-arch recesses.

The profile of the dome, like that of Imām Shāfiᶜī, is of the type that curves near the base. If the dome of Imām Shāfiᶜī proves not to be the original one, then the dome of al-Ṣāliḥ will become the earliest extant example of this type.

Since the domed chamber protrudes from the facade of the madrasa, all four of its windows, that is, the three on the facade and the one on the southern side, overlook the street. The lintels of the windows, like those of the nearby madrasa, are carved with intricate arabesques.

The entrance, which lacks all architectural enhancement, leads to a passage parallel to the mausoleum. It is surmounted by a slab which bears an inscription indicating the date of al-Ṣāliḥ's death (1249).

The Interior

The fact that the depth of the window recesses gradually decreases from north to south is an indication that the Mecca-oriented dome is set askew to adjust it to the street alignment.

The large iron-grilled windows were intended to give the passerby visual access to the Sultan's tomb, as well as a share in the blessing of Quran recitations performed at the windows for this very purpose.

The tall prayer niche preserves almost nothing of its original decoration, except a pair of marble columns with carved bell-shaped capitals and remnants of carved marble panels. Traces of glass mosaics in the conch, which could be seen until some years ago, indicated that the prayer niche was once decorated in the same manner as Shajarat al-Durr's own mausoleum.

The transitional zone of the dome consists of wooden trilobed squinches set within rows of stalactite niches. The windows set in the transitional zone are adapted to the profile of the squinches, each composed of three hexagonal lights, with stucco arabesque grills that include colored-glass bits.

The wooden cenotaph with geometrical inlay, together with some remnants of wooden shutters and doors, are original.

Bibliography

Creswell. *M.A.E.*, II, pp. 100 ff.
Maqrīzī. *Khiṭaṭ*, II, pp. 374 f.

THE MAUSOLEUM OF SHAJARAT AL-DURR (1250)

The mausoleum of Shajarat al-Durr at the cemetery of Sayyida Nafīsa is the only surviving structure of a complex she built there that included a madrasa. It is directly opposite the mausoleum of Sayyida Ruqayya and near the shrines of other female saints such as Sayyida Sukayna, Sayyida ᶜĀtika, and Sayyida Nafīsa in al-Fusṭāṭ's cemetery.

Pl. 64. The mausoleum of Shajarat al-Durr.

No Mamluk sultan's death is as famous as the death of the Sultana Shajarat al-Durr. She continued to wield power during al-Muᶜizz Aybak's reign, but soon lost power over her husband, who began to court the daughter of a ruler in Iraq. She killed him, whereupon his followers beat her to death and threw her body half naked from the Citadel, where it remained a few days until she was buried in her mausoleum. In time, her mausoleum, located in an area full of shrines, came to be venerated by the people living in the quarter. Today, the whole area is in rather dilapidated condition.

The Exterior

The most interesting feature of the mausoleum's dome is its profile, which like that of the mausoleum of the Abbasid Caliphs has a keel-arch curve, thus differing from that of al-Ṣālih's mausoleum. It also has a different facade treatment. The dome, with an entrance on every side except the qibla wall, makes an angle with the street alignment to which it is not adjusted. The building itself, with its three openings, must have been within an enclosure. The qibla wall with the prayer niche protruding outside and the southwest wall still have remains of ornaments: lozenges and medallions carved with flutes and keel-arched niches with fluted hoods.

The Interior

Inside the mausoleum of Shajarat al-Durr the three sides around the qibla are decorated with a stucco keel-arch niche set above each entrance. The qibla side is decorated with a keel-arched prayer niche. The keel-arched niches above the three entrances are shallow, fluted, with the flutes carved and radiating from a central panel. The frames of the niches are composed of stalactites, or two rows of carved small niches, and the spandrels of the niches are finely carved with floral motifs, appearing so lacy that the details are hardly recognizable. The whole is framed by an inscription band of naskhī script on an ornate background.

The transitional zone of the dome is reduced, compared to that of al-Ṣāliḥ, since the dome itself is smaller. Painting decorates the stucco squinches.

The prayer niche is concave; its conch starts above a wooden frieze that runs around the whole chamber above the three entrances. A stalactite triple frame borders the prayer niche, which is decorated inside with glass mosaics forming a tree with mother-of-pearl pieces set in the foliage, an allusion, perhaps, to the sultana's name, "Tree of Pearl." The wooden frieze running along the walls with carved inscriptions and arabesques is Fatimid in style and must have belonged to an earlier building. The upper inscription band underneath the transitional zone was once covered with a thick coat of black paint, no doubt by enemies of Shajarat al-Durr. It was later repainted in white, and carries her name and titles.

Pl. 65. The prayer niche at the mausoleum of Shajarat al-Durr.

Shajarat al-Durr's and al-Ṣāliḥ's Mausoleums Compared

The mausoleum of Shajarat al-Durr is attributed to the year 1250, the year she ruled, following the death of al-Ṣāliḥ, whose mausoleum she also built in the same year. It is thus interesting to compare the two structures.

The mausoleum of al-Ṣāliḥ was built near his madrasa, in the very heart of the city. Its architecture, as a structure added to the madrasa and also aligned with the street, and its facade whose keel-arch panels and carved lintels are similar to those of the madrasa emphasize its urban character. The mausoleum overlooks the street with large iron-grilled windows placed at a level that allows the passersby to look inside.

The mausoleum of Shajarat al-Durr was also part of a complex that included a madrasa and other structures, but it was built in a cemetery. The facade of the dome is not adjusted to the street, or lane, and the chamber was not directly accessible from the road but from another structure to which it was attached, as is suggested by the three entrances as well as the prolongation of the southwestern wall beyond the dome. The mausoleum chamber had three entrances and needed no windows.

In its urban context, the dome of al-Ṣāliḥ is thus an expression of the Sultan's royal status, while the mausoleum of Shajarat al-Durr, located in a venerated area of the cemetery, has more religious connotations.

Bibliography

Creswell. *M.A.E.*, II, pp. 135 ff.

Behrens-Abouseif, D. "The Lost Minaret of Shajarat al-Durr at Her Complex in the Cemetery of Sayyida Nafīsa." *Mitteilungen des Deutschen Archäologischen Instituts Abteilung Kairo*, 39 (1983), pp. 1 ff.

CHAPTER SEVEN

THE ARCHITECTURE OF THE BAHRI MAMLUKS

THE MOSQUE OF SULTAN AL-ẒĀHIR BAYBARS (1266-69)

The mosque of al-Ẓāhir Baybars is the earliest surviving royal mosque of the Mamluks in Cairo. Situated outside and northwest of the gates of the Fatimid city, in what was then the northern suburb of Cairo, it was built on the site of a polo ground, surrounded by greenery and overlooking the Khalīj. The quarter now called colloquially "al-Ḍāhir" takes its name from this mosque which, though in very dilapidated condition, still suggests the grand appearance it must originally have had.

The Exterior

Al-Ẓāhir Baybars' mosque shows influences from the mosque of al-Ḥākim: the protruding main entrance and its carved decoration; arched panels, carved lozenges and medallions at the portal, and the pointed arches of the interior standing on rectangular piers. Here, however, the arcades framing the courtyard, another arcade inside the sanctuary separating the maqṣūra dome from the rest, and the aisles of the three entrances are on piers. The other arcades were on columns; most of them have not survived.

The mosque was free standing, its massive walls supported by buttresses. It is little wonder that Napoleon's troops used it as a fortress. They may have contributed to its decay, but at the time they used it, most of the columns were already missing.

The main entrance, opposite the prayer niche, is in the form of a protruding cube and is decorated with keel-arched niches and lozenges. The entrance passage is covered by a shallow dome on pendentives, as at Bāb al-Futūḥ.

There are two side entrances, also protruding, but smaller in size, and their passages are roofed with cross-vaults as at Bāb al-Naṣr. The arch of the main entrance is adorned with a cushion voussoir, like the side arches at Bāb Zuwayla. The side-entrance arches are carved differently, one with zigzags and the other with scallops.

The main entrance used to have a minaret, a rectangular shaft decorated with keel-arch panels, whose stub is shown in an illustration in the *Description de l'Egypte*.

The exterior walls of the mosque have no decoration except for the pointed-arch windows with stucco grills and stepped crenellation.

The Interior

The mosque's sanctuary has a remarkable feature. In front of the prayer niche, which now has none of its original decoration, is a large area, the space of nine bays or three-by-three arch widths, which instead of being roofed with a ceiling like the rest of the mosque, or covered by a small one-bay dome as in earlier mosques, was covered with a dome as large as that of Imām Shāfiʿī. In royal mosques, the space in front of the prayer niche, called the maqṣūra, used to be enclosed and exclusively dedicated to the prayer of the ruler and his entourage. The dome of Baybars, made of wood, disappeared long ago. Baybars ordered the dome to be built and decorated with the wood and marble he brought as trophies from the Citadel of Yaffa, captured from the Crusaders. The dome thus commemorated Baybars' victory and the triumph of Islam. From the maqṣūra to the courtyard, Creswell has identified a transept, or triple aisle, higher than the rest and running perpendicular to the qibla wall instead of parallel to it.

A nine-bay dome over the prayer niche appeared first in Persian Saljūq architecture and was then repeated in eastern Anatolian mosques, from where it most probably was introduced to Egypt. Another notable feature at this mosque is the use of ablaq masonry, striped courses of light and dark stone, at one of the entrances. According to Creswell, this is the earliest extant example of ablaq, which becomes typical in later Cairene architecture. When applied on marble, ablaq masonry was made with two differently colored marbles. With stone, however, it was common to paint one course in red or black and leave the other with its natural stone color.

Pl. 66. The mosque of Sultan al-Ẓāhir Baybars.

The stucco window grills of the mosque are shaped in intricate arabesques covered with carving. Finely carved stucco panels and bands can still be seen inside the mosque though very little of this decoration remains.

Bibliography

Bloom, Jonathan. "The Mosque of Baybars al-Bunduqdārī in Cairo." *Annales Islamologiques*, 18 (1982), pp. 45 ff.
Creswell. *M.A.E.*, II, pp. 155 ff.
Maqrīzī. *Khiṭaṭ*, II, p. 300.

THE MAUSOLEUM-MADRASA AND HOSPITAL OF SULTAN AL-MANṢŪR QALĀWŪN (1284-85)

This complex, on what was the main avenue of medieval Cairo, opposite the madrasa of al-Ṣāliḥ and on the site of the western Fatimid palace, is one of the most outstanding monuments of medieval Cairo architecture and has several features without precedent in Cairo. Maqrīzī writes that the land on which the building was erected was acquired illegally by

Pl. 67. The facade of the madrasa-mausoleum of Sultan Qalāwūn with the sabīl of al-Nāṣir to the left.

Qalāwūn. Jurists thus questioned its status as a pious foundation, but Maqrīzī reluctantly adds that similar situations applied to many religious buildings. Originally, the complex included a madrasa, the mausoleum of the founder, and a hospital.

The Hospital

The hospital was known by the Persian word *māristān* or place of illness; originally, the name was *bīmāristān*, place of health (the prefix *bī-* forming the antonym), but the appellation was shortened. Having been cured at the hospital of Nūr al-Dīn at Damascus, Qalāwūn included a hospital in his complex, though he was not the first to do so in Cairo. Ibn Ṭūlūn, the Fatimids, and Ṣalāḥ al-Dīn had sponsored hospitals, but that of Qalāwūn is best known because it continued its functions as a charitable institution and center for studies and practice of medicine until the nineteenth century when modern medicine and hospitals were introduced by Muḥammad ʿAlī. The hospital of Qalāwūn was mentioned often by travelers. In the Middle Ages, Muslim medical knowledge and practice were very advanced, and Muslim medicine was taught in some parts of Europe until the eighteenth century.

As a philanthropic foundation, Qalāwūn's hospital was remarkable for its time, and even in comparison with modern times. Its foundation deed states that it was dedicated to all Muslims of both sexes and all ages, of whatever social or moral position, from any place in the world, with no distinction to be made except that priority should be given to those most in need of care.

The hospital was divided into sections for men and women, and each patient was entitled to a bed made of wood or palm slats, with pillows and covers. The administrator of the foundation, who also handled financial matters, took care that each patient was given proper food and medicine. He supervised the laboratories where medicines were mixed and bottled in adequate, but not excessive, quantities. The kitchen prepared juices and broth, chicken and meats for the patients, and each patient received his portion in an individual, covered vessel, fanned in the summer. Drinks were served in individual cups. Each patient had his own chamber pot. The laundry of the patient was done by the hospital. Physicians met to discuss each patient's case and his treatment, and followed up his progress. The ophthalmologists consulted the general physician. Doctors were present at all times at the hospital, together or in shifts. All services were generously provided and free of charge. Even funeral expenses, should the patient die, were assumed by the hospital foundation, and each person had a funeral according to his social standing. This applied even if the patient died in his own home after returning from hospital.

The building itself, which aside from a few walls, has not survived is described as having been beautifully decorated, with fountains trickling in marble basins. Curiously, the foundation deed itself refers to the beauty of the building, noting that it was intended to be one of the most magnificent in the world so that the foundation would have the dignity it deserved, and so that no one would be reluctant to make use of its services. The few remnants of wall decoration suggest how much care was lavished on this charitable institution.

Pl. 68. The minaret and dome of Sultan Qalāwūn.

The plan of the hospital must have been cruciform, with four large halls built along the four sides of a courtyard connected by a number of smaller rooms. It most likely was incorporated into the structures of the Fatimid palace. From the street only the facades of the madrasa and mausoleum were visible. A passage at the back led to the hospital.

The Facade

The facade of Qalāwūn's complex is fairly well preserved. Approaching from the south, the madrasa appears first, then the passage on whose left is the entrance of the madrasa, and on its right, the entrance of the mausoleum. The hospital is behind both. At the northern extremity of the facade, the minaret stands at the angle facing the pedestrian coming from Bāb al-Futūḥ and Bāb al-Naṣr.

The facade treatment was innovative for its time, enhanced by several recesses over the length of the whole building, and showing unprecedented verticality. These recesses have pointed arches. Unlike earlier architecture, however, no keel arches or stalactite recesses are visible on the facade. The only stalactites are a small row in the wall underneath the minaret. The recessed panels include three tiers of windows, giving the building the appearance of having three stories. The lower windows are large, rectangular, and have iron grills; the middle windows are smaller and pointed, and the uppermost windows are double windows with round arches separated by a column and surmounted by a small circular window. The lower part of each recess is flanked by a pair of elegant marble columns with fine pre-Islamic capitals. This row of columns along the facade is unique in Cairo's architecture.

Above the lower rectangular windows runs a band of inscription all along the facade, deeply carved in stone. This band, originally gilded, is called a *ṭirāz*, a term borrowed from textile arts designating an embroidered band in a ceremonial robe with the name and titles of a ruler.

The portal is composed of a round arch framed with interlacing bands of white and black marble ablaq. The earliest example in Cairo of this type of decoration is at one of the portals of the mosque of al-Ẓāhir Baybars. A beautiful original bronze door with geometric patterns still stands at the entrance, and a small iron grilled window above the door is attributed by Creswell to French craftsmanship, most likely by a Crusader.

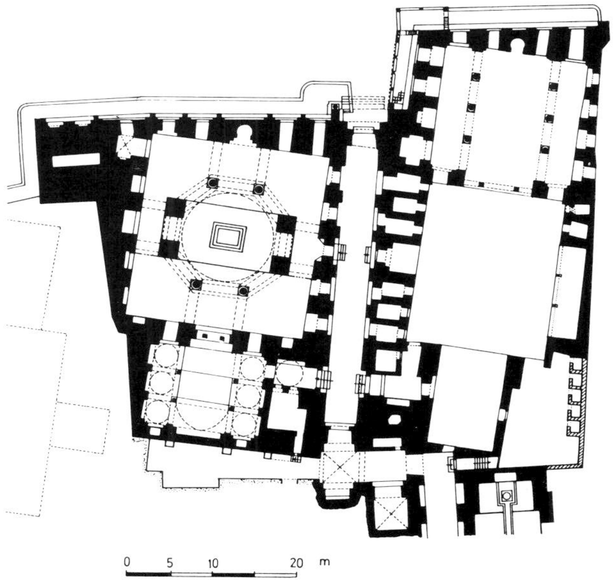

Fig. 20. The madrasa and mausoleum of Sultan Qalāwūn (Creswell).

The facade of the Qalāwūn complex clearly shows departures from local tradition. It lacks the keel-arches, stalactites, lozenges, and medallions of previous buildings. The pointed-arched panels with double windows and bull's-eyes have been interpreted as influences from Crusader architecture in Palestine. Creswell, however, finds their prototypes in Sicilian architecture of the same period. Sicily had close connections with the Muslim world in the medieval period and its own arts and architecture owe a great deal to the Fatimids. It is not unlikely that the transfer of styles traveled in both directions.

The Minaret

Qalāwūn's minaret is an imposing construction. The rectangular shaft and receding rectangular second story are built in stone; the third circular story is made of brick and decorated with stucco. The first story has horseshoe arches on cornices of stalactites on each side and is crowned with stalactites. The second story has horseshoe arches and cushion voussoirs. At this time horseshoe arches were typical of Andalusian and North African architecture. Lājīn's minaret restoration at the mosque of Ibn Ṭūlūn, done a few years after Qalāwūn's minaret, also shows influences of craftsmen who had immigrated to Cairo from western Islamic cities.

The third story of the minaret was constructed by Qalāwūn's son, Sultan al-Nāṣir Muḥammad, after the 1303 earthquake had demolished the original. Its lace-like stucco carving is not in harmony with the rest of the minaret. An interesting band with vertical moldings resembling ancient Egyptian reed motifs marks the end of the circular part. The helmet disappeared and was replaced at a later period by the present conical structure. Al-Nāṣir Muḥammad's restoration of the minaret, with a reference to the earthquake, is commemorated in the inscription band carved on the first story.

The Madrasa

The madrasa is today entered through a window opening. The original entrance, further back, was redecorated with moldings in the eighteenth century by Amir ᶜAbd al-Raḥmān Katkhudā.

The madrasa is not completely preserved, but can be reconstructed. The courtyard was surrounded by four īwāns of unequal size and between them, on several stories, were the students' cells. The largest of these īwāns is the sanctuary, on the qibla side, and it is the best preserved. The hall opposite is much smaller. On the lateral sides two recessed spaces flank the courtyard.

The prayer hall has a new type of facade, with a triple arch supporting a second story of arches, a device frequent in Byzantine architecture. The interior plan is that of a basilica, a central nave flanked by two smaller naves, from which it is separated by granite columns of ancient Egyptian origin. Stucco floral patterns and great numbers of marble colonnettes decorate the arches and upper walls. The ceiling is of painted and gilded wood. The prayer niche is richly decorated with marble, and its conch, like that at Shajarat al-Durr's mausoleum, is decorated with glass mosaics. Instead of a tree, however, a vase with plants is represented. No stucco carving was used in the prayer niche.

The Mausoleum

The mausoleum chamber is the best preserved part of the complex and is considered one of the most beautifully decorated medieval buildings in Cairo.

It is reached from a small courtyard surrounded by an arcade with shallow domes, perhaps of Byzantine inspiration. In the middle of the courtyard there was once a fountain. An arch carved in stucco frames the entrance leading to a rectangular hall. In the middle of this hall the dome rests on an octagonal structure, like the Dome of the Rock in Jerusalem, composed of two pairs of piers alternating with two pairs of columns. The original dome disappeared, and the modern dome is modeled after the mausoleum of al-Ashraf Khalīl, son of Qalāwūn, erected in 1288. Because it is mounted on an octagon, it has no zone of transition. A well-restored and preserved wooden screen, commissioned by al-Nāṣir Muḥammad, son of Qalāwūn, surrounds the octagonal part.

As the window recesses show, the facade of the building is aligned with the street, and the inner walls are set askew with the outer ones. Cupboards set in these walls, are fitted with wooden doors.

From top to bottom, the walls are covered with various types of decoration. Marble covers the lower parts, where the most remarkable feature are the numerous panels with inlaid marble, mother of pearl, and colored stones. A great variety of patterns are found, including for the first time in Cairo, square Kufic script repeating the name of Muḥammad. Bands of carved marble and a band of wood with relief inscriptions, painted and gilded, run along the walls. The coffered ceiling is painted and gilded, composed of sunken polygons similar to those first seen at the mausoleum of Imām Shāfiᶜī.

The outstanding feature of the mausoleum is the huge prayer niche, one of the largest in medieval Cairo. It is richly decorated with marble inlay and rows of niches with shell conchs, flanked with small colonnettes. The madrasa prayer niche also has these decorative arcades. Lavish use of mother-of-pearl with marble accentuates the decoration. As Meinecke has shown, Byzantine craftsmen must have been involved in these decorations, as many details, particularly the marble carving and inlay, resemble that of contemporary buildings in Constantinople. Indeed, Sultan Qalāwūn had friendly relations with the Byzantine emperor. The plan of the sanctuary of his madrasa also reveals Byzantine influence.

Qalāwūn's tomb became the site for celebrations of the appointment of amirs to be sent to Syria. Earlier they had taken place at the tomb of al-Ṣāliḥ, across the street.

Like the madrasa, the mausoleum chamber also housed a teaching program in the four rites of Islamic law. Qalāwūn's grandson, al-Malik al-Ṣāliḥ ᶜImād al-

Pl. 69. The mausoleum of Sultan Qalāwūn (German Archaeological Institute).

Pl. 70. The prayer niche of the mausoleum of Qalāwūn.

Dīn, intended to build a madrasa but died before he had done so, and a friend, Amir Arghūn, made the endowment to establish the madrasa at Qalāwūn's mausoleum. Readers of the Quran recited all day in the deeply recessed windows of the tomb. There was also a substantial library, and cupboards to house the sultan's robes. Sultan al-Nāṣir Muḥammad and other sons of Qalāwūn are buried there.

During the reign of Qalāwūn and his descendants endowments were increased and the mausoleum was the site of many celebrations and ceremonies. The sultan's private guards had the honor of living in and caring for the complex.

Bibliography

ᶜAbd al-Wahhāb. *Masājid*, pp. 114 ff.

Amīn, Muḥammad Muḥ. ed. Waqf of Qalāwūn's hospital published as appendix in Ibn Ḥabīb. *Tadhkirat al-nabīh fī ayyām al-Manṣūr wa banīh*. Cairo, 1976-86. I, pp. 295 ff.

Creswell. *M.A.E.*, pp. 191 ff.

Herz, M. *Die Baugruppe des Sultans Qalawun*. Hamburg, 1910.

Issa, Ahmed. *Histoire des Bimaristans (Hôpitaux) à l'Epoque Islamique*. Cairo, 1928.

Meinecke, Michael. "Das Mausoleum des Qalāʾun in Kairo — Untersuchungen zur Genese der Mamlukischen Architekturdekoration." *Mitteilungen des Deutschen Archäologischen Instituts Abteilung Kairo*, 27 (1971), pp. 47 ff.

THE MADRASA OF SULTAN AL-NĀṢIR MUḤAMMAD IBN QALĀWŪN (1295-1303)

This madrasa is adjacent to the complex of Sultan Qalāwūn. Its facade and minaret are visible only when one is quite close to them. The building was begun by al-ᶜĀdil Katbughā who ruled very briefly (1295/6) and was completed by al-Nāṣir Muḥammad, son of Qalāwūn. The madrasa taught the four rites of Islamic law.

The Exterior

The rather narrow facade includes the minaret above the entrance, to the right of which is the mausoleum of the founder. Al-ᶜĀdil carried out the construction up to the ṭirāz band, and the rest was done during the reign of al-Nāṣir Muḥammad. The mausoleum's wooden dome collapsed long ago, and only its octagonal wooden transitional zone with pendentives has survived.

The most remarkable feature of the facade is the portal, a trophy brought from a church in Akko during the Crusades by al-Malik al-Ashraf Khalīl and used later by al-ᶜĀdil Katbughā for his madrasa. It is a Gothic marble portal with pointed arch, at the apex of which was added the word, Allāh. Maqrīzī considered it one of the most magnificent portals in Cairo.

Above the portal stands the minaret. The first story of the rectangular brick shaft is covered with extremely fine stucco carving, giving a lace-like effect that contrasts with the shape of the shaft. The decoration is well preserved on the facade; little remains on the back and sides.

As in previous minarets, medallions, lozenges- and keel-arched niches and panels decorate the shaft, but here, the whole surface is completely covered with fine arabesques carved in high relief and on more than one level. The keel arches include lobed, smaller arches. Toward the top, there is a row of lobed arches filled with tiny geometrical shapes like the ones seen in the

Pl. 71. Stucco carving on the minaret of the madrasa-mausoleum of Sultan al-Nāṣir Muḥammad.

Mamluk restoration of the al-Azhar prayer niche, separated by pairs of colonnettes. A band of ornate Kufic runs across this arcade. Above the arcade of niches, an inscription band in naskhī commemorates the Sultan al-Nāṣir Muḥammad. Atop the shaft are stalactites which, unlike the simple cornice on Qalāwūn's minaret, are heavy bunches hanging like grapes.

The second story of the minaret is not contemporary with the lower part. Its style indicates it was added nearly a century later. It is octagonal in section with a keel-arch panel on each side framed by a molding running around the whole. We can still see remains of the blue faience balls used to decorate the loops of the molding. The faceted third story is made of wood, with a conical top, and so must be from the Ottoman period. The minaret is a light structure supported by the walls of the passage leading to the interior of the madrasa.

The Interior

Not much has survived inside the madrasa, but there is enough to indicate that the courtyard was once surrounded by four unequal halls, or that it was cruciform. The two larger īwāns are on the qibla side and the side facing it, which are vaulted. Between these īwāns were several stories of student cells.

The only decoration surviving in the interior of the madrasa is the carved stucco prayer niche: it is adorned with bosses, carved and pierced, that call to mind the repoussé technique of metalwork. The arabesque motifs of the background appear as carved, curving stripes in a very complex arrangement. The prayer niche is set within a larger arch also carved in stucco which includes a stucco window whose grill is of later date.

This prayer niche, which has no parallel in Cairo, is by a foreign hand. It shows similarities to Persian stucco work, which could have reached Egypt during the reign of al-Nāṣir Muḥammad. The sultan was married to a Mongol princess from Persia and had friendly relations with the Mongol court of Tabrīz. While the two countries exchanged ambassadors, Persian craftsmen came to Cairo and introduced the art of faience mosaic seen on other buildings. The minor arts were also influenced by these contacts.

It is possible that the madrasa's prayer niche was added at a later date. At the time it was built (1295-1303), Egypt's relations with Persia had not yet been fully developed, as they were later to become in al-Nāṣir's long, but twice interrupted, reign (1293-1341).

Bibliography

Creswell. *M.A.E.*, II, pp. 234 ff.

Michael J. Rogers. "Evidence for Mamluk-Mongol Relations 1260-1360." *Colloque International sur l'Histoire du Caire (1969)*. Cairo, pp. 385 ff.

THE KHANQĀH-MADRASA OF AMIR SANJAR AL-JAWLĪ (1303-4)

The founder of the madrasa/khanqāh of Sanjar al-Jawlī was one of the most powerful amirs during the reign of Sultan al-Nāṣir Muḥammad. The building commemorates his long friendship with Amir Salār, to whom he dedicated the large and more decorated of two mausoleums.

The Exterior

The building stands on Ṣalība street not far from the mosque of Ibn Ṭūlūn and is one of Cairo's most remarkable monuments. Perched on the rocks of Jabal Yashkur, the building is impressive to the viewer coming down from the Citadel, along one of the medieval processional roads. The facade is dominated by the unusual silhouette of a minaret flanked by two unequal domes, and the lower part of the building is paneled with window recesses as is usual in Mamluk mosques. The entrance, on an angle with the rest of the facade, is not particularly enhanced but is crowned like the windows with a stalactite cornice. A ṭirāz band runs along the facade. The mosque has another entrance at the rear with a stalactite portal.

The rectangular shaft of its mabkhara-type minaret is more slender and elongated than those built earlier.

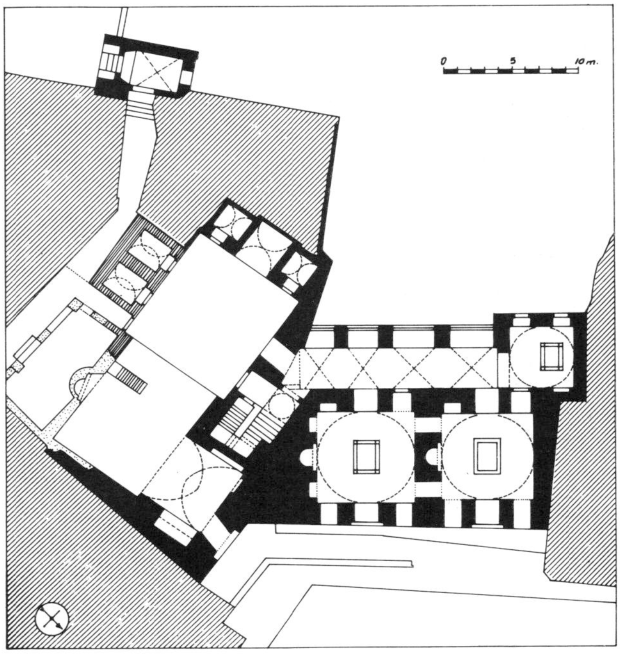

Fig. 21. The khanqāh-madrasa and double mausoleum of Amir Sanjar al-Jawlī (Creswell).

Pl. 72. The double mausoleum of the amirs Sanjar and Salār at the madrasa-khanqāh of Amir Sanjar.

Its decorations recall those of Qalāwūn's minaret, each side having an arched panel resting on stalactites and flanked with colonnettes; the horseshoe arch and double window with bull's-eye is also used here. The type of stalactites atop the rectangular shaft also recall those of Qalāwūn's minaret.

The upper structure is slender; the octagonal elongated section supports a cornice of stalactites and above it a ribbed helmet on a circular pavilion. A special feature of the minaret is a portal at its stairway entrance from the roof of the mosque with a trilobed arch and two small *maksalas* or benches on both sides. Only the minaret of Bashtāk, built in 1340, has a portal at the staircase entrance. The rectangular part of the minaret is made of stone, the upper part of brick.

The domes are similar but unequal in size. They are ribbed, but only as exterior decoration (the inner surface is plain), and they are decorated with a band of stucco at their drums with a Quranic inscription, a device widely used in the architecture of Bahri Mamluk domes. Their profile, unlike that of Baybars al-Jashankīr's khanqāh mausoleum, curves after about one-third of the dome's height.

The Interior

The entrance leads to a vestibule with a cross-vault, like most of the Mamluk entrance vestibules.

The interior is unusual. To the left is an irregular iwān, not oriented toward Mecca. The prayer niche, set askew on a side wall, is not the original. This īwān faces a courtyard (today covered) surrounded on three sides by cells. An arched, smaller īwān faces the main īwān. A stucco inscription band, nicely carved, runs along the walls that frame the courtyard. The cells are lit with openings with decorative grills, some of stucco and others of stone, pierced and carved in arabesque patterns.

The iwān with the cells is on the left side; to the right is a corridor, roofed with a line of cross-vaults. On the right side are the two doors of the two mausoleums, at the back of which is a dome built of stone, undated and unidentified. Judging from the style of its transitional zone, which resembles that of the dome added by Lājīn above the prayer niche of Ibn Ṭūlūn, it is one of the earliest stone domes of Cairo, if not the earliest.

Pl. 73a. Stone screen at the madrasa-khanqāh of Amir Sanjar.

Pl. 73b. Stone screen at the madrasa-khanqāh of Amir Sanjar.

On the left, the western side of the corridors, there are three pointed arches opening onto a courtyard that have quite special screens. There is a fourth such screen at a window between the covered courtyard and the open courtyard overlooked by the arches. These screens, which are stone panels that do not close the entire height of the arches, leaving an upper part bare, are pierced and carved. This technique is usually applied to stucco window grills. Panels made of stone and used as screens have no precedent in Cairo's architecture, though this type of work continued to be used and had an impact on minaret architecture.

Minaret balconies, formerly adorned with wooden parapets, were later to have parapets made of such stone panels, pierced and carved. The earliest extant examples can be seen at the minarets of Sultan al-Nāṣir Muḥammad at the Citadel (1318/35). There are more such panels, though smaller in size, decorating the walls of the corridor of the Sanjar double mausoleum, set between the arches as decoration. They are used again instead of stucco window grills to bring light into the students' cells.

Each of the four screens mentioned is carved with an individual, intricate floral design, one of them depicting grapes. Stylized palmettes, flowers and stalks are also used.

The Mausoleums

The two domed chambers are reached from the corridor through two doors on the right side, and they communicate with each other through doors inside the mausoleums. The first door leads to the larger of the two tombs which is also the more decorated. It has a prayer niche with fine geometric marble inlay designs like those in Qalāwūn's mausoleum. A wooden inscription band runs along the walls. The transition zone of the dome is made of an octagonal belt of niches and stalactites pierced by windows in niche forms. The inside of the dome is, unlike the exterior, not ribbed, thus differing from those of Sayyida Ruqayya and Yaḥyā al-Shabīh, where the flutes of the domes are structural.

Two openings opposite the prayer niche lead from Salār's to Sanjar's tomb. Here, the prayer niche has no colored marble, but the conch is ribbed, the ribs ending at the bottom of the conch with a row of small niches, a rare type of prayer niche decoration in Cairo. The transitional zone of both domes is treated in the same style.

Coming back to the corridor, the first of the four arches, which is smaller than the rest, opens onto a courtyard that includes several tombs. We do not know the exact function of this courtyard, today framed on two sides by modern buildings. On the wall that is part of the madrasa/khanqāh building, there is a small stucco carved prayer niche set in a corner, and a stucco inscription band runs along this wall. This courtyard, which has on this side the remains of cells could have been part of the living quarters of the community attached to the complex.

Functions

The exact function of Sanjar's foundation is unclear. Its own inscriptions do not specify whether it was built as a madrasa or a khanqāh; only the vague term, *makān*, or "place", is used. According to Maqrīzī, it was both a madrasa and a khanqāh. We find that in the thirteenth century, many mosques as well as madrasas were already performing Sufi rites indicating that Sufism was becoming increasingly widespread and was no longer restricted to a small, select community. On the other hand, many khanqāhs were integrating the teaching of law into their activities, thus adopting the madrasa's functions. With time, the madrasa/khanqāhs became the main form of religious institution.

The madrasa/khanqāh of Sanjar differs architecturally, however, from all others known in that it has no qibla-oriented main hall, while the double mausoleum is given the optimal location that makes it both Mecca- and street-oriented. The religious part of the complex is thus left without the main feature of a religious building, the qibla.

A mausoleum in itself is not a religious, but a secular building. By being attached to mosques, madrasas or khanqāhs, and by traditionally having a prayer niche, it acquired religious features. Thus, the double mausoleum of Sanjar and his friend Salār should be seen above all as a memorial building to both men and their friendship.

Bibliography

ᶜAbd al-Wahhāb. *Masājid*, p. 124.
Creswell. *M.A.E.*, II, pp. 242 ff.
Maqrizi, *Khiṭaṭ*, II, pp. 398, 421.

THE KHANQĀH-MAUSOLEUM OF SULTAN BAYBARS AL-JASHANKĪR (1307-10)

In Persian, *jashankīr* means "the taster," Baybars' position at the sultan's court before he became becoming sultan himself. His reign after the second reign of al-Nāṣir Muḥammad was very brief. During al-Nāṣir's absence to escape enemies, Baybars usurped power only to pay with his life when al-Nāṣir returned for his third, and longest, period of rule.

The khanqāh of Baybars al-Jashankīr in the Jamāliyya quarter is the oldest surviving khanqāh in Cairo. The one built by Ṣalāḥ al-Dīn disappeared long ago, and from the Khanqāh Bunduqdāriyya (1283/4), only the founder's mausoleum survives.

Like the madrasa, the khanqāh had living quarters attached, including a kitchen and other dependencies. The Sufis were expected to devote themselves to their mysticism and to learning. Every khanqāh also had

Pl. 74. The khanqāh-mausoleum of Sultan Baybars al-Jashankīr (Department of Antiquities).

accommodations for visiting Sufis, who generally were not allowed to stay more than three days.

The foundation deed of Baybars al-Jashankīr's khanqāh has survived, giving a detailed description of the regulations to be followed by the Sufis living there.

The Exterior

From a distance, the building appears to be a harmonious combination of dome and minaret and from nearby, the portal is impressive. The facade is dominated by the portal, composed of a great round arch with cushion voussoir framing a recess with a half-dome resting on two pendentives carved with stalactites. Niches are carved on both sides of the entrance recess and on the flanks. Their conchs are done in black and white marble ablaq, arranged in a sunrise motif. Beautiful engaged marble colonnettes with Gothic capitals decorate the corners of the recess. On both sides of the bronze door, the original door with geometric patterns, there is an inscription in white marble inlaid in a black-marble background. The threshold has a stone block with hieroglyphics, a feature found in many medieval mosques. They were not simply spoils from ancient monuments but had some kind of talismanic meaning.

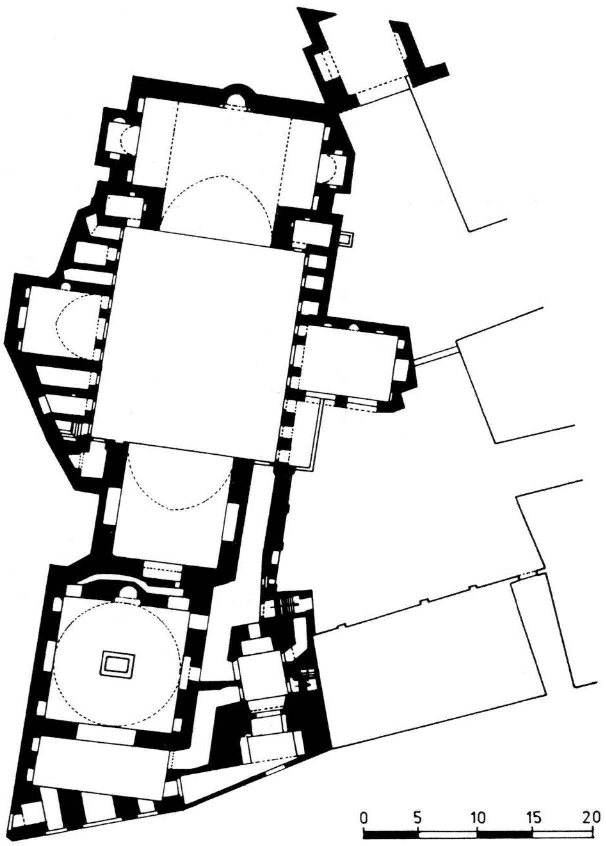

Fig. 22. The khanqāh and mausoleum of Sultan Baybars al-Jashankīr (Creswell).

The facade also has a ṭirāz band with the name and titles of the founder, but Baybars' titles were understandably obliterated by Sultan al-Nāṣir Muḥammad after he had recovered his throne and executed Baybars. The khanqah remained closed for twenty years.

The khanqāh was built first, and the mausoleum added later. A protruding wall with recesses and stalactites including iron grilled windows forms the left side of the facade. This is not the facade of the mausoleum itself, but a small room, or kind of vestibule, leading to it. The dome, like that of al-Ṣāliḥ Najm al-Dīn's mausoleum, curves from a low level.

The first story of the minaret is a rectangular shaft with keel-arch niches, topped with bunches of stalactites very similar to those on al-Nāṣir Muḥammad's minaret. The second story, for the first time, is circular and also ends with stalactites. A ribbed helmet on a open circular pavilion crowns the minaret. The helmet shows the remnants of green tiles that once must have covered it entirely. The minaret thus lacks the octagonal part seen in other mabkhara-style minarets, and is one of a very few minarets without an octagonal transition between the rectangular and circular sections.

The Interior

One reaches the courtyard of the khanqāh through a bent entrance. The plan of the khanqāh is cruciform. The main īwān on the qibla side is vaulted, with two smaller arched recesses on its sides, each communicating with an air shaft. There is no decoration on the walls except for the two columns flanking the prayer niche, perhaps suggesting the simplicity needed for Sufi prayer.

Two smaller, unvaulted, īwāns are on the lateral sides of the courtyard, and the fourth īwān is vaulted but smaller than the main īwān. Between these four unequally sized īwāns there are three levels of cells. The upper floors' cells have windows overlooking the courtyard. The cell windows form the main decoration of the courtyard and their recesses are topped with either keel- or pointed-arch niches with radiating hoods, or with stalactites of different patterns. Some windows are inside lobed arches. The khanqāh housed two hundred Sufis, but the living quarters, apart from these overlooking the courtyard, have not survived.

The Mausoleum

The sanctuary of the khanqāh is rather austere, with no wall decorations; the mausoleum of the founder, in contrast, has rich marble mainly black and white paneling.

The prayer niche is inlaid with two-colored marble, but, unlike the exterior niches, the radiation starts not from the lower part of the conch but from the apex of its arch. The marble dadoes or lower wall panels, though less rich and colorful than those in Qalāwūn's mausoleum, are in the same style, as is the wood inscription running along the walls and framing the prayer niche.

Unlike all other royal mausoleums in medieval Cairo, this one does not open directly onto the street. Instead the protruding vestibule mentioned above is set between the domed chamber and the street, which it overlooks from large iron-grilled windows. The large window of the vestibule is said to have been removed from the palace of the Abbasid Caliph in Baghdad; it was taken to Egypt in the Fatimid period along with the turban of Caliph al-Qāʾim, who had been overthrown in a rebellion. The window had been incorporated into the Fatimid's viceroyal palace, on the site where Baybars' khanqāh was erected. Ṣalāḥ al-Dīn had resided in this palace before it was turned into a khanqāh.

Bibliography

ᶜAbd al-Wahhāb. *Masājid*, pp. 131 ff.
Creswell. *M.A.E.*, II, pp. 249 ff.
Maqrīzī, *Khiṭaṭ*, II, p. 416.

THE MADRASA-MAUSOLEUM OF AMIR SUNQUR AL-SAᶜDĪ (1315)

Originally, Amir Sunqur al-Saᶜdī's foundation consisted of a madrasa, the founder's mausoleum, and a *ribāṭ*, a type of convent for women. In the Ottoman period it was used by Sufi dervishes of the Mawlawī order.

Pl. 75. The madrasa-mausoleum of Amir Sunqur al-Saᶜdī (Department of Antiquities).

The entrance has a stalactite portal, a half-dome resting on bunches of stalactites. The conch of the half-dome is treated with ablaq masonry in the form of sunrise motifs that radiate from three points at the base of the conch. There are the usual *maksala*s or benches at the door. Joggled lintels like those at Baybars al-Jashankīr's khanqāh adorn the entrance. The windows are typically included in recesses crowned with stalactites. Above the portal arch there is a band of interlaced geometrical shapes whose origins go back to Fatimid prayer niches, which we also see on the south minaret of al-Ḥākim's mosque and Imām Shāfiᶜī's mausoleum.

The Minaret

The mabkhara minaret is unusually slender and is decorated typically with stucco keel-arched niches. Its upper structure with heavy cascades of stalactites gives it a special character. Lobed arched openings within keel arches cover the octagonal zone. Its finial is in the shape of a Mawlawī turban, which must have been added in Ottoman times.

The Dome

The dome is unique in its exterior stucco decoration. The entire transitional zone is framed with carved bands forming rectangles, within each of which is a medallion. The drum of the dome is lavishly carved with inscriptions and arabesques that cover the whole area of the windows. The interior is remarkable, for although it is covered by a dome, it is rectangular not square. The prayer niche is one of the largest in Cairo's medieval buildings.

The dome inscription is not Quranic, but a carved text from the *Maqāmāt* of al-Ḥarīrī, the popular twelfth-century collection of stories in rhythmic prose. The texts selected for the mausoleum deal with death.

A further unique feature in this inscription is that the date (721 A.H.) is given in numbers, not words, as is the case in all other medieval buildings of Cairo. As on the exterior, the window zone of the dome (at the drum) is included in a ring of dense stucco ornament.

Of the madrasa, only one īwān has survived, but one may assume that the plan was cruciform. The rest was rebuilt in the Ottoman period by the Mawlawī dervishes as a theatre for their whirling performances. The building is currently undergoing restoration.

Bibliography

Creswell. *M.A.E.*, II, pp. 267 ff.
Maqrīzī. *Khiṭaṭ*, II, p. 397.
Muḥammad, ᶜAbd al-Raḥmān Fahmī. "Bayna adab al-maqāma wa fann al-ᶜimāra fī al-madrasa al-saᶜdiyya," *Majallat al-majmaᶜ al-ᶜilmī al-miṣrī*, 52 (1970-71), pp. 39 ff.

THE MOSQUE OF SULTAN AL-NĀṢIR MUḤAMMAD AT THE CITADEL (1318-35)

The mosque of Sultan al-Nāṣir Muḥammad is the royal mosque of the Citadel, in fact, of Cairo, for it was there that the sultans of Cairo performed their Friday prayers, except on religious feasts, when prayer took place in a large gathering at the hippodrome beneath the Citadel walls.

The Citadel included a mosque from the time of its foundation, and the mosque of Sultan al-Nāṣir, like

Pl. 76. The minarets of Sultan al-Nāṣir Muḥammad at the Citadel.

most of the buildings the Sultan erected at the Citadel, was built on the site of a previous construction. There were several mosques within the Citadel, but this was one of the most glamorous in Cairo until the original dome over the prayer niche, covered with green tiles, collapsed in the sixteenth century and the marble was carried off by the Ottoman conquerors.

The Exterior

The mosque, according to an inscription at the northern entrance, was founded in 1318. We are told by Maqrīzī that it was pulled down and rebuilt on a larger scale in 1335. However, its masonry shows that it was only built higher, and its roof rebuilt. Traces of the walled-up earlier crenellation on the exterior indicate where the original level was.

The hypostyle mosque is built as a regular free standing rectangle around a courtyard with a large dome covering the prayer niche area. There are three entrances, one on the northeastern side with a trilobed shallow recess and another on the northwestern wall with a stalactite portal. The third entrance is on the southern wall and is enhanced by a pointed arch including a sun-rise motif in ablaq masonry. Neither entrance has a *maksala* or bench making them the exceptions to the rule in Cairo. There are two minarets, at the northeast corner and at the northwest portal.

Unlike the mosques of the city, but like the mosque of al-Ẓāhir Baybars, its facades are not paneled and have no decoration except crenellation. Its appearance is rather austere except for the exotic minarets decorated with blue and green faience mosaics.

The Minarets

The positions of the two minarets and two asymmetrically located portals are dictated by the situation of the mosque, which faces the nothern enclosure of the Citadel on one side with its official and military buildings, and adjoins the residences of the sultans on the west and south.

The minaret to the north directed its call to prayer to the officers and soldiers dwelling there; the other minaret faced the sultans' palaces. The northern minaret is the higher of the two, most likely so that it could be seen by the palace residents some distance away. Both minarets are built entirely of stone.

The western minaret is conical, its shaft carved with a deep zigzag motif that is vertical on the first story and horizontal on the second. Its top is unique in Cairo; it has no openings and has a garlic-shaped bulb resting on a ribbed, tapering cylinder. The whole upper structure is covered with green, white and blue faience mosaics like those found at al-Nāṣir's sabīl attached to the madrasa built by his father Qalāwūn. A Quranic inscription band made of white faience mosaic adorns the neck of the bulb.

The minaret at the northeastern corner of the mosque is a different shape. The base is rectangular and the second story cylindrical, and both are without carving. Its upper part has an open hexagonal pavilion that supports the top structure, which is similar to the top of the western minaret. Both minarets have balconies adorned with parapets made of stone panels pierced with arabesques and carved in the same technique used to make the screens of Sanjar.

We know that a craftsman from Tabrīz came to Cairo during the reign of al-Nāṣir Muḥammad and that he built other minarets covered with faience, as was then the fashion in Persia. Not only the faience mosaic technique, but also the bulb shape, seems to have come from Tabrīz. Meinecke has found a thirteenth-century miniature painting of the city of Tabrīz with garlic-shaped minaret tops.

Both minarets have another feature distinguishing them from all other Mamluk minarets: their base is below the level of the roof of the mosque. This indicates that when the roof of the mosque was rebuilt after the walls were made higher, the minarets were already standing.

On the northern wall of the mosque underneath the minaret is a small balcony reached by a staircase inside the mosque. Its function is not known, but one may speculate that it was intended for prayers or recitations addressed to overflow crowds of worshipers outside the mosque.

The Interior

The walls supported by the arcades have a row of arched windows that give the building a special character. These windows must have been added when the roof was raised. The openings help reduce the thrust carried by the arches, admit light, and are ornamental as well. The voussoirs of the mosque's arcades are composed of ablaq masonry of the same stone, but painted.

The crenellation around the courtyard is of the stepped type, differing from the outer crenellation composed of rectangles with rounded tops like those of the city and Citadel walls. At the corners near the crenellations of the courtyard are four decorative structures similar to the mabkhara minaret tops.

A special collection of pre-Islamic capitals crowns the marble columns of the mosque. The two pairs of Coptic capitals at the main entrance are most remarkable. Their white marble is carved with a basket pattern. Originally, the mosque had a number of large iron-grilled windows that are now walled up. It was also paneled with a high marble dado which was later removed by Sultan Selim and shipped to Istanbul with other marbles from the palaces. The ground level inside the Citadel has risen, and the mosque must have originally been at a much higher level and reached by a staircase.

Pl. 77. The mosque of Sultan al-Nāṣir Muḥammad at the Citadel.

Following the example of al-Ẓāhir Baybars' mosque, there is a dome above the prayer niche, though this one is much smaller and was covered with green tiles. The present dome is modern. The dome is carried by granite columns like those of the Citadel palaces; they were taken from ancient Egyptian temples. As the transitional zone is made of wood, we may assume that the original dome, like many others in Cairo, was made of plastered wood. The transitional zone consists of pendentives carved with stalactites. They, together with the inscription band referring to the founder, were painted and gilded.

During the later Mamluk period, we find that stalactite squinches are supplanted by stalactite pendentives. Pendentives are triangles at the corners of the transitional zone of a dome that transfer the thrust of the dome to the corners of the four walls. The squinches are arches or quarter-domes that transfer the thrust into the middle of each of the four walls. When pendentives were adopted, the transitional zone no longer had the appearance of an uninterrupted ring of niches, as is seen in earlier domes. In the absence of squinches, no niches were used in the transitional zone, and windows were no longer divided to resemble pierced niches; a new, arched style of windows appears. In al-Nāṣir's mosque three arched windows alternate with each pendentive.

Al-Nāṣir Muḥammad's mosque has another interesting feature, a small loggia located above the northwestern entrance, reached by the staircase that leads to the roof. It is perhaps a *dikkat al-muballigh*, like the bench on columns in the sanctuary of other mosques that is used for call to prayer, recitations and Quran readings.

Bibliography

Meinecke, Michael. "Die Mamlukischen Faience Dekorationen: Eine Werkstätte aus Tabriz in Kairo (1330-1355)". *Kunst des Orients*, 11 (1976-77), pp. 85 ff.

THE ZĀWIYA OF SHAYKH ZAYN AL-DĪN YŪSUF (1298-1325)

Almost all the religious buildings dealt with in this introduction to Cairo's Islamic architecture were sponsored by members of the ruling class—caliphs, viziers, sultans, amirs, or governors. They functioned either as mosques, madrasas, or khanqāhs, or a combination of these.

There are, however, a few other buildings of which not much survives today, founded by members of the religious establishment, usually Sufi shaykhs. Maqrīzī also mentions a few mosques, built by the wealthy bourgeoisie. In his enumeration of Cairo's religious foundations, Maqrīzī mentions a number of zāwiyas of which only one from the Bahri Mamluk period is extant, that of Shaykh Zayn al-Dīn Yūsuf. A few from the Circassian period and several more from the Ottoman have survived.

The zāwiya of Shaykh Zayn al-Dīn Yūsuf is the only foundation of the Bahri Mamluk period to carry an inscription identifying it as a zāwiya. Shaykh Zayn al-Dīn Yūsuf, whose genealogy is inscribed upon the building, is identified as a descendant of the Umayyad caliphs; thus he had the same Qurayshī Arab origins as the Prophet. Originally from Mosul, he migrated to Syria where he was offered an honorary title of amir and a fief, but he rejected these and lived in a luxurious castle, served by mamluks and slave girls. He surrounded himself with treasures, owned fine horses and sumptuous clothes, and celebrated banquets in royal style.

Pl. 78. The zāwiya of Shaykh Zayn al-Dīn Yūsuf.

The importance of his status is shown in an episode related by Maqrīzī. Sultan al-Ashraf Khalīl, son of Qalāwūn, once sent him two of his highest ranking amirs to solicit his oath of allegiance. The Shaykh let them stand one hour talking with him while he remained seated, and when he invited them to sit, they knelt at his feet. He then gave him his oath of allegiance and a generous gift of 15,000 dirhams. His order, called the ᶜAdawiyya after one of his ancestors, became powerful in Syria and politically suspect. When Sultan al-Nāṣir Muḥammad began to persecute the ᶜAdawiyya, Zayn al-Dīn, also in trouble with other members of his family, fled to Egypt, where he introduced the order. His status, equal at least to that of an amir, is reflected in the architecture and superlative decoration of the zāwiya and his mausoleum.

The Exterior

The zāwiya is in the southern cemetery between the Citadel and the mausoleum of Imām Shāfiᶜī. It has a portal that now stands detached and to the east of the building, dated later than the rest (1336). Its inscriptions give the genealogy of the Shaykh and the term

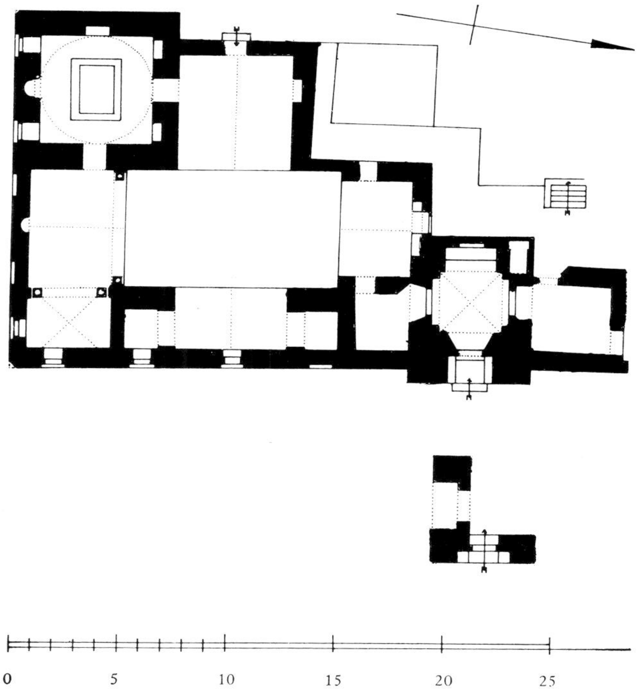

Fig. 23. The zāwiya of Shaykh Zayn al-Dīn Yūsuf (Creswell).

zāwiya is used. The portal has a rectangular recess with stalactites.

The building itself, on the west side of the cemetery road, has a rather low facade, with only one level of windows and a stalactite portal at the north side. The windows are set in recesses whose form and decoration are quite distinctive. The eastern facade has four windows, the two at the extremity set within a trilobe-arched recess, the upper part of which is framed by a molding. The two in the middle are crowned with stalactites and also framed in the upper part by a molding.

The south facade's windows are crowned with keel-arched niches. Remarkable stone carved lintels with arabesques and inscriptions also decorate the windows.

The dome is attached to the prayer hall, on its west side, which is not the street side. At that time, mausoleums in the cemetery, unlike those in the city, were not always street oriented. However, the dome is high enough to be quite visible from the road above the low facade. Its windows overlook the street on the south side. The dome is of the elongated and ribbed type, and the exterior transitional zone is decorated with bands of carved stucco that frame all of its facets as well as the twenty keel-arched windows of the drum. Above the windows is another stucco inscription band. There is no minaret.

The Interior

The stalactite portal, carrying an inscription assigning the zāwiya to the year 1298, on the north edge of the facade, leads through a vestibule to a cruciform interior. The courtyard is surrounded by four vaulted īwāns. The cruciform plan differs from others, however, in not having cells between the īwāns. There were formerly a few cells on the upper floor that were removed during restoration work. Another irregularity is that the side īwāns are unequal in size, and the qibla īwān is relatively shallow. Layla Ali Ibrahim, who studied the architecture of this building, assumes that the cruciform layout was introduced in the interior at a date later than that of the mausoleum and facade construction. An inscription slab at the mausoleum entrance carries the date 1325, but does not specify the event it commemorates. The two dates and the irregularity of the plan suggest that the zāwiya was not built according to a comprehensive plan.

The decoration of the zāwiya interior is composed of a band of carved stucco running around the whole building and framing the prayer niche, including within arabesque borders rows of cartouches, one oblong and the next circular, with inscriptions. This band also frames the entrance to the mausoleum dome adjoining the qibla iwān to the west.

As the qibla īwān is relatively shallow, the mausoleum is wider than the īwān's depth and thus protrudes into the west side īwān which it also directly joins, as there are no cells between.

The Mausoleum

The lower part of the domed chamber is decorated with a polychrome marble dado and inlaid panels with square Kufic inscriptions. The upper wall decoration has disappeared, but that of the dome survives and is quite exceptional. The dome is ribbed inside and out, with flat carved ribs that spring from a central inscription medallion at the apex. At the base, each rib ends in a niche with a carved conch flanked by two colonnettes. The arabesque pattern carved on the ribs recalls the soffits of Qalāwūn's mausoleum. The stucco was painted, and the frames of all twenty drum windows together with the composite squinches are carved stucco, giving the dome's interior an extremely lavish appearance. The window stucco grills are formed with arabesque patterns and filled with colored glass.

Bibliography

Ali Ibrahim, Layla. "The Zāwiya of Shaikh Zain al-Dīn Yūsuf in Cairo". *Mitteilungen des Deutschen Archäologischen Instituts Abteilung Kairo*, 34 (1978), pp. 79 ff.
van Berchem. *C.I.A.*, pp. 148 ff.
Creswell. *M.A.E.*, pp. 229 ff.
Maqrīzī. *Khiṭaṭ*, II, pp. 435 ff.

THE SABĪL OF SULTAN AL-NĀṢIR MUḤAMMAD (1326)

On the left side of the entrance to Qalāwūn's madrasa is an arcade of four pointed arches running around the corner of the building, forming an L-shape (s. Pl. 67). Its roof has a small octagonal structure which must have been the base of a small dome no longer there. The structure is a sabīl, added by Sultan al-Nāṣir Muḥammad, a public fountain for the thirsty visitor.

The name sabīl comes from the expression, *fī sabīl Allāh*, which is equivalent to "for the sake of God", or charity. The Quran has many references to the obligation of giving water to the thirsty. Such fountains were often sponsored by rulers as charitable, pious deeds.

Providing water in medieval Cairo, far from the Nile, was no small task. Houses of the rich had their own wells or cisterns, as did all important foundations such as mosques, madrasas, and khanqāhs. The cisterns were cleaned yearly and treated with aromatic herbs to give the water a fresh flavor, and filled by caravans of donkeys from the Nile. Common people bought water for general purposes from water carriers, but the sabīls, of which al-Nāṣir Muḥammad's is the earliest surviving example, were for drinking water only. The sabīl had a cistern, and a man in charge of cleaning and maintaining the facility and handing out water to the thirsty.

The shape of this sabīl is unusual; it is an arcaded building on a corner. The octagonal structure upon which a dome must have once stood is decorated with colored faience bits, ceramic pieces set like mosaics in patterns. Unlike common mosaics which are of uniform pieces, here the tessera are cut in larger or smaller pieces according to the requirements of the patterns of the letters, which are set on a plaster background. Today, these mosaics are hardly visible beneath the dust, but some brown, green and white pieces can be seen. This technique of architectural decoration originated in Mongol Persia during the same period, whence it came to Egypt and was used here and there but never to the extent that it was in Persia. In Cairo, carved stucco and stone were preferred to the more colorful ceramic decoration.

Bibliography

Creswell. *M.A.E.*, II, pp. 274 ff.
Meinecke. "Faience."

THE MOSQUE OF AMIR ALṬINBUGHĀ AL-MĀRIDĀNĪ (1340)

Amir Alṭinbughā was the cup-bearer and the son-in-law of Sultan al-Nāṣir Muḥammad. The mosque he erected is in the southern outskirts outside Bāb Zuwayla, in the quarter called Tabbāna.

The Exterior

The mosque has a hypostyle plan like the mosque of al-Nāṣir, but its exterior walls are treated in the usual urban Mamluk style, with recesses crowned with stalactites including double-arched windows.

Pl. 79. The mosque of Amir al-Māridānī.

The mosque has three entrances, one on the axis of the prayer niche which has a stalactite portal with a medallion of faience mosaic, and two on the sides. The main street is on the north side; hence the minaret and main entrance are also on the north side of the mosque.

The main portal is a deeply recessed pointed arch, with a richly decorated wall facing the street. Carved and inlaid two-colored marbles are topped by a stalactite cresting. There is a small window with colonnettes above the door, and maksalas flank both sides of the entrance. On the left side of this entrance passage stands the minaret. The wall under the minaret has an obvious irregularity: the ṭirāz band starting on the right side of the entrance vault that runs along the whole facade is interrupted underneath the minaret, and the colonnettes at the facade's other corners are missing at this corner. A close look at the buttress of the minaret reveals that different types of stone are used, meaning that this part of the wall has been rebuilt. The crenellation is missing above the entire portal and the buttress of the minaret.

The south side entrance and northern axial entrance are decorated with blue and white faience mosaic patterns on window grills, medallions and panels.

The Minaret

The mosque provides the first example of a minaret that is octagonal from top to bottom. It also has the earliest extant top that is not the mabkhara type, but a pavilion of eight columns carrying above a crown of stalactites a pear-shaped bulb. This composition will be seen to characterize all later Mamluk minarets. We know from Maqrīzī that the architect of this minaret, Muᶜallim al-Suyūfī, Sultan al-Nāṣir Muḥammad's chief architect, also built the minaret at Aqbughā's al-Azhar madrasa. That minaret has an octagonal first story, but the second is circular; the third is missing.

The Interior

Like the mosque of al-Nāṣir at the Citadel, this is a hypostyle mosque and its columns have a variety of pre-Islamic capitals. Ancient Egyptian granite columns support the dome above the prayer niche. This dome is similar to al-Nāṣir's royal mosque dome at the Citadel and has the same type of transitional zone.

The facade of the courtyard is remarkable. The pointed arches are framed with a continuous molding forming a loop at the apex of each arch. Above the arches, keel-arched niches alternate with a lozenge above a medallion, all carved in stucco. The stepped crenellation is also carved in stucco arabesques. Decorative structures of mabkhara shape are set at the corners and in the middle of each wall of the courtyard facade, each carrying a bulb of blue glass.

The main feature of the courtyard facade is the wooden mashrabiyya that secludes the prayer hall from the courtyard. It has a large inscription and pleasantly filters light from the courtyard. This and the screen at the mosque of al-Ṣāliḥ Ṭalāʾiᶜ, originally also in the sanctuary, are the only surviving examples of such wooden screens in mosques. There is a similar screen at the mausoleum of Qalāwūn around the cenotaph area.

The interior of the sanctuary is richly decorated. In addition to the colored marble dado on the walls, there are panels of inlaid marble like those at the mausoleum of Qalāwūn, also with decorative square Kufic script repeating the name of Muḥammad. The prayer niche is inlaid with marble and has rows of niches separated by blue glass colonnettes. Carved stucco once covered the walls with a series of medallions and naturalistic tree representations unique in Cairo architecture.

The pendentives of the dome and its inscriptions are made of painted and gilded wood. Stucco arabesque grills filled with colored glass decorate the windows. The pulpit, which is original, has geometric star patterns, and the bulb at its top is similar to that of the minaret. Above all these doors inside are panels with

Pl. 80. The sanctuary of the mosque of Amir al-Māridānī.

Pl. 81. Mashrabiyya at the sanctuary of al-Māridānī.

blue and white faience mosaics. The ablution fountain in the courtyard is not part of the original mosque.

On the northern wall of the sanctuary is an inscription panel of white marble carved and inlaid with green gypsum-like paste.

Bibliography

ʿAbd al-Wahhāb. *Masājid*, pp. 147 ff.
Maqrīzī. *Khiṭaṭ*, II, p. 308.

THE MOSQUE OF AMIR AQSUNQUR (1347)

The mosque built by Amir Aqsunqur, a son-in-law of Sultan al-Nāṣir Muḥammad, and the husband of his widow, stands in the Tabbāna quarter between Bāb Zuwayla and the Citadel. It has a hypostyle plan like the mosque of Amir Alṭinbughā al-Māridānī, though it differs in many other respects.

Because it is situated on a thoroughfare, the mosque has a ground plan that is not quite regular. It has three entrances, the main one opening onto the western arcade opposite the sanctuary, and two side entrances, one into the southern arcade and the other at the corner between the northern and western arcades.

The primary irregularity of the ground plan is the presence of a mausoleum dome on the street side that predates the foundation of the mosque and which was incorporated into its masonry. The mausoleum is not Mecca-oriented, which is unusual in Cairo mausoleums; instead it follows the street alignment.

Pl. 82. The sanctuary of the mosque of Amir Aqsunkur.

When integrated with the mosque, the western arcade acquired a triangular shape to cope on one side with the street alignment and to be parallel on the other side to the Mecca-oriented sanctuary. Thus, the entrance bay is set askew to the rest of the mosque, as it is at al-Aqmar.

The Exterior

The tall circular minaret at the southwestern corner of the mosque is visible to the passerby coming down from the Citadel long before he reaches the door of the mosque. This minaret, because of its location in relation to the winding street and other buildings, was frequently illustrated by nineteenth-century artists and photographers. In three of these illustrations, we see a remarkable feature that characterized this minaret before it was restored—it originally had four, not three, stories. Unfortunately, when the minaret was restored at the beginning of this century, the third floor was not rebuilt, and it has thus lost its uncommon feature. The first story is circular and plain, the second circular and ribbed, the third was octagonal, and the fourth is composed of the usual pavilion of eight columns supporting a bulb like the top of al-Māridānī's minaret. The minaret is remarkable in its elegance and in being one of the few Mamluk minarets with a circular shaft.

The main portal is composed of a large pointed arch with corbels at the springing of the arch. The mausoleum on the north side of the portal has two facades on the street.

This mausoleum contains the graves of several sons of Sultan al-Nāṣir Muḥammad. We know that the first deceased son died in 1341 so the mosque must already have been standing at that time. The mausoleum was known, however, by the name of Sultan ʿAlāʾ al-Dīn Kujuk, another son of al-Nāṣir Muḥammad, who ruled a brief time between 1341 and 1342. He was first buried elsewhere and then brought to this mausoleum two decades later, during the rule of his brother Sultan Ḥasan. Aqsunqur, himself related by marriage to the Qalāwūn family, incorporated the mausoleum into his own mosque and built a mausoleum for himself next to it where he and his son are buried. A sabīl and a kuttāb have completely disappeared.

The Interior

The interior presents a rather incoherent layout, as part of the arcades are carried by piers supporting cross-vaulted bays while others are carried on columns supporting a flat wooden ceiling. Originally, the mosque must have been built only on piers supporting cross-vaulted bays. Meinecke identifies this feature as Syrian. Aqsunqur had been governor of Tripoli in Syria and Maqrīzī writes that he supervised the construction of the mosque himself, even to carrying materials along with the masons. The piers supporting the cross-vaults remain unique in Egyptian medieval architecture, with no later imitations. The prayer niche is enhanced by a one-bay dome on plain squinches, an archaic feature in 1347, though the combination is also found in brick in the same mosque in Kujuk's mausoleum. The stone version is seen at the mausoleum domes of Umm al-Sulṭān Shaʾbān and the two domes of Tankizbughā (1359 and 1362). The prayer niche is quite remarkable with its carved white marble conch that was originally painted. The lower part is paneled with polychrome marble. The pulpit is one of the few marble ones and is a masterpiece, decorated with carved bands and on both sides with large patterns inlaid with colored stones. The pulpit door's stalactites and the bulb on four columns at the top are all carved in marble.

The *dikka* facing the courtyard from the sanctuary has Western style capitals that may be Crusader trophies. The mosque was in poor condition by the early fifteenth century, since its endowments in Syria had by then been lost. An amir added an ablution fountain in the center of the courtyard in 1412 but because of lack of funds, the mosque was used only on Fridays and special occasions.

Amir Aqsunqur's masons, apparently not familiar with the vaulting system applied in the mosque's architecture, must have done a poor job of building them, for in 1652 the Amir Ibrāhīm Aghā Mustaḥfiẓān made important structural restorations of the arcades and the roof, using columns to support the southern arcaded hall. At the same time, he redecorated the sanctuary with the tiles that have given the mosque its modern touristic name, "the Blue Mosque."

In the Ottoman period many sponsors of religious foundations restored old mosques that had fallen into decay or built upon their foundations and walls, rather than building new ones. Such mosques then acquired the name of the restorer, and this mosque, after restoration, was sometimes called the mosque of Ibrāhīm Aghā.

The tiles are of seventeenth-century Turkish Iznik style. They are blue and green with typically Ottoman floral motifs, such as vases with carnations and tulips, and cypress trees. Some motifs are applied individually on each tile; others form compositions on a set of tiles. The Cairo craftsmen were not quite familiar with the art of tile paneling, and the tiles are inexpertly applied to the walls.

Ibrāhīm Aghā used the opportunity to add in the southern arcade a mausoleum for himself, also paneled with marble in Mamluk style and including a prayer niche whose decoration is quite faithful to the Bahri Mamluk marble-inlay tradition.

Bibliography

ʿAbd al-Wahhāb. *Masājid*, pp. 152 ff.

Maqrīzī. *Khiṭaṭ*, II, p. 309.

Meinecke, Michael. "Die Moschee des Amirs Aqsunqur an-Nasiri in Kairo," *Mitteilungen des Deutschen Archäologischen Instituts Abteilung Kairo*, 29 (1973), pp. 9 ff.

Meinecke-Berg, V. "Die Osmanische Fliesendekoration der Aqsunqur-Moschee in Kairo. Zur Entwicklung der Iznik Fliesen des 17. Jahrhunderts." *Mitteilungen*, 29 (1973), pp. 39 ff.

THE MOSQUE AND THE KHANQĀH OF AMIR SHAYKHŪ (1349, 1355)

The mosque and khanqāh of Amir Shaykhū, a leading amir under Sultan Ḥasan, face each other on Ṣalība Street with similar facades and minarets, giving the complex an interesting appearance. Six years separate the foundation of Shaykhū's mosque from that of the khanqāh.

The architectural combination appears today as unique, but at one time it was not. A few years earlier (1340), Amir Bashtāk built a mosque and a khanqāh facing each other across a street, with a bridge connecting them. The complex of Amir Manjaq al-Silāḥdār near the Citadel (1349) also consisted of a mosque on one side of the street and a khanqāh on the opposite side, of which only ruins remain. Some complexes in the cemetery, such as those of Barsbay, Qāytbāy, and Qurqumās, were also composed of structures on both sides of the street.

The Mosque: The Exterior

The lintel and threshold of the mosque are taken from ancient Egyptian temples. A stalactite portal surmounted by the minaret leads to the vestibule. The minaret is octagonal throughout and has a special feature: rather than stalactites underneath the balconies, it is decorated with carving consisting of

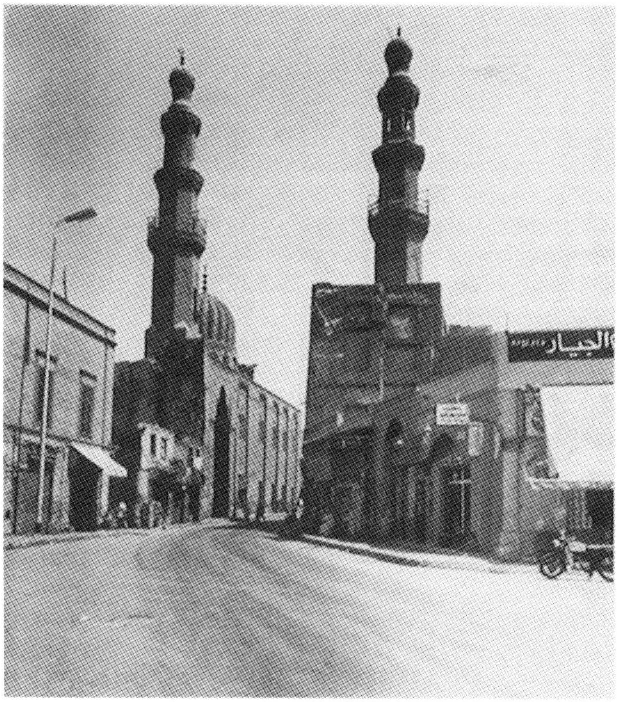

Pl. 83. The mosque (left) and khanqāh of Amir Shaykhū.

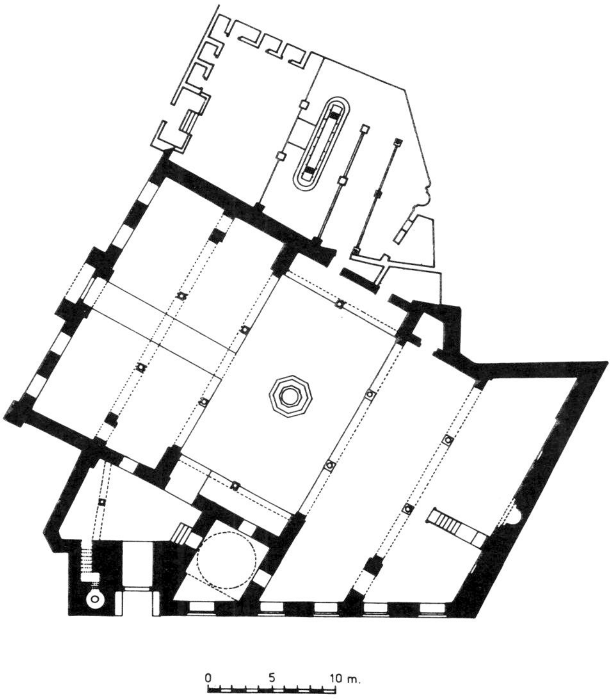

Fig. 24. The mosque and mausoleum of Amir Shaykhū (Department of Antiquities).

horizontal moldings at the first balcony and vertical ribs at the upper balcony. The vertical ribs are similar to those at the top of Qalāwūn's minaret, added by his son al-Nāṣir. Creswell compared this pattern to ancient Egyptian reed motifs. Only one other minaret in Cairo, that of Manjaq al-Silāḥdār, has this type of decoration.

Except for their transitional zones and some details in the carved arabesques of the shaft's first story, the two minarets are identical. Their bulbs are carved in an almond-shaped pattern and Quranic inscriptions encircle the necks of the bulbs.

The facade of the mosque has a small ribbed mausoleum dome next to the minaret. The entrance to the mausoleum is from the vestibule; the entrance to the mosque, also from the vestibule, is bent. In the vestibule are pieces of polished black stone in the walls that must have served as mirrors.

The Interior

The mosque of Shaykhū was severely damaged when the last Mamluk sultan, Ṭūmānbāy, hid there during battles between the Mamluks and Ottoman conquerors. Some parts were burned, including a dome that was above the prayer niche. Little of the original decoration has survived. The prayer niche is paneled with marbles of no special interest; it may have been restored during the Ottoman period. The lower part of the prayer niche has seventeenth-century Tunisian tiles.

The plan of the mosque is hypostyle, though it differs from the plan typical of its time in having only two riwāqs or arcaded halls. On the lateral sides are recesses facing the courtyard with a double arch supported by one column. Thus, the features of the classic hypostyle plan are combined with the cruciform pattern. The prayer hall is not a regular rectangle, but follows without accommodation the shape of the ground space available.

The pulpit of the mosque is made of stone and though most of its decoration has disappeared, what remains shows the style of Sultan Qāytbāy's reign. A similar, and better preserved, example is that at the khanqāh of Faraj Ibn Barqūq. The *dikka*, or bench used for recitations, is also made of stone rather than the usual wood or marble. It is covered with carvings different from those of the pulpit and is dated A.H. 963 (1555/6).

The Khanqāh (1355)

The portal and minaret are repetitions of the patterns used in the mosque facade six years earlier. Ancient Egyptian stones are also used here for the lintel and the entrance threshold. The vestibule leads through a bend to the khanqāh, whose plan differs from that of the mosque in having several stories of living units for the Sufis surrounding the courtyard on three sides. The prayer hall is hypostyle and has a prayer niche whose only decoration is the ablaq masonry in the conch.

The plan follows the street alignment and is thus irregular, making the interior of the sanctuary a trapezoid instead of a rectangle. Shaykhū was buried at

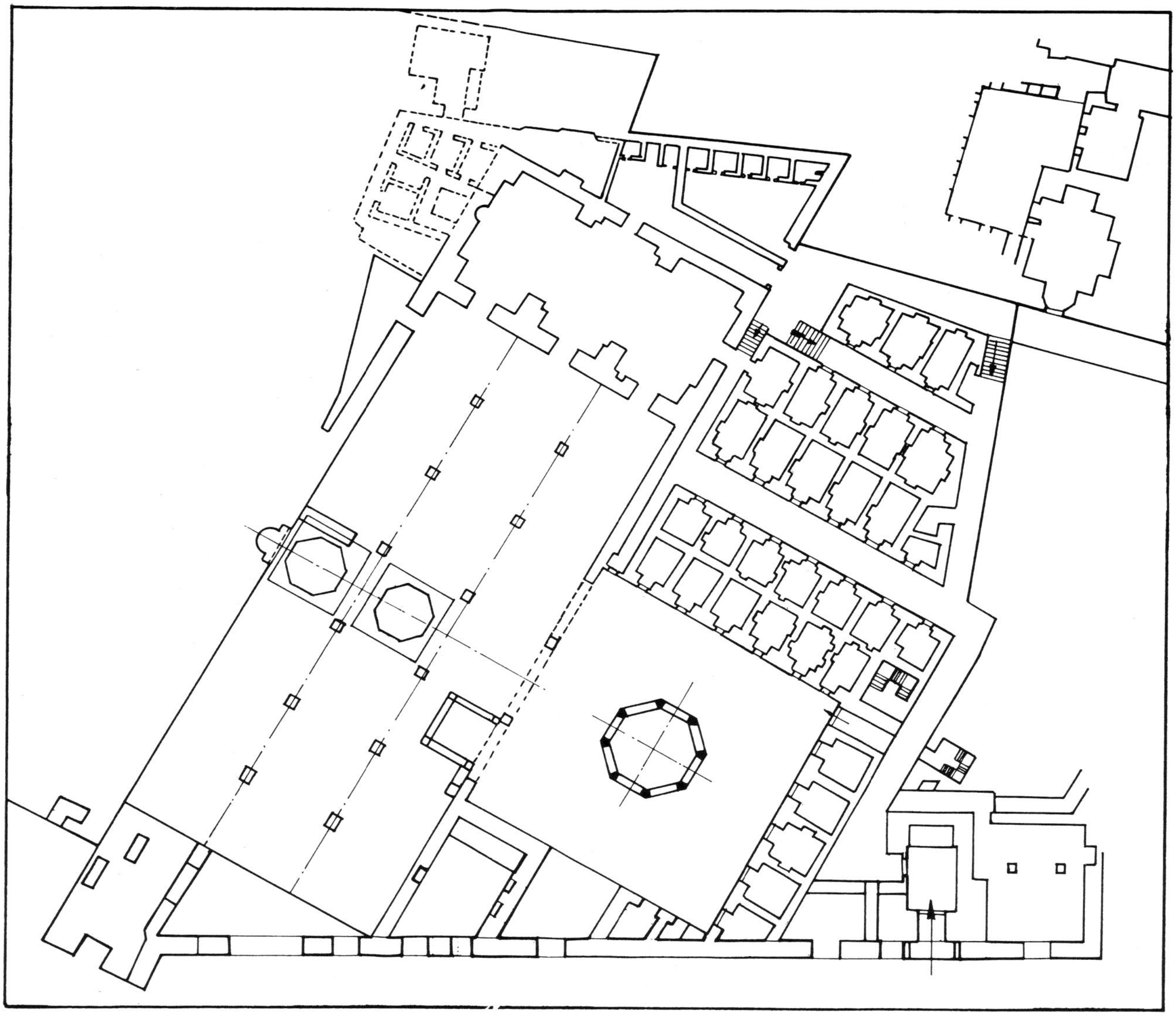

Fig. 25. The khanqāh of Amir Shaykhū (Department of Antiquities).

Pl. 84. The interior of the khanqāh of Amir Shaykhū.

the corner on the northeastern or street side rather than in the mausoleum he had attached to the mosque, and the first shaykh of the khanqāh is also buried there. In the Ottoman period, wall paintings representing the Ka^cba in Mecca were added to this part of the sanctuary.

The fourth (north) side on the street, has a small īwān and is very irregular. In fact, it seems to have functioned primarily as a screen wall between the street and the interior. Its ground plan is triangular. This gave the courtyard a regular rectangular plan, unlike the sanctuary.

There is a bulbous wooden dome in front of the prayer niche which may or may not be original. The beautiful ceiling paintings in blue and white were done in the eighteenth century, as an inscription notes.

A foundation inscription slab, originally at the entrance but now in the sanctuary, is interesting in that it gives the founder's name without the usual series of titles and attributes. Only the phrase, "the humble servant of God," is used, suggesting that Shaykhū considered himself a Sufi. The text further implies that the khanqāh was also intended to house pilgrims on their way to Mecca, for interestingly, the text of the inscription on the khanqāh minaret is from the sūra referring to pilgrimage. The khanqāh of Shaykhū, according to Maqrīzī, included the teaching of theology and the four rites of Islamic law, making it equivalent to a madrasa.

To the south of the sanctuary is a qā^ca or reception hall, today in very dilapidated condition though its plan is recognizable. Sufi foundations often had residential structures attached where the founder spent time with the Sufis in order to receive their blessings.

The Living Units

The cells surrounding the courtyard of the khanqāh are supplemented by a large complex of three-storied cells on the south side of the building that overlooked a passage between them and the khanqāh. According to Maqrīzī, the khanqāh originally covered an area of one *feddan*, or over four thousand square meters. Attached to the khanqāh were two public baths, shops, and living units, providing income for the upkeep of the foundation. The Sufis attached to the foundation were given bread, meat, oil, soap and sweets. This was one of Cairo's largest pious foundations.

Bibliography

ᶜAbd al-Wahhāb. *Masājid*, pp. 156 ff.
Maqrīzī. *Khiṭaṭ*, II, pp. 313, 421.
van Berchem. *C.I.A.*, p. 232.

Pl. 85. Gallery in the living quarters at the khanqāh of Amir Shaykhū.

Pl. 86. The facade of the madrasa-mausoleum of Amir Ṣarghitmish (Department of Antiquities).

THE MADRASA OF AMIR ṢARGHITMISH (1356)

Amir Ṣarghitmish, whose career began under Sultan al-Muẓaffar Ḥājī, died during the reign of Sultan Ḥasan. He built his madrasa adjoining the mosque of Ibn Ṭūlūn on Ṣalība Street. The madrasa taught the Ḥanafī rite, and its students were Persians. The building has several remarkable features.

The Exterior

The southwestern facade facing the mosque of Ibn Ṭūlūn has shops underneath, but the main facade is on the west side, with a stalactite portal and an octagonal minaret with carved bulb on its left. The portal stalactites differ from others of their time in having pendentive triangles at the two corners between the semi-dome and rectangular recess. The minaret is decorated with two-colored inlaid masonry forming a sunrise motif on the first story, and a zigzag motif on the second story. There is only one of the small decorative balconies on the second story where there are usually four, one on every second facet of the octagon.

Projecting onto the street on the southwestern side of the building is a mausoleum that does not adjoin the prayer hall, so that it can face the main street.

The dome is unusual with its particularly high drum, remains of an inscription band, and a cornice of stalactites underneath the dome. This is the earliest extant example of a dome with stalactites on the exterior. The transitional zone of the dome is not visible from the exterior and the profile of the dome differs from the common type in lacking a pointed top. It is double shelled, with the inner shell quite a bit lower than the outer, a device used in the mausoleums of Samarkand beginning in the Timurid period (early fifteenth century).

The Interior

The madrasa plan is cruciform with four unequal īwāns, between which are living units. Some of the living units overlook the street; others open onto the courtyard. An unusual feature in Cairo cruciform plan plan madrasas is the large dome over the prayer niche. The original dome collapsed and has since been rebuilt using an old photograph as guide. This dome does not have a double shell, as the dome of the mausoleum though it has a similarly high drum. We do not know whether the original dome had a double shell or not. The dome is carried on wooden pendentives and covers the central bay of the prayer hall. Two flat-roofed bays are on each side of the domed area.

The prayer hall has carved marble slabs, some of which are in the Islamic Museum, and others in another mosque in the neighborhood. The decorations on these slabs are floral; one of them has an interesting composition of arabesques with two hands holding stalks, a lamp, and birds. Ḥasan ʿAbd al-Wahhāb writes that marbles with animal representations and grapes were found under the floor of the madrasa.

One of the slabs near the prayer niche has a medallion at its center and an inscription with the founder's name as well as a blazon, or emblem, of Ṣarghitmish, a handkerchief, symbol of his function as *jamdār*, or amir in charge of the royal wardrobe.

In the Bahri Mamluk period, the functions of the various amirs were represented in their blazons, or emblems applied to their buildings, residences, and objects they used. These blazons symbolized their functions at the royal court: a sword on the gate of the sword-carrier Manjaq al-Silāḥdār (1346/7); polo sticks carved at the mosque of Amir Ālmalik al-Juqandār, the polo master (1319); a cup at the madrasa of Iljāy al-Yūsufī (1373), and the wakāla of Qūṣūn (1341), cup bearers. The earliest example of a blazon on a Cairo building is the pair of lions facing each other on al-Ẓāhir Baybars' madrasa at Naḥḥāsīn; in this case, the emblem was of his name, *baybars* meaning lion.

In the middle of the marble paved courtyard is an ablution fountain in the shape of a pavilion of eight marble columns which most likely once had a dome, like that on the Sultan Ḥasan mosque.

The domed mausoleum is reached from the western īwān opposite the prayer hall. The domed area does not directly overlook the street; adjoining it is a rectangular space that is cross-vaulted and has windows. A similar device is used at the mausoleum of Baybars al-Jashankīr. In both cases, this is explained by the street alignment on one side and the Mecca orientation of the dome and its relationship to the rest of the building on the other side, where there is a fine marble cenotaph. The transitional zone of its double-shell dome differs from that of the prayer-niche dome in being composed of several tiered squinches, as is usual in brick domes.

The Domes

The exotic character of the domes of Ṣarghitmish's madrasa might be associated with its dedication to Per-

Pl. 87. The madrasa-mausoleum of Amir Ṣarghitmish and the minaret of Ibn Ṭūlūn.

sian students. Though several similar domes are found at Samarkand in Transoxania (today in the Soviet Union), all examples are of a later date, built around the year 1400. There is no doubt, however, that these domes had a foreign prototype and did not belong to a Cairene tradition, for they appear suddenly in Cairo architecture with no signs of a previous evolution. Furthermore, double-shell domes were common in Persia. A common prototype in Persia could have been the origin of both the Samarkand and Ṣarghitmish domes, though no examples have survived there.

A similar situation is seen in the mosque of Ibn Ṭūlūn, where features taken from Samarra mosques have very few surviving precedents, and in the minarets of al-Nāṣir Muḥammad at the Citadel, whose Persian origins cannot be demonstrated in surviving structures. The double-shell dome was built once more in Cairo, at the Sulṭāniyya mausoleum.

Bibliography

ʿAbd al-Wahhāb. *Masājid*, pp. 106 ff.
Maqrīzī. *Khiṭaṭ*, II, p. 403.
Meinecke. "Faience."

THE MOSQUE OF SULTAN ḤASAN (1356-61)

Although it was never completed, the mosque of Sultan Ḥasan has always been praised as one of the major monuments of the Islamic world. Its founder, Sultan Ḥasan, was not one of the major rulers of Egypt; he came to power as a child, and authority was in the hands of his regents. His rule was interrupted (1347-51 and 1354-61), and when he was killed, his body was hidden and never found again. Cairo's greatest mausoleum was empty until an amir was buried there more than a century later.

Pl. 88. The madrasa-mosque and mausoleum of Sultan Ḥasan.

The mosque of Sultan Ḥasan was a madrasa for the four rites of Islamic law, and for the first time in Cairo, the madrasa had also the status of a congregational mosque for the Friday sermon.

The foundation was ambitious in every respect. In architectural proportions it is the most gigantic of Cairo's mosques, built to house four hundred students. The cost of the building and decoration became so high that the work had to be left uncompleted. It is reported that Sultan Ḥasan said he would have abandoned the whole scheme but for the shame it would bring if people could say that an Egyptian sultan was not able to complete a mosque he had started.

The Site

The mosque of Sultan Ḥasan was erected on the site of a palace that was pulled down, overlooking the square where the hippodrome and horse market were located, beneath the royal residences of the Citadel. It was thus one of the most prestigious sites in Cairo, and the centerpiece of the panoramic view from al-Qaṣr al-Ablaq with its huge gilded window grills. The entire architectural conception of this gigantic building responded to the privileged character of the site.

Its location was, however, also a liability, for with its massive walls and proximity to the Citadel, it suffered in ways that no other mosque in Cairo did. During the reign of Sultan Barqūq, rebels occupied the mosque and fired at the Citadel from its roof, whereupon Sultan Barqūq destroyed the staircases in order to prevent any repetition of that event. Later, another sultan had to send soldiers to occupy the mosque to prevent rebels from entrenching themselves in it, and once again, Sultan Jaqmaq blocked the staircases. Sultan Jānbalāṭ took the surprising decision in 1500 to destroy the mosque to prevent its being used for military uprisings, and a team of workers set about the demolition until criticism forced him to abandon it.

In the Ottoman period, the mosque was again involved in warfare. Bullet holes pierced the dome, so weakening it that it was demolished to prevent its accidental collapse. The collapse of one of the two minarets, taking away part of a buttress with its stalactites, could also have been a consequence of battles. In the eighteenth century, the mosque was reopened after having been closed for half a century for security reasons.

The Facades

The mosque is free standing and has three facades. The fourth, western, side has the large commercial complex and other dependencies belonging to the waqf of Sultan Ḥasan which financed the foundation. A waterwheel is still in place.

The facade as seen from the Citadel presented a dome flanked on each side by a minaret. The dome was that of the mausoleum, which collapsed in 1661. According to a traveler's description, it was huge and bulbous, built of wood and covered with lead as is the dome of Imām Shāfiᶜī. The fact that it is described as bulbous recalls the mosque of Ṣarghitmish, built only a few years earlier. The present dome of Sultan Ḥasan is modern and is a misinterpretation of the original design.

One of the two original minarets has survived, the highest minaret of medieval Cairo at eighty-four meters. It is octagonal throughout, like the minarets of al-Māridānī, Shaykhū, and Ṣarghitmish. Its shaft also has geometric patterns made of inlaid stone, and its top is composed of a bulb on eight columns. Its silhouette is massive compared to other minarets of the same period. The second minaret collapsed in 1659 and was replaced shortly afterward by the inferior structure we see today on the north corner of the mausoleum.

The facade of Sultan Ḥasan's mosque that is seen from the Citadel today is thus quite irregular. The domed square of the mausoleum protrudes on three sides and is also particularly high, over thirty meters. At its top is a projecting stalactite cornice in carved stone running along the facade of the building; it has no parallel in any other Cairene mosque.

The center of each of the three mausoleum facades is decorated with a medallion with a bull's-eye in the center, framed by interlaced bands in two colors. There also two rows of windows, the upper ones inserted in recesses crowned with stalactites surmounted by a shallow conch, an arrangement similar to portal treatments. The shallow conch like the medallions is decorated with interlaced bands.

Pl. 89. The northern facade and portal of Sultan Ḥasan.

The lower windows are inserted in recesses that have a stepped pyramidal profile and were once decorated with faience mosaics, of which there are still traces on the south side. These mosaics show that the craftsmen from Tabrīz who came during the reign of Sultan al-Nāṣir Muḥammad, Sultan Ḥasan's father, must have had their workshops in Cairo for several decades.

Finely carved columns with stalactite capitals and bases grace the corners. The twisted carved motif on the shaft of the columns is also seen on the colonnettes decorating the facade of the al-Aqmar mosque, a motif going back to Byzantine tradition. The southern facade of the complex has eight horizontal rows of windows, each two corresponding to one story of student cells. This composition gives the facade the appearance of a modern highrise not seen in any other medieval building in Cairo. The northern facade, with the mosque's portal, is also characterized by a multitude of windows.

The Portal

The portal occupies the whole length of the facade, making it by far the largest in Cairo. Its most remarkable feature is that it is set at an angle to the rest of the facade. It may have been set askew so that it is visible from the Citadel, or perhaps simply to suit the street alignment. The portal is dominated by a cascade of dripping stalactites surmounted by a fluted half-dome.

The architecture of the portal has been compared to that of the Gök madrasa in Anatolia built under Saljūq rule (1271/2), with medallions flanking the stalactite vault, the carved bands framing it, and the panels filled with geometric patterns. The similarity also extends to the original plan of the mosque, with two minarets at the portal as in Anatolian mosques and at the Gök madrasa. The original plan called for four minarets: one was built at the portal, but it collapsed before the second was erected, and the plan to build minarets at the portal was abandoned. The resemblance between the portals of Sultan Hasan's mosque and the Gök madrasa cannot be explained by their having the same architect, as the Gök madrasa was built much earlier. However, the Sultan Ḥasan portal could have been designed by a Cairo craftsman who had been in Anatolia and was impressed by the portal of the madrasa, or it could have been made by an Anatolian craftsman in Cairo who was inspired by the same building. According to Maqrīzī craftsmen from all over the world worked on the mosque of Sultan Ḥasan.

The portal of Sultan Ḥasan's mosque is superlative not only in size, but also in the quality of the craftsmanship involved in its decorations. The decoration was never completed, though work on the mosque continued for years after Sultan Ḥasan's death. Prayer, however, was inaugurated as soon as the prayer hall was completed. Because the prayer hall dictated the orientation of the main part of the mosque, it was the part completed first. The carved bands adorning the portal are not continued above, and the stages of work can thus be seen: the carvings below are completed and the patterns above them are incised but not carved out, showing that work began on the lower part and moved upwards. The uppermost part of the portal is devoid of decoration and seems to be lacking its facing.

The carved, but not completed, decoration at the portal of Sultan Ḥasan is of great interest, as it presents Chinese flower motifs such as chrysanthemums and Chinese lotus flowers. These patterns were common in Mamluk fourteenth-century minor-art objects, but this is the only known example in architecture. The patterns do not imply that Chinese craftsmen worked on the mosque, but that the craftsmen who did were familiar with Chinese art motifs. Trade between the Far East and the Islamic world flourished during the fourteenth century, promoted by the opening of land routes between the Mediterranean and China, under the Mongols' Asian hegemony. Chinese porcelains and silks, highly cherished in Egypt, must have inspired Cairene artists to enlarge their decorative repertoire with these exotic designs.

On the right side of the entrance is a narrow, very curious carved panel with architectural designs, such as a Gothic portal and a domed structure with gabled roof of Western, probably Byzantine, origin, possibly a craftsman's signature in disguise. In fact, the layout of the vestibule, with a stone dome on pendentives flanked with three half domes dripping with stalactites, is Byzantine in style. The domed structure has been interpreted as the Dome of the Rock.

Before entering the vestibule, there is a handsome inlaid marble inscription and two marble niches inlaid with geometric designs, whose conchs are decorated with stalactites as in Anatolian prayer niches. The vestibule has a large stone bench that may have been used by Quran readers, and also has medallions of inlaid marble with intricate geometric patterns and carved stone niches.

The original bronze door of Sultan Ḥasan's mosque is now at the mosque of Sultan al-Muʾayyad at Bāb Zuwayla. Al-Muʾayyad acquired it, illegally, from Sultan Ḥasan's foundation, along with a huge bronze chandelier that is now at the Islamic Museum.

The Interior

Through a bent entrance, passing beneath the student living quarters, we reach the courtyard framed by four unequal and enormous vaulted halls or īwāns. In the center is an ablution fountain completed in 1362, composed of eight marble columns carrying a bulbous wooden dome decorated with an inscription band in relief. This is perhaps a replica of the missing mausoleum dome that was also wooden, and bulbous.

The great size of the four īwāns leaves no space for the cells to overlook the courtyard, and as has been noted, their many windows overlook the street on the southern and northern facades. The other cells have windows onto light shafts.

Between the four īwāns are the four entrances to each of the madrasas. The entrances are decorated with rich multicolored marble inlay work. The largest madrasa, on the right side of the prayer hall, was that of the Ḥanafī rite, to which the Mamluks adhered. Next largest, on the left side of the sanctuary, was that of the Shāfiʿī rite, which most Egyptians at the time followed. The Mālikī and Ḥanbalī madrasas are on the opposite

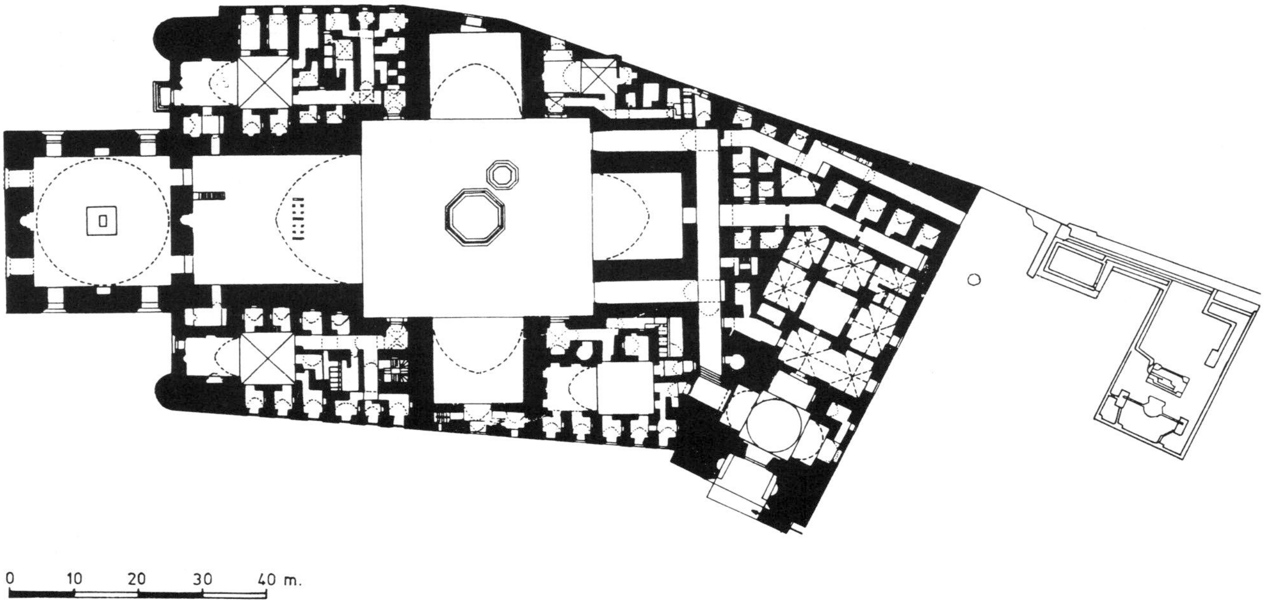

Fig. 26. The madrasa-mosque of Sultan Ḥasan (Department of Antiquities).

side. Each madrasa has a courtyard with ablution fountain, a qibla-oriented īwān, and four stories of living units. Some cells are larger than others, and a number of latrines are included in the living quarters. Each cell on the street side has two large windows, one above the other, making the interior very light and giving the inhabitants a view outside.

Some features of the plan of Sultan Ḥasan's mosque, such as the location of the cells in relation to the four īwāns, may have been inspired by the madrasa of Ṣarghitmish. However, the madrasa of Sultan Ḥasan locates most of the cells on the street, the only Cairene madrasa to do so, leaving the courtyard dominated by the four huge vaults. At the madrasa of Ṣarghitmish, some cells overlook the courtyard and others open onto the main and side streets, but the windows are not so organically integrated into the architecture of the facade as they are at Sultan Ḥasan.

The marble pavement of the courtyard is modern. There is no decoration of the īwāns except that of the sanctuary. This īwān is the largest vaulted hall of the medieval Muslim world and is reported by Maqrīzī as being even a few cubits larger than the īwān of Kisrā at Ctesiphon. The īwān of Kisrā, or vault of Cyrus (Khusraw), still standing not far from Baghdad, was part of a gigantic palace built at Ctesiphon, the Sassanian capital, and attributed to the emperor Cyrus. It is the largest single-span brick vault in the ancient World (twenty-six meters width by twenty-nine meters height), as famous in the past as at is today.

The īwān of Sultan Ḥasan is richly decorated. The qibla wall is paneled with a large polychrome marble dado, as is the prayer niche, flanked with columns whose style indicates that they must be trophies from Crusader buildings in Palestine.

A marble *dikkat al-muballigh*, the bench standing in the sanctuary near the courtyard, is adorned with remarkable columns composed of different colored stones. The pulpit for the Friday sermon is one of the few made of marble. It is topped by a carved bulb and has a portal leading to the steps with stalactite cresting and a beautiful bronze door with openwork bosses in the repoussé technique. There are several other bronze doors leading to various rooms that are masterpieces of medieval metalwork, particularly the one at the window between the sanctuary and the mausoleum, inlaid with silver and gold and bearing the names and titles of Sultan Ḥasan.

The most remarkable feature of the qibla īwān is the large inscription band that runs along its three walls, made of stucco with ornate Kufic script on a background of floriated scrolls with Chinese lotus blossoms.

Pl. 90. Stucco inscription at the sanctuary of Sultan Ḥasan.

There is a similar band in the īwān of the Ḥanafī madrasa, but there is nothing else similar in Cairo architecture. The style is, however, typical of Quran illuminations of the period, and the architect must have been inspired by these to translate the designs into stucco.

Close to this band on the right is the signature of a *naqqāsh* or decorator called ʿAbd Allāh Muḥammad ʿAlī. Ḥasan ʿAbd al-Wahhāb's interpretation of another signature found on the inscription band of the Ḥanafī madrasa as that of the architect is contradicted by historical sources, for the signature is that of the *shād al-ʿamāʾir*, or supervisor of works, who was usually an amir, not a craftsman.

The Mausoleum

The domed chamber of the mausoleum is reached by a door on the left side of the prayer niche and is thus located just behind the sanctuary, an unusual plan in Cairo. Only the mosque of Amir Ḥusayn (1319) and the mosque of Maḥmūd Pasha (1568) have the mausoleum behind the prayer hall. Usually, if attached to the qibla wall, the mausoleum is to one side of the prayer hall so that worshipers do not pray toward the founder's mausoleum. The unconventional location of Sultan Ḥasan's domed mausoleum is most likely explained by the urban setting of the building, built to impress the viewer from the Citadel with the mosque's grand scale and exotic dome. Because of the location, the mausoleum is free standing on three sides and its windows open onto the street though the structure still adjoins the prayer hall. The concession made to gain these advantages was the unconventional, perhaps unorthodox, but apparently not forbidden, placement of the dome. In fact, building a mausoleum for a founder is in itself unorthodox in Muslim religion, as is even the decoration of mosques. None of the medieval historians, however, seem to have been upset by the location of Sultan Ḥasan's mausoleum.

The chamber, the largest domed mausoleum in Cairo, thirty meters to the top of the rectangle, is twenty-one meters wide. Its wooden inscription band, whose high relief is painted white, is easily read from below. The wooden stalactite pendentives formerly carried a wooden dome higher than the present one. In the upper part of the transitional zone are inscriptions with the name of Sultan Qāytbāy, indicating that restorations must have been carried out during his reign. Restorations were also made in 1671-77, as stated in an inscription.

The Islamic Museum in Cairo houses a large collection of glass enameled lamps that once hung in the mosque, as well as gigantic and splendid bronze chandeliers. Many chains still hang from the ceiling, but the lamps have gone.

Bibliography

ᶜAbd al-Wahhāb. *Masājid*, pp. 165 ff.
Amīn, Muḥammad Muḥ. ed. Waqf of the madrasa of Sultan Ḥasan published as appendix in: Ibn Ḥabīb. *Tadhkirat*, III, pp. 349 ff.
Herz. *La mosquée du Sultan Hassan au Caire*. Cairo, 1899.
Maqrīzī. *Khiṭaṭ*, II, pp. 316 ff.
Rogers, J. M. "Seljuk Influence in the Monuments of Cairo." *Kunst des Orients*, 7 (1970-71), pp. 40 ff.
Wiet, Gaston. "Sultan Hasan." *La Revue du Caire*, June 1938, pp. 86 ff.

THE SULṬĀNIYYA MAUSOLEUM (1360's)

Located in the Suyūṭī cemetery beneath the southeastern side of the Citadel, this mysterious double mausoleum is undated and unidentified. Its popular name, "the royal" or "sultan's" mausoleum, indicates only that it belonged to a person of royal rank. It is composed of two similar domes with a vaulted īwān between them, and the whole is built in stone. At a short distance, and now not connected with it, is a minaret that must have belonged to the building, most likely at a corner of the enclosure attached to the mausoleum.

The domes, like those of Ṣarghitmish, have a very high drum, and the transitional zone is not visible from the outside. Also as at Ṣarghitmish, they are both adorned with stalactites, but here these form the base from which ribs grow toward the apex, decorating the dome. The domes' profiles are pointed, and they have a bulbous shape. The northern dome has square Kufic script carving in the drum, otherwise seen only in marble decorations; the other dome lacks this feature. Both drums are pierced with windows which, unlike the usual pattern, do not alternate with blind windows. The interiors are also different. The northern one has concentric masonry in the inner shell; in the southern dome, the stone courses radiate from the apex of the dome.

The prayer niche of the īwān is made of carved stone and is similar to the two niches flanking the portal of Sultan Ḥasan, a conch with stalactites, a motif often seen in Turkish Anatolian architecture. The prayer niches of the domes are plain. The minaret is octagonal, similar in design to that of Sultan Ḥasan, but more slender. Its decorations of inlaid masonry forming geometrical shapes also recall the style of Sultan Ḥasan. With these parallels to Ṣarghitmish and Sultan Ḥasan, the building can be dated in the 1360's.

Like the domes of Ṣarghitmish, those of the Sulṭāniyya have parallels in the Central Asian architecture of Samarkand. The mausoleum of Tīmūr built in 1403/4 has a high drum with square Kufic inscription, a double-shell dome, and ribbed exterior ending in stalactities above the drum, but is made of brick covered with colored ceramics, mainly blue. Its profile is similar to the Sulṭāniyya's dome, but is not pointed. Here again, the examples at Samarkand cannot have been the prototype, as they are later than the period suggested by other features of the Sulṭāniyya mausoleum. These features must have a common source from the northwestern province of Persia.

It is interesting to note here another example of Cairo architects translating foreign patterns originally done in brick into stone. The Sulṭāniyya, the minarets of al-Nāṣir at the Citadel, and the earlier minaret of Ibn Ṭūlūn, all show this translation into stone of prototypes built of brick. One more dome was built in this style, with high drum, ribbed, and with stalactites at the base of the ribs, that of Yūnus al-Dawādār near the Citadel (1382). However, this one is so elongated that it is sometimes mistaken for a minaret, and it has only one shell. Moreover, the transitional zone is visible from the outside.

Bibliography

Meinecke. "Faience."

Pl. 91. The Sulṭāniyya mausoleum and the minaret of Amir Qūṣūn on the right.

THE MADRASA OF UMM AL-SULṬĀN SHA^cBĀN (1368/9)

Sultan Sha^cbān was a grandson of al-Nāṣir Muḥammad. His mother, Khawand (Lady) Baraka, was a wealthy and pious woman. The madrasa associated with both names is situated at Tabbāna, between Bāb Zuwayla and the Citadel.

The inscriptions on the building say that Sultan Sha^cbān dedicated the foundation to his mother. The sultan was, however, still a child when the building was erected, and we may assume that Lady Baraka was the founder. In Muslim societies it was not unusual for a woman to erect a religious foundation. We have seen that Shajarat al-Durr founded a madrasa, and there are a number of other foundations created by women including the madrasa of Fāṭima Khātūn, wife of Qalāwūn (1283/4); the khanqāh of Umm Anūk, wife of al-Nāṣir Muḥammad (1363/4); the mosque of Sitt Miska, housekeeper at the court of al-Nāṣir Muḥammad (1340); the mosque of Fāṭima al-Shaqrā (1469); the mosque of Khadīja bint Dirham wa Niṣf (1520); the mosque of Aṣalbāy, wife of Sultan Qāytbāy at Fayyum (1499); and the mosque of the Ottoman princess Malika Ṣafiyya (1610). The royal ladies at the Mamluk courts were often extremely wealthy, and sometimes quite powerful.

The Exterior

The madrasa of Umm al-Sulṭān Sha^cbān, founded in 1368/9 for both the Shāfi^cī and Ḥanafī rites, had a

Pl. 92. The madrasa-mausoleum of Umm al-Sulṭān Shaᶜbān (Department of Antiquities).

portal built in a style alien to Cairo but typical of Saljūq Anatolia. Instead of a conch above the stalactites, there is a deep stalactite vault with a triangular profile. If an architect came from that area to Cairo to work on the mosque of Sultan Ḥasan, he might have designed this portal as well, but we know almost nothing of the architects of this period.

Another interesting feature of this mosque is the upper composition of an octagonal minaret with a zigzag carved shaft next to two unequal domes built of stone and ribbed. This minaret is one of the earliest examples of a carved shaft instead of inlaid masonry ablaq decoration. The ribs of the domes end at the base with rows of festoon-like curves. The composition here is quite different from that of Sanjar's double mausoleum. The minaret is on the left side of the portal, the larger dome is to its left, and the second dome is at the corner, both separated by the prayer hall so that from the street one cannot see the three elements at one time, as one can at Sanjar's mausoleum.

On the main facade of the building, occupying the corner between a main and a side street, a large grilled window to the left of the portal belongs to a sabīl. All mosques had sabīls for the thirsty, though not all of these have survived. On the right side of the portal was a watering trough for animals and above it, an arcaded loggia that was a kuttāb or primary school for boys, which like the sabīl was a charitable service of the mosque. As Muslim law does not allow children inside the mosque, so the kuttāb was always in a separate structure. Children were taught a basic knowledge of the Quran along with reading and writing. The kuttāb here is reached from the vestibule.

Pl. 93. The portal of the madrasa-mausoleum of Umm al-Sulṭān Shaᶜbān.

The Interior

A bent entrance leads through a long passage to the cruciform madrasa, the awkward layout is a result of the street orientation of the mosque and two mausoleums. There is not much remaining of the original decoration in the building except for some marble in the rather small sanctuary and remains of a painted wooden ceiling in one of the side īwāns. Unlike the madrasa of Sultan Ḥasan, the īwāns are not vaulted, but have a wooden ceiling. One either side of the qibla īwān is a domed mausoleum.

The northern dome next to the minaret is the larger of the two. In it, Lady Baraka and a daughter are buried. This mausoleum has a prayer niche between two windows overlooking the street. The smaller, southern mausoleum includes the graves of Sultan Shaᶜbān and his son al-Manṣūr Ḥājjī. Because of its disadvantageous location at the corner, it could not have both a prayer niche and a window onto the main street, and the window was given preference. Thus, this is one of the very few cases of a mausoleum without a prayer niche.

Both the stone domes have an interesting feature: they are not carried by triangular pendentives or several tiers of squinches as was usual during this period, but by plain squinches in the form of an arch at each corner. We see this feature also in the domes of the mosque of Aqsunqur (1347) in brick, and the mausoleum of Tankizbughā (1362) in stone. It is an archaic feature, since this type of transitional zone was used in the early Fatimid period, as in the dome of al-Ḥākim, and later replaced by the more composite two (or more) tiered squinches.

Bibliography

ᶜAbd al-Wahhab. *Masājid*, pp. 182 ff.
Kessler. "Mecca oriented ...."
Maqrīzī. *Khiṭaṭ*, II, p. 390.

THE MADRASA OF AMIR ILJĀY AL-YŪSUFĪ (1373)

Iljāy al-Yūsufī was one of the amirs of Sultan Shaᶜbān and was married to Lady Baraka after the death of her husband, Sultan Ḥusayn. He built a madrasa with Friday prayer at Sūq al-Silāḥ, the Weapons Market, on a street on the north side of the mosque of Sultan Ḥasan.

The Exterior

The facade has a trilobed stalactite portal framed by a molding. Near the entrance we see the blazon of Iljāy al-Yūsufī, a cup in the middle of a circle divided by three horizontal lines. On the left side of the portal is a sabīl surmounted by a kuttāb, both on the corner. The kuttāb is a loggia with columns at the corner and an arch on each side. At the madrasa of Umm al-Sulṭān Shaᶜbān, the sabīl was on the left and the kuttāb on the upper right side, but here the evolution has gone a step further, with sabīl and kuttāb forming an architectural unified composition that henceforth characterizes all mosques. The advantage of having the sabīl at a corner is that it allowed better ventilation, to keep the water fresh, and at the same time provided access to more people to stretch their hands through the grill to have their cups filled by the sabīl attendant.

Pl. 94. The madrasa-mausoleum of Amir Iljāy al-Yūsufī.

Between the recesses crowned by stalactites that decorate the facade of the building, there are also two recesses that have keel-arched niches at their tops.

The minaret and the dome are particularly elegant. The minaret is octagonal and circular with inlaid decoration once painted in ablaq. The bulb looks as if it is resting on a flower, the petals of which are represented by carving on the lower part of the bulb. The ribs of the dome, which are the only exterior carving, do not follow the usual vertical pattern from base to apex, but instead follow oblique lines, giving the dome a twisted appearance. We see this pattern sometimes carved on columns on the facades of mosques. The earliest example is on the facade of the al-Aqmar mosque, but this type of column decoration was used in the Byzantine period much earlier.

The Interior

The vestibule has two very noteworthy features: it is roofed by an elaborate groin vault carved in stone, which gives it the appearance of the inside of an umbrella, and the back wall has a trilobed arch also above a groin vault. The interior of this cruciform madrasa is characterized by its strict symmetry in the arrangement of windows. The qibla wall has two rows of pointed-arched windows. Curiously, the prayer niche is plain except for ablaq masonry in the conch.

The courtyard has windows at the corners of the four īwāns, set in recesses with a special type of stalactite at their tops. The students' living quarters have windows overlooking a side street. Here, as at Ṣarghitmish, the mausoleum overlooks the street but does not adjoin the prayer hall.

Bibliography

ʿAbd al-Wahhāb. *Masājid*, pp. 188 ff.
Maqrīzī. *Khiṭaṭ*, II, p. 399.

CHAPTER EIGHT

ARCHITECTURE OF THE CIRCASSIAN MAMLUKS

THE MADRASA-KHANQĀH OF SULTAN AL-ẒĀHIR BARQŪQ (1384-86)

This building stands next to the madrasa of Sultan al-Nāṣir Muḥammad at Naḥḥāsīn on the street called al-Muʿizz. Its founder, Sultan Barqūq, was of Circassian origin, recruited under the Turkish Bahri Mamluks. He himself recruited Circassian Mamluks from the Caucasus, and the next period is thus known as the Circassian Mamluk period. The Circassian Mamluks were garrisoned in the Citadel and were therefore also called the Burjī (from the fortress) Mamluks.

This foundation endowed a madrasa teaching the four rites, a Friday mosque, and a mausoleum, but unlike Sultan Ḥasan's madrasa, it was also a khanqāh for Sufis. It was a large foundation, housing one hundred twenty-five theology students and sixty Sufis, with living quarters for the teachers and stables for their mounts.

The Exterior

The facade is characterized by its trilobed stalactite portal, next to which on the north is a large dome flanked by a minaret. The facade is paneled as usual with recesses topped by stalactites. The upper windows are in pointed arches and have wooden grills, rather than stucco with painted glass. This style is seen in several mosques of the Bahri Mamluk period, such as that of Aydumur al-Bahlawān (1346) and of Ulmas (1329/30). A ṭirāz band runs along the facade.

Though the dome next to the minaret is not original, the two features are nicely composed. The original dome, a wood and plaster structure, collapsed in the nineteenth century, but the building had been illustrated often, making it possible to reconstruct the dome rather accurately. The present dome is of brick. The dome's surface is plain but has a cornice of stalactites at the base, a feature seen at the mausoleum of Ṣarghitmish, the Sulṭāniyya, and the mausoleum of Yūnus al-Dawādār (1382) near the Citadel; this is the latest surviving example.

Pl. 95. The religious-funerary complex of Sultan Barqūq.

The minaret is octagonal throughout but differs from most fourteenth-century minarets in that its shaft is carved. There are intersecting circles where white marble has been inlaid in the stone. These circles may have been inspired by the intersecting arches atop the minaret of Qalāwūn, which was built during al-Nāṣir Muḥammad's reign. The facade has on its lower part, as at Qalāwūn's mausoleum, columns attached to the wall. These columns with their capitals are carved parts

Pl. 96. Carved capital with a ram's head on the facade of the religious-funerary complex of Sultan Barqūq.

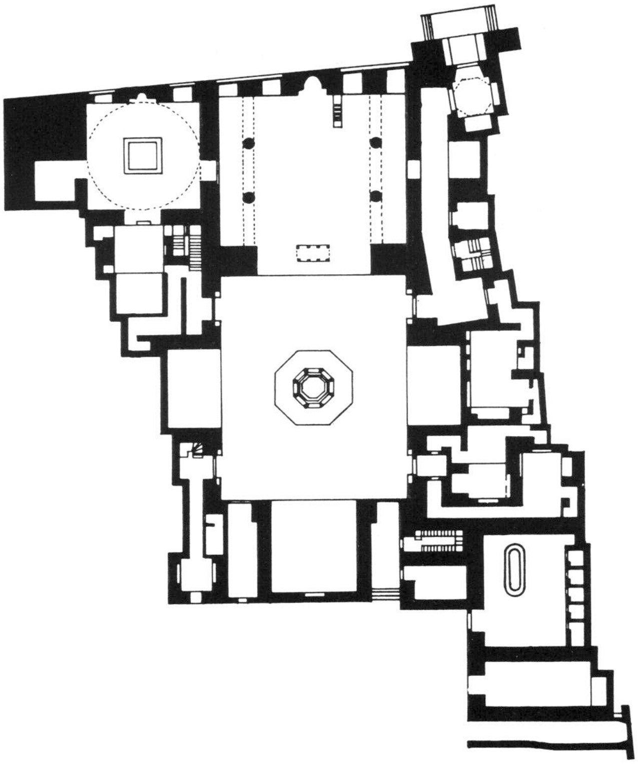

Fig. 27. The religious-funerary complex of Sultan Barqūq (Department of Antiquities).

of the wall masonry, not true capitals. The capitals have quite unusual patterns, with palmettes in high relief. One of them displays a motif of a stylized ram's head.

The Interior

The vestibule imitates that of Sultan Ḥasan's mosque, though on a much smaller scale, and has a stone dome flanked by stalactites. The original bronze door with geometric stars is still in its place. The recess of the portal is decorated with a large rectangular panel with inlaid marble geometrics, reminiscent of that at Sultan Ḥasan's vestibule.

The bent entrance leads through a passage to the cruciform interior. On the left side of the vaulted passage is a recess no doubt for water jugs, kept fresh by a wooden lattice door that is no longer there. The four īwāns facing the courtyard have four large, pointed arches. The sanctuary is not vaulted but has a wooden ceiling. Above the arches is a large inscription band carved in stone.

The ablution fountain in the center of the courtyard has a bulbous wooden dome on eight marble columns, similar to that at the mosque of Sultan Ḥasan. At that time the traditional inauguration ceremonies of a mosque the sultan attended the first day of prayers. It is recorded that at the inauguration of Sultan Barqūq's mosque, the ablution fountain was filled with sugared water, and sweetmeats were distributed to the congregation.

The sanctuary's composition is tripartite, like that of Sultan Qalāwūn's mosque, with two pairs of granite columns on each side separating the central, larger aisle from the side aisles. The gorgeous painted and gilded ceiling was restored in modern times, and the qibla wall is decorated with a marble dado and a marble prayer niche.

The entrances to the four madrasas are pierced in recesses, the upper part of which form round arches with zigzag carved voussoirs, a device seen at the Rawḍa Nilometer, though there, the arches are pointed.

The doors inside the building have a new feature: rather than the whole surface being faced with a bronze sheet, there is a central bronze medallion and four quarter circles of medallions at the corners, leaving the wood background to contrast with the bronze. The bronze appliqués are also pierced, showing the wood background. This pattern of decoration, common in carpets, was originally adopted from book bindings.

The living units for the students all open onto interior passages, as there is no space on the facade or the courtyard.

On the north, or left, side of the prayer hall a door leads through a vestibule with a stone bench to the domed mausoleum. The dome has wooden pendentives, painted and gilded, and the usual decorations. The mosque has a number of its original windows, doors, and other furniture.

Bibliography

ᶜAbd al-Wahhāb. *Masājid*, p. 192.
Maqrīzī. *Khiṭaṭ*, II, p. 418.
Mostafa, Saleh Lamei. "Madrasa, Hanqa und Mausoleum des Barquq in Kairo mit einem Beitrag von Felicitas Jaritz." *Abhandlungen des Deutschen Archäologischen Instituts Abteilung Kairo, Islamische Reihe*, 4 (1982), pp. 118 ff.
Mubārak, *Khiṭaṭ*, VI, p. 4.

THE KHANQĀH OF SULṬAN FARAJ IBN BARQŪQ (1400-11)

Sultan Barqūq, though he built a mausoleum for himself in the city, wanted to be buried near the tombs of the Sufis in the northern cemetery. His son and successor, Sultan al-Nāṣir Faraj, fulfilled his father's wish, building a large khanqāh and double mausoleum near the Sufis' tombs and the mausoleum of Anaṣ (1382), father of Sultan Barqūq. The mausoleum, with a ribbed brick dome, still stands.

The northern cemetery is on the eastern, desert outskirts of the Fatimid city of al-Qāhira. During the reign of Sultan al-Ẓāhir Baybars, there was a hippodrome where the sultan, a great soldier himself and fond of chivalric sports, attended tournaments and encouraged his amirs in these contests. Later, under Sultan al-Nāṣir Muḥammad, this hippodrome was abandoned in

Pl. 97. The khanqāh-mausoleum of Sultan Faraj Ibn Barqūq.

favor of others, and the amirs begans to build religious and funerary structures on its site.

Sultan Faraj, while erecting the khanqāh, planned at the same time to urbanize the site. He transferred the donkey and camel market and had other commercial plans, but died before realizing them, and the donkey and camel market returned. It should be kept in mind that a Muslim medieval cemetery was never totally a place of the dead. Palaces and residences were also built for the rich to stay in during feasts and other occasions when they visited their dead. There was also a good deal of traffic produced by those who came to visit the tombs of saints and other venerated persons. The religious foundations and great tombs always had residential structures attached to them for the founders and their families, as well as for Sufis and students.

The khanqāh took eleven years to complete. The sultan was dethroned twice in the meantime. The latest inscription on the building is 1411, but according to Maqrīzī, the khanqāh was inaugurated in 1410. Forty Sufis were appointed to it. As no foundation deed exists, we do not know how far this khanqāh also performed the functions of a madrasa.

The Exterior

Having plenty of space and no restrictions of prior development in the cemetery, the architect could afford to design a very symmetrical structure that is rare in Mamluk architecture of this period. The building is free standing, with four interesting facades. At the southwest corner is a trilobed portal flanked to the left by a sabīl-kuttāb. This facade has a ṭirāz band at the top and twin minarets. The north facade also has a portal, with a sabīl-kuttāb on its western corner. The two portals, though not identical, have a conch on stalactites and on both sides, the round blazon of the founder. The northern facade shows one of the two minarets mentioned above and to the left, one of the two domes, the same combination seen from the southern side of the building. The eastern facade shows the two huge stone domes and between them, a smaller ribbed brick dome which is above the prayer niche.

On the northern side of the complex is an arcade that starts on the left side of the portal and leads almost to the mausoleum of Barqūq's father, Anaṣ. This arcade appears to have been a *muṣallā*, or open prayer place for the dead. According to Islamic law, the dead are not to be brought inside the mosque when the funeral prayers are said.

Pl. 98. The northern entrance of the khanqāh of Sultan Faraj Ibn Barqūq with a sabīl-kuttāb to its right.

The minarets on the northwestern facade are identical, beginning as rectangles, with the second story receding and circular and without a transition between the two stories. The middle of the shaft is carved with intersecting lines. The plan of these minarets was used earlier, in those of Baybars al-Jashankīr, and the northern minaret of al-Nāṣir Muhammad at the Citadel.

The domes are the largest Mamluk stone domes in Cairo, with a diameter of over fourteen meters, not much less than that of Imām Shāfiʿī, which is wooden. They are carved with a zigzag pattern, and their transitional zones on the exterior are treated in a novel manner. Instead of being simply stepped, they are carved with one step concave and the next convex, a device applied earlier at the minaret of Bashtāk (1336).

The Interior

Barqūq's structure is a hypostyle mosque on stone piers. The sanctuary is flanked on each side by a domed mausoleum. The side riwāqs have only one aisle each, with cells behind. Both lateral sides had upper floors of cells, but they no longer exist. There are more cells on the northern side of the building; the dependencies are on the south side. This was the first hypostyle mosque plan to have living units attached to it; the plan had earlier been used only for plain mosques. When mosques were being replaced by a combination madrasa-mosque, or even madrasa-khanqāh-mosque, at first, it was the madrasa plan that was maintained. Here, we find a new architectural combination.

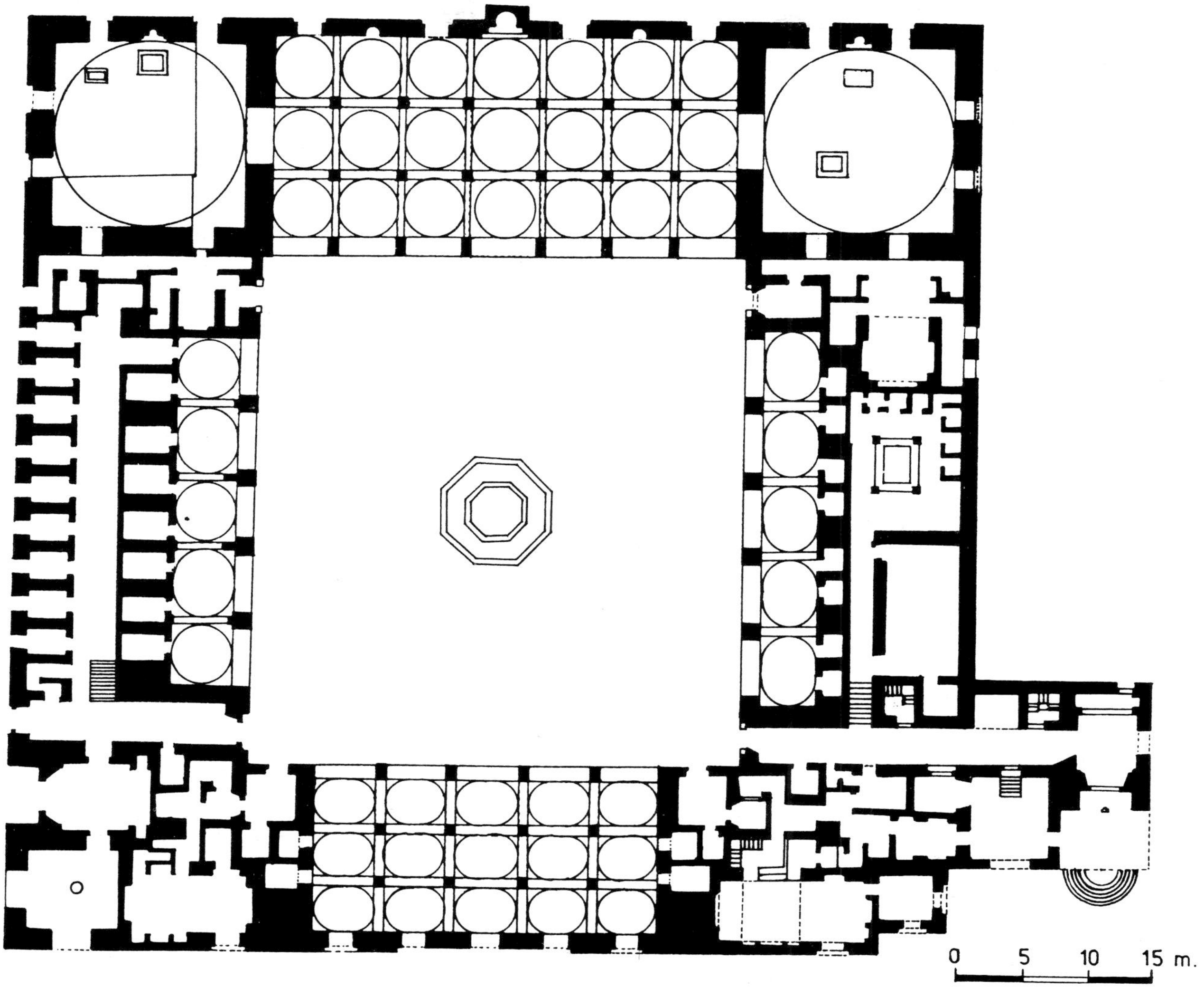

Fig. 28. The khanqāh and mausoleum of Sultan Faraj Ibn Barqūq (Department of Antiquities).

The arcades have pointed arches supporting a roof composed of shallow brick domes, each dome above a bay.

The courtyard has the remains of an ablution fountain. At the four corners of the courtyard are arched recesses with doors that are treated with round arches with zigzag voussoirs exactly like those of Barqūq's madrasa.

The sanctuary is strikingly simple, with no marble and no painted wood. Only the windows are decorated, with stucco grills and colored glass. The prayer niche is of plain stone and two smaller prayer niches are to the left and right. The main one has on the marble column flanking it to the left a carving in the shape of a mosque lamp. A stone pulpit was added by Sultan Qāytbāy, carved with panels in various geometrical and floral patterns which imitate wood carvings. As at Sultan Ḥasan, it has a portal with stalactite cresting and a carved bulb at the top. At the upper step, on the back of the seat of the preacher (*khaṭīb*), a lamp flanked by a pair of candlesticks is carved.

The Mausoleums

The northern mausoleum is for Barqūq and his son Faraj; the southern mausoleum for his wife and daughter. Both mausoleums are entered through wooden lattice screens. The mausoleums, in contrast to the khanqāh, are richly decorated with marble dadoes. Like most Mamluk stone domes, these are carried on pendentives carved with stalactites.

The use of the triangular pendentive rather than squinches led to a different device for the windows of the transitional zone. This style became standard and is found at the madrasa of Iljāy al-Yūsufī. It consists of a triple-arched window surmounted by three bull's-eyes, one over two.

Bibliography

Mostafa, S. L. *Kloster und Mausoleum des Farağ Ibn Barquq in Kairo*. Glückstadt, 1968.

THE MADRASA-KHANQĀH (1416-21) AND MĀRISTĀN (1418-20) OF SULTAN AL-MUʾAYYAD

The Madrasa-Khanqāh

This madrasa-khanqāh of Sultan al-Muʾayyad included a Friday mosque, two mausoleums, and a madrasa for the four rites dedicated to Sufi students, and is thus a hybrid madrasa-khanqāh.

Because of its site, the mosque, or at least its minarets, became a landmark of Cairo. Originally, the site had unpleasant associations. There was a prison adjoining Bāb Zuwayla which al-Muʾayyad, when an amir, was lucky to leave alive. Once he became sultan, he decided to pull it down and establish a pious foundation in its place. Numerous donkeys were occupied for days carrying away loads of bones of the dead found in the prison.

Originally, the mosque had three minarets, the twins we see above the towers of Bāb Zuwayla, and a third one of different appearance, located near the western entrance, which disappeared in the nineteenth century. The twin minarets, though they represent no innovation in the evolution of minarets, are particularly slender and elegant with their zigzag carved shafts. They do also have a very noteworthy feature: the signature of the architect, al-Muʿallim Muḥammad Ibn al-Qazzāz, is carved on a cartouche above the entrance to their staircases on the northern side of each shaft, with the dates 1419 and 1420. This is so far the only known signature of a Mamluk architect on a building. We do not know to what extent he was involved in building the rest of the complex.

The mosque originally had four facades and four entrances. The two main facades are the one parallel to Bāb Zuwayla on the site of the Fatimid southern city wall which was rebuilt in the nineteenth century, and the facade perpendicular to Bāb Zuwayla on its left, with the main portal.

The Portal

The portal is of grand proportions and is enhanced by a *pishtāq*, or wall above the entrance higher than the rest. A conch rests on a large vault where dripping stalactites have been lavishly used. A band of carved

Pl. 99. The portal of the religious-funerary complex of Sultan al-Muʾayyad.

stone inlaid with marble and colored stones frames the doorway.

The door, a masterpiece of metalwork, was taken, together with a bronze chandelier, from the mosque of Sultan Ḥasan against payment of a sum to the waqf of Sultan Ḥasan—which, however, did not change the illegality of the deed. Islamic law prohibits the acquisition of land or other properties for a new foundation already endowed upon a previous religious foundation. Once endowed, a property cannot change owners. Maqrīzī, however, mentions many such illegal acts connected with the foundation of religious buildings and makes a resigned and bitter comment about "one thief stealing from another."

The Interior

The vestibule is covered by a magnificent groin cross-vault flanked by two half-domes on stalactites. It is perhaps the most remarkable feature of the architecture of this complex. Today we enter the mosque through the mausoleum, but originally there was direct access into the courtyard. The mausoleum dome, whose exterior is similar to that of Faraj Ibn Barqūq, is smaller and has two cenotaphs, one larger than the other, with remarkable Kufic inscriptions in marble crafted during the Ikhshidid or early Fatimid period. Their texts are Quranic, and they must have been taken from an earlier building. Sultan al-Muʾayyad and his son are buried there.

On the top part of the northwestern wall of the mausoleum, on the side facing the courtyard, there are two blind windows with very intricately carved stucco decoration in the Andalusian style.

The hypostyle plan of the mosque is similar to that of the khanqāh of Faraj Ibn Barqūq, but on columns instead of piers. There is an ablution fountain in the middle of the courtyard. Of the four īwāns, only the

Pl. 100. The facade of the hospital of Sultan al-Muʾayyad.

sanctuary has survived. It was planned to be flanked on either side by a domed mausoleum, only one of which was built. The site is occupied by the tombs of female members of the family, but there is no mausoleum.

The sanctuary is lavishly decorated with a high marble dado and a polychrome marble prayer niche with a row of inlaid niches separated by blue glass colonnettes. A painted and gilded wooden ceiling, stucco grilled windows and beautiful doors inlaid with wood and ivory in addition to the marble columns with their pre-Islamic capitals, contribute to the richness of the decoration. The prayer hall was restored in the nineteenth century, and again in recent times. The mosque also has its original wood and ivory pulpit.

The living units of the Sufi students were not around the courtyard as they are at Faraj's khanqāh, but formed a separate structure, a courtyard surrounded by several stories of living units. It no longer exists.

On the western side of the mosque, Sultan al-Muʾayyad built a ḥammām. The pendentives in it that once supported a dome have remarkable stalactites.

The Māristān

Although the hospital of Qalāwūn was still functioning at the time, Sultan al-Muʾayyad decided to build one of his own. It was built on the site of a former mosque, near the Citadel. It was used only a short time, however, and after the sultan died, the building was used by foreign residents and was later turned into a residence for ambassadors visiting Egypt. Still later, it was transformed into a Friday mosque. As it was originally built on the site of a mosque, the cruciform construction was already oriented toward Mecca, so it needed only a new prayer niche.

Although now in ruins, the building has preserved its splendid facade, one of the finest in Cairo. It is quite symmetrical, the middle part enhanced by the pishṭāq with a pointed arch above the recess of the stalactite portal. Along the facade, running horizontally and vertically, is a carved molding in high relief in a pattern resembling a chain, the only such decoration in Cairo.

Two keel-arched panels flank the portal recess, composed of inlaid masonry with inlaid square-Kufic Quranic texts. Further to the right and left on the facade, on each side of the keel-arched panels, are medallions of inlaid marble. Above the entrance is a double-arched window within a keel arch. The whole makes an unusual facade composition. The interior has a cruciform plan, but is today in quite dilapidated condition.

Bibliography

ᶜAbd al-Wahhāb. *Masājid*, pp. 207 ff.
Maqrīzī. *Khiṭaṭ*, II, pp. 328; 408.
Mubārak. *Khiṭaṭ*, V, pp. 124 ff.

THE MADRASA-KHANQĀH OF SULTAN BARSBĀY IN THE NORTHERN CEMETERY (1432)

Shortly after his accession to the throne, Sultan al-Ashraf Barsbāy had built in 1425, a madrasa-khanqāh at the ᶜAnbariyyīn or amber market, south of the Qalāwūn complex now in the street of al-Muᶜizz, the royal avenue where so many sultans before had established their foundations. This complex was planned to accommodate sixty Sufi students. The building, which is architecturally typical of this period, has the usual Mamluk facade with a sabīl-kuttāb on the left side of the portal. The portal has a ribbed conch on a small cornice of stalactites and pendentives at the corners. The minaret, almost identical to those of Faraj Ibn Barqūq, flanks the small zigzag ribbed stone dome. The minaret and dome make an angle with the facade following the Mecca orientation of the interior, most likely for architectural rather than religious reasons.

The interior does not differ much from that of Barqūq's madrasa, aside from its being less well preserved. The inscription running above the arches of the four īwāns, however, includes fragments of the waqf document stating what has been endowed upon the foundation, most likely as a precaution against illegal dealings. The small mausoleum has windows onto the street but has no prayer niche.

A few years later, in 1432, the sultan founded a khanqāh-madrasa in the cemetery, also with a mausoleum. The foundation in the city was a madrasa for the four rites, built to accommodate sixty Sufi students; the one in the cemetery was for only seventeen Sufis, of whom four were students, and only ten were housed on the premises. The complex, occupying both sides of the street south of the khanqāh of Faraj, covered a large area, but many of its structures have not survived.

The Exterior

The decoration of the domes with star patterns has already been discussed. The larger, and most likely the earlier, of the carved mausoleum domes included in this complex is that of the sultan, attached to the mosque. On its north side there is a smaller mausoleum, and on its eastern side another, open on

Pl. 101. The religious-funerary complex of Sultan Barsbāy.

three sides, dedicated to amirs and relatives of the sultan. A fourth carved dome has disappeared. The enclosure included a number of other tombs. Today, we see the facade with a dome and a later and unattractive minaret flanked to the south by the ruins of an apartment complex.

Although it has been restored, it is obvious that the portal was not built in the stalactite-vaulted style of the time. A trilobed vault was used, including groins instead of stalactites. This pattern was again used in the late Mamluk and the Ottoman period, along with continued use of the stalactite portal.

The original minaret did not survive, though we may assume that its first story was rectangular, forming the lower part of the present structure.

The Interior

The cross-vaulted vestibule leads through a bend to the prayer hall that also differs from its contemporaries in style. It is neither a cruciform nor a hypostyle mosque, but an oblong hall whose roof is carried on two pairs of columns with three arches, each running parallel to the qibla wall and thus forming three aisles. The floors of the two side aisles are raised slightly above the level of the central aisle. Windows on both the east and west bring light into the covered hall. On the northern side of the mosque, opposite the entrance, the central aisle leads to the door of the mausoleum.

The Mausoleum

The mausoleum, due to the plan of the mosque, has the ideal location; it is open on three sides while at the same time attached to the prayer hall. Its dome's transitional zone is composed of stalactite pendentives. On the outside, it is carved in an undulating pattern similar to that on the domes of Sultan Faraj. The other two domes of the complex are treated differently, one with a stepped exterior transition, and the northern one with a pyramidal structure at each corner leading from the rectangular to the octagonal part. Sultan Barsbāy is buried in this mausoleum, and not in the mausoleum he built in the city.

Decoration

The decoration of the sanctuary is unusual. While the walls are bare, the floor is richly covered with inlaid polychrome marbles of high quality. The prayer niche is of plain stone, and windows with stucco and colored glass are the only ornament on the walls. The painted wooden ceiling appears to have been redone in the Ottoman period. The pulpit has a star geometric pattern of ivory inlaid in wood, but the pattern is unusual in having curved segments.

In the mausoleum, the quality of the marble inlays of the prayer niche, with rows of niches running across the conch reminiscent of the thirteenth and early fourteenth centuries, arouses the suspicion that Sultan Barsbāy used materials from earlier buildings. This also applies to the floor pavings of the mosque, which seem to have been originally intended for doors and windows.

Other Structures

Next to the mosque on its south side are the remains of the student living quarters. According to the foundation deed, there were ten units. These, however, unlike earlier accommodations, are not single rooms, but apartments in two-storied duplexes, each with a latrine. Each upper room has a window onto the main road. These dwellings appear to have been quite comfortable, and it is likely that the Sufis, who were each entitled to a whole unit, were also allowed to have their families with them. The foundation deed does not stipulate that Sufi students must be unmarried, as was the case in earlier foundations. There was also a hall on the upper floor for Sufi gatherings, of which all that remains is a prayer niche.

The complex of Sultan Barsbāy extended along both sides of the road. On the other side, there is today only a large domed structure, designated in the foundation deed as a zawiya for the Rifāʿī order. The khanqāh appears to have been independent of any particular order of Sufis. The zāwiya is a smaller structure where the ideology of one shaykh and his order (*ṭarīqa*) is practiced and propagated.

Interestingly, its architecture is quite distinct from that of contemporary funerary structures, and in fact the domed building was not intended for burial. The height of the dome is not increased, and instead of the usual pendentives, it is carried by squinches that start within, not above, the rectangular space. The squinches were remodeled at a later date, and today they have a trilobed shape, reminiscent of the portal treatment at the khanqāh of Barsbāy. The dome is built in brick with a plain exterior surface. There was another zāwiya on the same side of the street, but it was not a domed structure.

There were two sabīls, remnants of one of which can be seen, and other structures including large apartments and various dependencies.

The complex of Barsbāy, with fewer but larger living units than earlier ones, and with two zāwiyas, which is unprecedented in previous complexes, signals a new development in Cairene religious life. It shows a trend toward a less monastic type of Sufism, in which the Sufis' daily lives were less regulated. These later khanqāhs, combining the activities of khanqāh and madrasa, prepared their members for professional and administrative positions and thus their Sufis were more active than those who devoted themselves to mysticism and worship in seclusion.

The Tomb of Umm al-Ashraf

South of the complex of Sultan Barsbāy, in the cemetery on the west side of the street, is a brick dome carved with interlaced bands similar to the minarets of Sultan Barqūq. Apart from the usual ribbing, this pattern is the only one used to decorate brick domes. Today the tomb is surrounded by modern buildings. The mausoleum is neither dated nor identified except by its popular name, Khadīja Umm al-Ashraf. Al-Ashraf was a title of Sultan Barsbāy. Another dome carved in the same manner, that of Amir Taghrībirdī on Ṣalība street between Ṣarghitmish's madrasa and Shaykhū's complex and dated 1440, suggests that this dome was built for Barsbāy's mother sometime between 1430 and 1440.

Bibliography

Darrag, Ahmad. *L'Acte de Waqf du Sultan al-Ashraf Barsbay*. Cairo, 1963.

Fernandes, Leonor. "The Evolution of the Khanqah Institution in Mamluk Egypt." Ph.D. dissertation, Princeton University, 1980, pp. 223 ff.

—. "Three Sufi Foundations in a 15th Century Waqfiyya." *Annales Islamologiques*, 17 (1981), pp. 141 ff.

Mubārak. *Khiṭaṭ*, IV, pp. 57 ff.

THE RELIGIOUS-FUNERARY COMPLEX OF SULTAN AL-ASHRAF ĪNĀL (1451, 1454, 1456)

Sultan al-Ashraf Īnāl's funerary complex stands to the north of the khanqāh of Sultan Faraj Ibn Barqūq, on the west side of the road that crosses the cemetery. At first glance, the great irregularity of its facade composition is striking.

The Eastern Facade

The eastern facade is of a mosque with groin-vaulted portal, on the left of which, not attached but connected only by a wall, stands a minaret. On the right side, also not attached but connected only by a wall, is a mausoleum. Its dome's rectangular base is lower than the roof of the mosque. In the usual Mamluk facade, the base of the minaret and the dome are above roof level. An exception is provided by the minarets of al-Nāṣir Muḥammad at the Citadel, but that is because the mosque was remodeled after they were built.

The epigraphy in the architectural group confirms the impression given by the facade, that the complex was not built at one time.

The Mausoleum

The stone zigzag-carved dome of unpretentious proportions has an additional ornament: the carved loops that adorn the base of the dome are filled with balls of blue glass paste. These balls are also seen on the second story of the minaret of al-Nāṣir Muḥammad's madrasa and were added later, and on the mabkhara structures decorating the corners of the facade of the Māridānī mosque. This mausoleum is dated 1451, at which time Sultan Īnāl was only an amir. As the minaret's and dome's bases were built at the same level, we may assume that they were built at the same time.

The Minaret

The shaft is completely of stone, lavishly carved, a development in minarets that took place during the fifteenth century. The base is almost totally covered with decorative carved panels. The first story has a molding running along its eight facets and framing the keel-arched niches. The space between these niches is also carved with arabesques and several colonnettes are set between them. There are also, as on the minarets of al-Muʾayyad, three inscription bands, two on the first and one on the second story.

The carving on the second story, where the minaret mason always shows most of his innovations, has an interesting design. The zigzag pattern is not applied on a plain circular shaft as usual, but the shaft at this level has a section like a multiple-pointed star, its own profile dented like a zigzag, so that the zigzag carving appears to be three-dimensional.

The Northern Facade

The mausoleum dome occupies the corner between the eastern and the northern facade. On the left side,

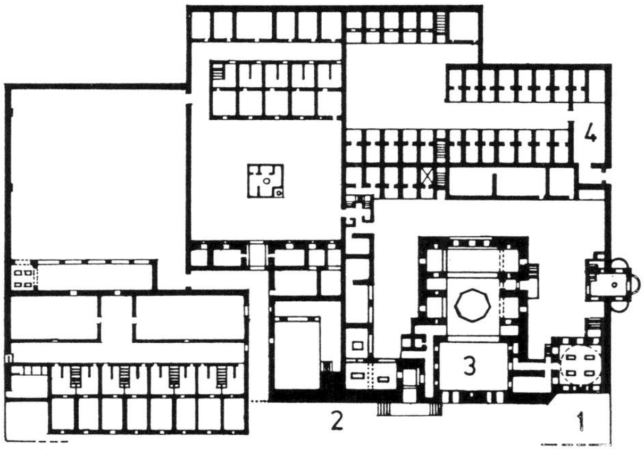

Fig. 29. The religious-funerary complex of Sultan Inal (Department of Antiquities).

Pl. 102. The religious-funerary complex of Sultan Īnāl.

the mausoleum is separate from the mosque by an open space. This facade of the mosque also has a portal, not groin vaulted but a conch on stalactites. To the right side of the mausoleum on the same alignment, a protruding structure is identified as a sabīl-kuttāb whose upper structure is missing.

Further to the right, on the western edge of the complex, is a building with its own entrance, identified by its inscription as a khanqāh built in 1454, or later than the mausoleum; by that time, Īnāl had become Sultan. The khanqāh is in ruins, but we can still tell that it was an important foundation, judging from its large number of duplex living units and dependencies, among which are latrines with running water. As at the khanqāh of Barsbāy, each living unit has its own latrine. There are also the remains of a qāᶜa or hall for gatherings.

The Madrasa

The mosque, designated by its inscription as a madrasa was built in 1456. It is built above a row of rooms that might have been cells for students, or storerooms. The epigraphy in the building indicates that Īnāl built a mausoleum for himself while still an amir, which most likely had a sabīl-kuttāb attached to it. Usually tombs have a prayer hall attached, so there must have been a building on the site before the madrasa was added, and the minaret already existed since its architecture fits with that of the mausoleum. Once he became sultan, Īnāl added the khanqāh, and later rebuilt the mosque. Ibn Iyās writes that the expenses were taken care of by Amir al-Jamālī Yūsuf, who also added a zāwiya, following the example of Barsbāy. It must once have been quite a luxurious building. The prayer niche of the mosque of Īnāl is made of carved stone with a molding comprising a sunrise motif filling the conch.

The small mosque has two facades, one on the road and the other on a courtyard, and a modified cruciform plan. The reduced inner courtyard is the type usually covered by a wooden dome or lantern and paved with marble, rather than the larger courtyard open to the sky with an ablution fountain in the center.

The roofed cruciform plan is that of the qāᶜa, or the reception hall, in residential architecture. In residential architecture, however, the central space was occupied by a marble fountain, usually octagonal, like the octagonal lantern above it that protrudes above the ceiling of the īwāns. The palaces of the Citadel, and perhaps other palaces as well, had domes in their centers. Even the large, open courtyards were covered against the summer midday sun, usually by tenting stretched on ropes. The earlier mosque of Aṣlam al-Bahāʾī (1345) is cruciform with a roofed courtyard, but we do not know how many of the mosques with small courtyards were roofed.

In the second half of the fifteenth century, large mosques were no longer needed. With the inner space reduced and the living units concentrated in an independent structure, the smaller, covered courtyard was adopted, and mosques came to resemble residential reception halls. Already, in Fusṭāṭ during the Fatimid period, the īwāns in the qāᶜa of a house were closed by doors and the courtyard was open to the sky, but no doubt protected by tents. The adoption of the qāᶜa plan was not the only borrowing from residential architecture. The double-storied living units themselves, as we see at the khanqāhs of Barsbāy and Īnāl, have a plan that is borrowed from the rabᶜ or apartment building.

Bibliography

Van Berchem. *C.I.A.*, p. 394.
Ibn Iyās. II, pp. 331, 334.

THE RELIGIOUS-FUNERARY COMPLEX OF SULTAN AL-ASHRAF QĀYTBĀY (1472-74) AND HIS MADRASA AT QALᶜAT AL-KABSH (1475)

The Religious-Funerary Complex

Sultan Qāytbāy was much given to founding religious institutions and his reign, like that of al-Nāṣir Muhammad in the fourteenth century, was long and stable enough to give a style a chance to develop in the various important monuments he sponsored.

The architecture of this period was not gigantic but tended rather toward refinement of proportions, and it was a golden age for stone carving. Marble work, especially on facades, also played a prominent role in architectural decoration. Compared to architecture during the reign of al-Nāṣir Muḥammad, the style of the Qaytbay period was more homogeneous, undisturbed by new ideas, foreign elements and daring innovations. It was a period of consolidation rather than of innovation.

The Mosque

Like most of the other religious funerary complexes, Qāytbāy's was composed of several structures, not all of which have survived. The main and best preserved

Pl. 103. The religious-funerary complex of Sultan Qāytbāy.

is the mosque, also called a madrasa, with the founder's mausoleum.

It is a relatively small structure with two free standing facades. The south side has a trilobed portal with a groin vault decorated with ablaq inlay and some stalactites (s. Pl. 19), with a sabīl-kuttāb to its left and the minaret to the right. Projecting from the southeast side of the building is the magnificent, though not large, mausoleum dome.

The minaret, slender and elegant, is of stone, carved with stars in high relief. Its bulb has a carved, twisted band on the neck. The sabīl has a richly painted and gilded wooden ceiling, and in the vestibule are a stone bench and cupboard with doors inlaid with wood and ivory.

The Interior

A particularly handsome umbrella-like groin vault, is above the passage leading to the interior, next to the recess with wooden lattice doors where water jugs were kept cool. The interior is a qaᶜa, with two unequal īwāns and two recesses, all richly ornamented with marble floor, polychrome marble dadoes, and stucco with colored glass windows. The vividly painted wooden ceiling and wooden lantern above the central area have been restored along with the rest. The prayer niche is of stone, with albaq inlaid patterns similar to those of the portal conch. Keel-arched niches with windows decorate the corner recess around the covered courtyard. An inscription band frames the central upper space.

The mausoleum is reached from the courtyard. Its prayer niche is of paneled, carved and painted stone. The stalactites of the stone pendentives are finely carved.

None of the living units has survived, though the foundation deed refers to various apartments for the Sufis and others attached to the foundation. Though the foundation deed calls the building a madrasa, it does not refer to any systematic curriculum of instruction in Islamic law. It is noted that Sufis should attend sessions in the mosque, but no reference is made to their being boarders, and there was no kitchen attached to the structure. The term madrasa must have been used simply by tradition, rather than as referring to a particular function. It was an ordinary Friday mosque, and such mosques normally had sessions for Sufis.

On the west side of the mosque is the small mausoleum built by Qaytbay before he became a sultan. It has arabesque carvings. There are other funerary structures and a *maqᶜad* or loggia, this one pierced by a row of windows within blind arches opening onto the exterior of the complex. As usual in an important funerary complex, there were residential buildings. On the north side of the mosque the remains of an animal watering trough can be seen, decorated with keel-arched carved niches. Further north is the facade of the rabᶜ belonging to Qaytbay.

The Rabᶜ

The rabᶜ of Qāytbāy, as the portal shows, is buried more than two meters under the present street level. It has a magnificent groin-vaulted trilobed portal flanked by the sultan's blazon. Though the shops are now

Pl. 104. Interior of the mosque of Sultan Qāytbāy.

buried, an idea can be had of the architecture of the apartments, whose wooden ceilings were painted.

A rab^{c} may be built above storerooms or workshops of a complex called a wakāla, qaysariyya, or khān. Usually, the living units of a rab^{c} have windows onto the street, unless they are built around a courtyard and have windows over the courtyard, as at the wakāla of Sultan al-Ghūrī (s. Pl. 35). Qāytbāy built another wakāla with a rab^{c} above it near Bāb al-Naṣr, and another which is now in ruins, near the mosque of al-Azhar.

The Madrasa at Qal^{c}at al-Kabsh

This madrasa, built by Qāytbāy, is in the quarter called Qal^{c}at al-Kabsh, on the eastern side of the mosque of Ibn Ṭūlūn. It is a free-standing building, with two entrances enhanced by two portals of different styles.

The minaret stands on the northeast corner near the northern entrance which has a trilobed portal whose conch is carved with a geometric pattern with no other decoration. The other portal, on the southeastern side, is for this period almost old fashioned, with its semi-dome above bunches of stalactites.

The minaret is unusual in that it has only two stories. Its lower balcony rests on a carved octagonal base rather than upon stalactites, and the carved circular shaft above it is surmounted by a columned pavilion.

An interesting feature of the facade is the style of the upper windows, the type hitherto used in the transitional zone of domes, a double arch surmounted by a bull's-eye. No marble decoration was used.

The interior is the qa^{c}a plan with a plain prayer niche made of stone. The wooden ceiling is richly painted with arabesque patterns.

Bibliography

Ali Ibrahim, Layla. "Middle-class."
Mayer, L. A. *The Buildings of Qaytbay as Described in His Endowment Deeds*. London, 1938.
Mubārak. *Khiṭaṭ*, V, pp. 69 ff.

THE SABĪL OF SULTAN QĀYTBĀY (1479)

On Ṣalība street, between the complex of Shaykhū and the right-hand side of the square below the Citadel, stands a handsome sabīl-kuttāb built by Sultan Qāytbāy. It is a free-standing structure with a trilobed portal on its western facade, and large iron-grilled windows.

Pl. 105. The sabīl-kuttāb of Sultan Qāytbāy at Ṣalība.

The upper structure, which must have been a kuttāb, is a modern restoration.

The facades of the sabil are all richly decorated with polychrome marble inlay and carved stone in the same style as was used later at the mosque of Qijmas al-Isḥāqī. After its ablaq painting was renewed, making the inlaid pattern and carved details more visible, the groin-vaulted trilobed portal regained its original glamor. Cairo's dust has taken care of applying the patina. The portal vault is flanked on both sides by carved medallions with the name and epithet of Sultan al-Ashraf Abū 'l-Naṣr Qāytbāy.

The lintels are not simply joggled like those of the Bahri Mamluk period, but the inlaid blue and white marble forms a variety of intricate arabesque patterns on the facade. Each window is surmounted by two such decorative slabs, one above the other, and both are surmounted by medallions inlaid with arabesques in the same style and framed by carved moldings. Bits of red stone and ceramic enhance the effect of stone and marble interaction.

This is the earliest free-standing sabīl-kuttāb, not attached to a mosque, a combination that came to predominate in the Ottoman period.

THE CISTERN OF YA^{c}QŪB SHĀH AL-MIHMANDĀR (1495/6)

The domed cistern (*ṣihrīj*) built by Ya^{c}qūb Shāh al-Mihmandār at the foot of the Citadel, facing it from

Pl. 106. The cistern of Amir Yaʿqūb Shāh al-Mihmandār.

the east, is not just a structure to store and provide water, but a memorial building of very special interest. Its founder, Yaʿqūb Shāh was not a prominent amir, but he owed much to his master Sultan Qāytbāy, to whose glory he dedicated this building, as its inscription, unique in Cairo's Mamluk epigraphy reveals. The inscription running along the whole facade as its sole decoration commemorates in glowing terms the victory of Mamluk troups over the Ottomans and the capture of their general at the battle of Adana in 1486, years before the completion of the cistern. These facts are recorded in a literary style, unconventional for architectural epigraphy but comparable to that of medieval epics.

Domes in medieval architecture were not restricted to religious or funeral architecture; they also surmounted all types of secular buildings. The undecorated cistern is surmounted by a small dome occupying half its width. A shallow trilobed portal leads through a cross-vaulted vestibule to the domed room. The inscription refers to two domes and two cisterns, but only this domed structure survives.

Bibliography

Van Berchem. *C.I.A.*, pp. 547 ff.

Rogers, J. M. "The Inscription of the Cistern of Yaʿqūb Shāh al-Mihmandār in Cairo." *Fifth International Congress of Turkish Art*. Budapest.

THE MOSQUE OF QĀḌĪ ABŪ BAKR IBN MUZHIR (1479/80)

This mosque, erected in a quarter on the west ṣide of al-Muʿizz street, is typical of the style of the time, a small architectural jewel. Its minaret is located at the corner where the west and south facades meet and is carved with star patterns. The conch of the trilobed groin-vaulted portal rests on two, instead of the usual three, arches and thus recalls the squinches of the Fadāwiyya Dome.

The interior uses a qāʿa plan with a variation: the two larger īwāns, instead of facing the covered courtyard with a large arch, have a triple arch supported by

Pl. 107. The mosque of Qaḍī Abū Bakr Ibn Muzhir, the qibla īwān.

Pl. 108. Window spandrel with marble inlay and signature of the craftsman at the mosque of Abū Bakr Ibn Muzhir (drawing "The Mosques of Egypt").

a pair of columns. The side recesses have one arch each. A marble medallion covers the central part of the floor.

Another distinctive feature of the interior is the marble decoration on the qibla wall. The spandrels of the window arches and of the prayer niche itself are of finely inlaid marble, not as seen before with stones and marbles that dictate geometric patterns, but with a dark gypsum-like colored paste that allows delicate curved lines, very finely drawn as on Persian carpets. The craftsman, ᶜAbd al-Qādir al-Naqqāsh, *naqqāsh* meaning decorator, deservedly proud of his work, placed his signature in the same medium in a prominent place in the middle of a carved field above a window. The mosque of al-Māridānī has a marble inscription slab executed in this technique, on the north wall of its sanctuary; the inscription is made of green paste inlaid into the marble surface. Its vigorous style differs, however, from the work of ᶜAbd al-Qādir.

Bibliography

Mubārak. *Khiṭaṭ*, V, pp. 113 f.

THE FADĀWIYYA DOME (1479-81)

For its period, the square domed building standing in the modern quarter of ᶜAbbāsiyya, once the northern outskirts of the medieval city between Ḥusayniyya and Raydāniyya, is in many respects an architectural surprise. Its popular name, Qubbat al-Fadāwiyya, dates from the Ottoman period. It is called in medieval sources Qubbat Yashbak. It once stood near a hippodrome amidst gardens and residences, overlooking an artificial pool dug by the founder to enhance the view. Amir Yashbak min Mahdī al-Dawādār was one of the most powerful and wealthy amirs during Sultan Qāytbāy's reign. Yashbak also built for himself a mausoleum not far away, which is no longer extant. The building, part of a complex the rest of which has disappeared, is often mentioned in the chronicles of Ibn Iyās and always in connection with excursions, banquets, and processions of the sultan and his amirs.

Pl. 109. The Fadāwiyya Dome or Qubbat Yashbak.

The Exterior

Although domed, the building is not a mausoleum but a mosque. We do not know if there ever was a minaret, but there is no architectural trace of one on the structure now extant. As a mosque entirely covered by a dome, it is of special interest, and it is also the largest brick dome of Mamluk Cairo. The domed chamber measures 14.30 meters to a side.

The exterior is unusually plain, with one upper and two lower windows, except on the south side. The windows are not in their usual, recesses and the walls are therefore undecorated. The dome itself is also undecorated, starting from the cubic building without any exterior transitional zone.

The portal is a shallow recess crowned with stalactites in a rectangular frame with an inscription band on each side of the door. The inscription refers to Sultan Qāytbāy as the founder, but historic accounts leave no doubt that Amir Yashbak began its construction. He died before completing it and the Sultan saw to its completion.

The Interior

Another particular feature of this building is that the prayer hall is built above a vaulted first story. The most extraordinary feature about the dome of Yashbak is that the entrance to the domed area, or prayer hall, was not reached as it is today by a flight of steps, but was originally connected to the Ḥusayniyya quarter by a long passage built on an arcade. The exact function of this long elevated passage is not clear, but it might have been connected with the hippodrome once located nearby.

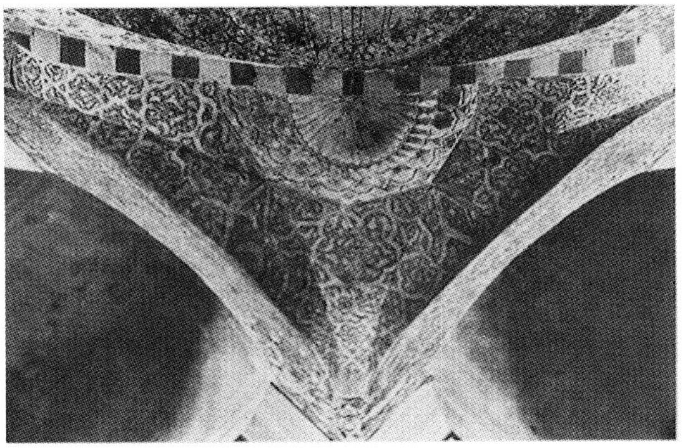

Pl. 110. Squinch at the Fadāwiyya Dome (Creswell).

The portal leads directly into the prayer hall without bend or vestibule. The interior space is impressive, owing to the height and width of the dome. The transitional zone of the dome, as we have seen from the outside, does not rest above the rectangular part, but within its walls, so that the dome proper begins immediately above the cube. The transitional zone differs from the usual type and has large trilobed squinches, each set within a large pointed arch. This trilobed squinch is reminiscent of the trilobed groin vaulted portals of the fifteenth century and was no doubt influenced by them, as the structural principle of transition from a rectangular to a spherical space is the same. The zāwiya for the Rifāᶜiyya order built by Sultan Barsbāy near his mausoleum is a domed hall on similar squinches, and there were other zāwiyas of this type of architecture which have not survived.

Under each of the squinches are two windows at the corner. The space between the squinches is filled with a pointed blind arch on each wall, to make the transitional zone homogeneous. The drum of the dome is pierced with a row of windows.

Decoration

The decoration is also extraordinary, for the entire interior except for the marble dado and marble prayer niche, of which only traces remain, is covered with carved stucco, once also painted and gilded. A large variety of patterns cover the transitional zone, each section differently treated, partly with geometric designs and partly arabesque. These patterns have no parallel in contemporary architectural decoration, and indeed, except for this dome and the mosque of Sultan Qāytbāy in Rawḍa, no other building of the period is decorated with stucco. At the mosque in Rawḍa, however, very little of the decoration has survived.

There are two inscription bands, also of stucco, underneath the dome, one directly above the squinches and the other above the drum. The lower inscription is Quranic, the upper one commemorates the pilgrimage of Sultan Qāytbāy in 1480. The entire interior of the dome has repetitive stucco arabesques, some of which still have fine paint and gold. The patterns recall the carved decoration on the dome of Qānibāy al-Rammāḥ.

Bibliography

Behrens-Abouseif, D. "Four Domes of the Late Mamluk Period." *Annales Islamologiques*, 17 (1981), pp. 157 ff.

—. "The Northeastern Expansion of Cairo under the Mamluks." *Annales Islamologiques*, 17 (1981), pp. 191 ff.

—. "The Qubba, an Aristocratic Type of Zawiya." *Annales Islamologiques*, 19 (1983), pp. 1 ff.

ᶜAbd al-Wahhāb. *Masājid*, pp. 269 ff.

THE MOSQUE OF AMIR AZBAK AL-YŪSUFĪ (1494/5)

The mosque of Amir Azbak al-Yūsufī occupies a corner between two streets, has a sabīl-kuttāb, and is built on a side street off Ibn Ṭūlūn's Ṣalība. It has a carved minaret; the pattern in the middle section is similar to that of the minaret of Sultan Qāytbāy at Qalᶜat al-Kabsh. The facade, including the portal, is richly decorated in the usual Qāytbāy style.

There is no dome. Though the founder is buried inside, there is no particular architectural enhancement of his tomb, which is located in the east side recess to the left of the entrance. A noteworthy feature, however, is the window connecting this funerary īwān with the entrance vestibule, and thus with the street, so that the passer-by may see inside.

The *dikkat al-muballigh* is attached to the wall of the western īwān, facing the prayer niche.

Residential structures were located near the mosque as the remains of a qāᶜa there indicate.

Bibliography

Herz, M. "La mosquée d'Ezbek al-Youssoufi." *Revue Egyptienne*, I (1899), pp. 16 ff.

Mubārak. *Khiṭaṭ*, IV, p. 55.

THE MOSQUE OF AMIR QIJMAS AL-ISḤĀQĪ (1479-81)

The mosque of Amir Qijmas al-Isḥāqī is popularly known by the name of Shaykh Abū Hurayra who was buried there last century. It is a congregational (Friday) mosque located in the Darb al-Aḥmar quarter south of Bāb Zuwayla. The mosque stands above a row of shops, has three facades, and occupies a triangle in a bifurcated street. An elevated passage connects the mosque with the ablution fountains. The sabīl-kuttāb is a separate structure across the street from the north side of the mosque and has only one large facade. Although the building had to be squeezed into a narrow plot, the architect dealt successfully with these restrictions.

The Exterior

The facade of this mosque is among the most characteristic of the late Mamluk period, with dense ornamentation in a relatively small space. The windows on the three sides of the facade are on two levels, placed close together and occupying most of the facade. The lower ones have lintels of polychrome inlaid marble. The treatment of these lintels with a great variety of complicated patterns, as at the sabīl of Sultan Qāytbāy at Ṣalība, has no parallel in earlier architecture and forms a characteristic feature of Qāytbāy's decorative style. Stone panels with a net-like motif contribute to the facade ornamentation, as do the richly carved engaged columns at the corners.

The portal of the mosque, located on the southeast side of the facade, has a trilobed groin-vaulted arch with ablaq inlaid masonry. The central part of the portal recess also has an inlaid medallion. In contrast to the heavily decorated facade, the dome and the minaret are unadorned, which is quite unusual for this period. The dome is a narrow, plain brick construction, and the minaret is not carved in the middle portion as it usually is. The three rings of stalactites and keel-arched niches of the octagonal first story are the only ornaments.

Pl. 111. The mosque of Amir Qijmas al-Isḥāqī.

The Interior

The interior, a qāᶜa plan, is colorful and differs little from other mosques of the period except in the details of the decoration. ᶜAbd al-Qādir al-Naqqāsh worked here also, decorating the spandrels of the qibla windows. The prayer niche under the conch is masterfully decorated with panels of white marble inlaid with a dark-colored paste forming extremely fine scrolls or arabesques. In the very center of the decorated field, the artist proudly put his signature, as he did at the

Pl. 112. The prayer niche at the mosque of Qijmas al-Isḥāqī with the signature of the craftsman.

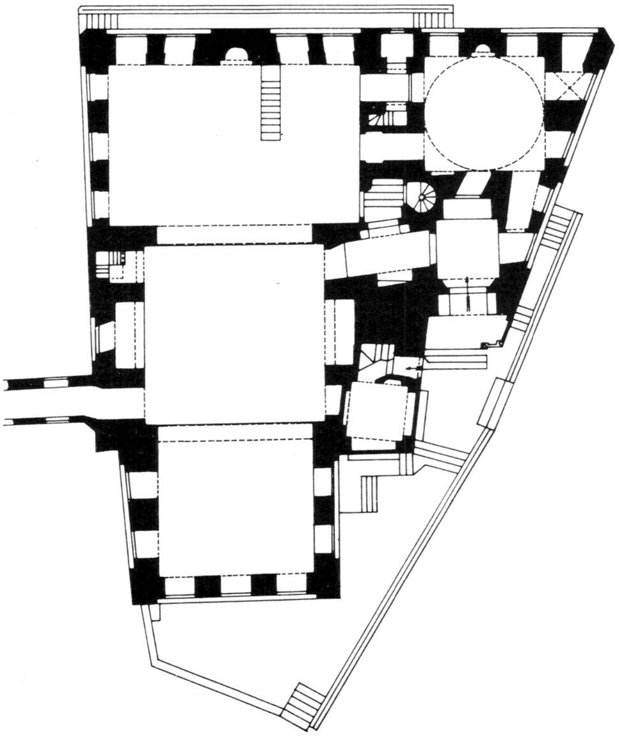

Fig. 30. The mosque of Amir Qijmas al-Isḥāqī (Department of Antiquities).

mosque of Abū Bakr ibn Muzhir, in a scroll, written twice symmetrically from left to right and right to left. This device, common in North African art, can be seen in one of the windows of the mosque of al-Ḥākim, though in quite a different style. This type of marble work, which must have been the creation of ᶜAbd al-Qādir, is one of the last innovations in the medieval decorative arts of Cairo.

In the western īwān, opposite the qibla, a thick cornice of painted and gilded wooden stalactites, runs along the upper part of the wall just underneath the ceiling. The dome, next to the qibla īwān, has an extended transition zone and is so small that it looks from the inside like a tower. Another notable feature in this mosque is the use of sliding doors in the vestibule, the only known example in the Mamluk period. It appears that the architect devised this solution to cope with the rather restricted space available for doors.

Bibliography

Mubārak. *Khiṭaṭ*, IV, pp. 48 ff.

THE MOSQUE OF AMIR QĀNIBĀY AL-RAMMĀḤ (1503)

The foundation deed calls the mosque of Amir Qānibāy a madrasa, but it functioned as a mosque with the usual Sufi services. A rabᶜ in its neighborhood endowed the foundation and at the same time provided housing for the staff attached to it. The mosque included a library, a room near the sanctuary, served by a librarian.

The extraordinary facade of this building deserves special mention. The architect made ample use of the large site on a hill overlooking the hippodrome, the mosque of Sultan Ḥasan and the horse market, creating a facade that is notable among Cairo monuments.

The long facade has, from left to right, a sabīl-kuttāb at the western corner, a rectangular double-headed minaret, a trilobed groin-vaulted portal to the right of the minaret, and on the eastern side and corner, a stone mausoleum dome carved in a repetitive arabesque pattern. The whole facade is reached by a ramp. Its composition is altogether quite harmonious.

A double-headed minaret was built by Sultan al-Ghūrī at al-Azhar. Qānibāy himself built another mosque in the Nāṣiriyya quarter which also has a rectangular double-headed minaret.

The interior reveals some variations on the qāᶜa plan. The īwān with a prayer niche, instead of having a flat ceiling, has a shallow vault on spherical pendentives, the type seen at Bāb al-Futūḥ. The stone courses are alternately painted to give an ablaq effect. The lowest course has a carved inscription and blazons. The windows above the prayer niche are also unusual, for

Pl. 113. The religious-funerary complex of Amir Qānibāy al-Rammāḥ.

instead of being set in pointed arches, they are like those usually found on the transition zone of domes, three round surmounted by three circular ones, or bull's-eyes. The prayer niche is made of stone and its conch has ablaq inlay. The īwān opposite the qibla is cross vaulted.

The four īwāns open onto the central space through a pointed arch with ablaq voussoir. The mausoleum dome is entered from the covered courtyard and is connected by doors to the qibla īwān.

Bibliography

ʿAbd al-Wahhāb. *Masājid.*, p. 281.

THE MADRASA AND KHANQĀH OF SULTAN AL-GHŪRĪ (1503/4)

Though the reign of Sultan al-Ghūrī followed shortly after that of Qāytbāy, it witnessed a clear decline in quality of craftsmanship, particularly in the stone carving and marble inlay that so richly embellished Qāytbāy's monuments. Some innovations, however, did appear in minaret architecture.

The funerary complex of Sultan al-Ghūrī, in the Faḥḥāmīn quarter (charcoal market) in al-Muʿizz street, is interesting as an architectural composition built on both sides of a street. The western side includes a Friday madrasa-mosque built on the qāʿa plan, and the eastern side includes a khanqāh and mausoleum as well as a sabīl-kuttāb.

The Madrasa

The western facade has a trilobed stalactite portal, a ṭirāz band, and a minaret projecting at its south edge. The minaret is four-storied, a rectangular structure from bottom to top, with arched panels on each side. The top originally had four bulbs instead of just one, and they were made of brick and covered with green tiles. The present top with five bulbs is a modern addi-

Pl. 114. The religious-funerary complex of Sultan al-Ghūrī.

tion, and a misrepresentation of the original. There were already minarets with double bulbs, such as those at the mosques of Qānibāy al-Rammāḥ and that of al-Ghūrī at al-Azhar. When Muḥammad Bey Abū'l-Dhahab built his mosque he crowned its minaret with five bulbs.

The interior is richly paved and paneled with black and white marble. Stone carving covers the walls but it is of poor quality, shallow and repetitive. Of interest are the stalactites that frame the upper walls of the covered courtyard, underneath the skylight.

The Khanqāh and Mausoleum

This structure also has a trilobed stalactite portal and a ṭirāz band. On its northern edge a sabīl-kuttāb projects into the street with three facades. The mausoleum on the south side of the interior now has only its rectangular base and transition zone. The dome, made of brick and covered completely with green tiles, collapsed at the beginning of this century. We know that the mausoleum dome of Imām Shafi^{c}ī was also covered at one time with green tiles, perhaps after al-Ghūrī's restoration. The transitional zone is made of stone pendentives.

On the left or north side of the entrance vestibule is a qā^{c}a that is called a khanqāh, though no living units were attached to it. The waqf deed says that Sufis should have their meetings there, but does not refer to any living accommodations provided for them. A few living units are attached to the madrasa across the street.

This building, unlike all previous royal foundations along the street, has its facades unadjusted to the street alignment. They instead make an angle, leaving the space between the two facades widening into a sort of square. The square was rented for market stalls, the income contributing to Sultan al-Ghūrī's endowment. David Roberts' nineteenth-century engraving shows a textile market there, and today there are still shops and booths on both sides of the street, the rent of which is collected by the Ministry of Waqfs and used in maintaining the religious buildings and their personnel.

Bibliography

^{c}Abd al-Wahhāb. *Masājid*, p. 286.
Mubārak. *Khiṭaṭ*, V, p. 61.

THE RELIGIOUS-FUNERARY COMPLEX OF AMIR QURQUMĀS (1506/7)

The funerary complex of Amir Qurqumās included a Friday mosque with Sufi services. Its layout is very similar to that of Sultan Qāytbāy's mosque, with the minaret at the right of the portal, the sabīl-kuttāb at the left side, and the dome on the southeast corner of the building adjoining the qā^{c}a-plan prayer hall.

The dome has carved lozenges in the lower part and a zigzag pattern on the upper part. The minaret has lozenges carved on the faceted middle section and a zigzag profile like that of the mosque of Sultan Īnāl.

An interesting feature preserved in this complex is the *qaṣr*, the term used in the waqf deed to designate the hall on the south side of the mausoleum. This was a residence overlooking the cemetery to the south, east and west from large iron-grilled windows surmounted by arched openings in pierced stone rather than stucco. There are latrines and bedrooms near it. The founders of large religious foundations often attached residential structures to their buildings, particularly if the foundation was for Sufis, like the khanqāh of Shaykhū, or was located in the cemetery where the founder went for feast days and other occasions. The complex of Barsbāy has apartments attached to it, and that of Qāytbāy still has a *maq^{c}ad* or reception loggia.

The complex of Qurqumās had apartment complexes as well, occupying sites on both sides of the cemetery road. A rab^{c} on one side has survived, with living units built on two floors and a latrine on both floors of each apartment. The foundation deed states

Pl. 115. The religious-funerary complex of Amir Qurqumās with the minaret of Sultan Īnāl to its right.

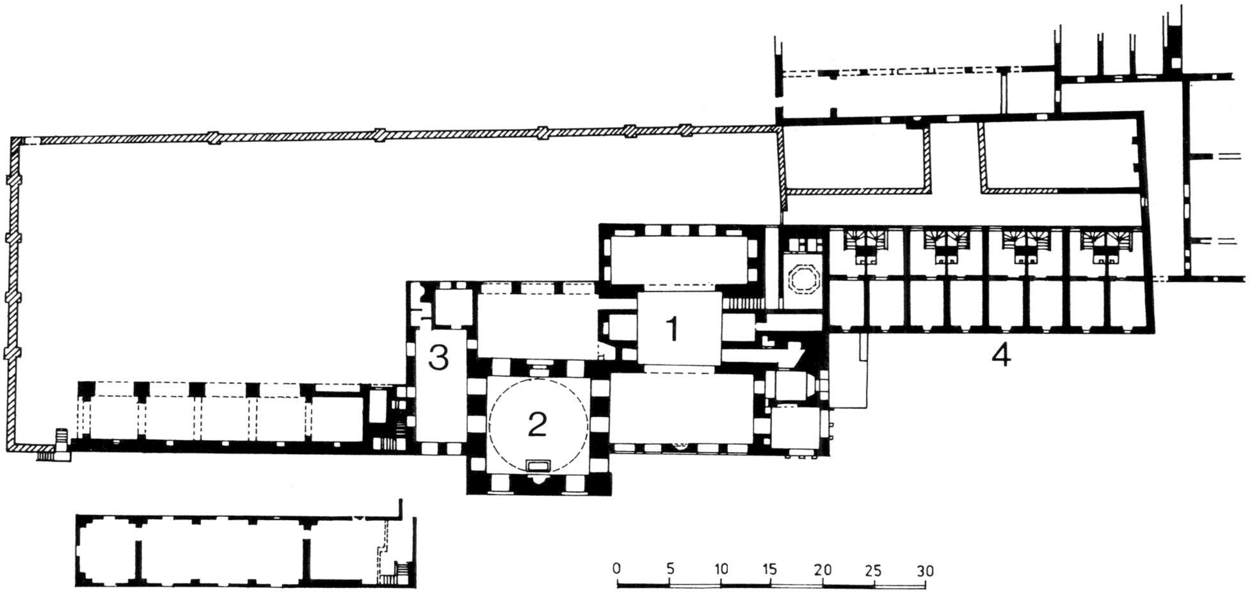

Fig. 31. The religious-funerary complex of Amir Qurqumās (Department of Antiquities).

that these dwellings could be occupied by members of the foundation's staff, as well as others, meaning that the inhabitants might be families with women and children. Like most of the foundations of its time, the complex of Qurqumās was a mosque with multiple functions, not a khanqāh with a monastic community.

Bibliography

Misiorowski, Andrzej. *Mausoleum of Qurqumās in Cairo: An Example of the Architecture and Building Art of the Mamlouk Period.* Warsaw, 1979.

THE MADRASA-MOSQUE OF AMIR KHĀYRBAK (1520-21)

Amir Khāyrbak was the governor of Aleppo during the reign of Sultan al-Ghūrī. As a reward for betraying the sultan and cooperating with the Ottoman conquerors, he became the Ottomans' first governor of Egypt after their conquest in 1517. He built his mosque in 1520/21.

The Exterior

The building that stands at Tabbāna reveals to the passerby coming down from the Citadel to Bāb Zuwayla a carved stone dome and carved brick minaret. The dome is covered with a repetitive arabesque pattern and the minaret has a geometric stucco design carved on the brick shaft; the top has been lost, but old illustrations show that it was of the usual pavilion type.

The facade of the building is not regular. On the south side under the dome, the wall is on an angle. On the western or street side, the wall is adjusted to the street alignment between the mausoleum and the ruins of the palace. On the eastern side of the dome there is an arch including an interior staircase connecting the palace with the mausoleum. This palace was built by Amir Alīn Aq in the late thirteenth century and was subsequently inhabited by various amirs, including Khāyrbak. The facade of the mausoleum has arched windows in pairs surmounted by circular windows. The lower windows are rectangular. Carved stone panels and joggled lintels decorate the facade.

A trilobed groin-vaulted and marble inlaid portal leads through a corridor into a courtyard from where the mosque is reached, an uncommon approach to a mosque. To the left side of the portal, across an entrance passage, is a sabīl-kuttāb. The courtyard on the east side of the mosque is occupied by a tomb and is bordered by Ṣalāḥ al-Dīn's eastern city wall, separating it from the cemetery of Bāb al-Wazīr.

Pl. 116. The madrasa and mausoleum of Amir Khāyrbak.

The Interior

The interior of the mosque is not a qāʿa plan, but a hall consisting of three cross vaults supported by pointed arches. The central vault has an octagonal opening to admit light. The eastern wall, with the prayer niche, paneled like the rest of the wall with a polychrome marble dado with a conch of plain stone, shows an awkward feature. The windows above the prayer niche are partly hidden by the curve of the central arch supporting the vault, as if the architect had begun the walls with the intention of roofing them as usual with a wooden ceiling, but then changed his mind after the qibla wall was erected and instead added arches for the vault.

A shortage of wood might explain this anomaly. Egypt always had to import its wood, and in Sultan al-Ghūrī's time, it would have been imported from Anatolia. At the time this building was erected, Egypt was already embroiled in the disturbances caused by the Ottoman conquests, and thus the importation of timber may have been difficult.

The *dikka*, a loggia made of wood, is placed on the western wall opposite the prayer niche. This wall, adjusted to the street alignment by irregular thicknesses of the wall, includes recesses. The qibla wall is not properly oriented to Mecca, as is the prayer niche in the mausoleum. The irregularity is most likely due to lack of space, raising the question of whether the space occupied by the mosque was originally planned for another purpose and later adapted for a religious building.

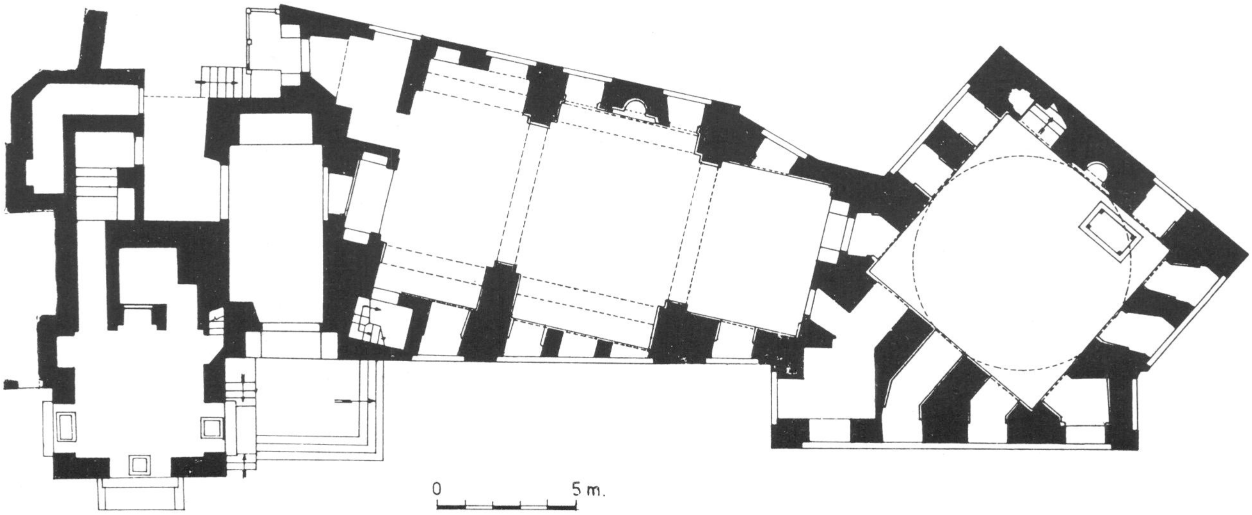

Fig. 32. The madrasa and mausoleum of Amir Khāyrbak (Department of Antiquities).

The Mausoleum

At the back of the prayer hall, facing the entrance, is a trilobed portal with a groin vault decorated with ablaq masonry and stalactites in the two side arches. It leads into the mausoleum. A special feature of this building is the treatment of the mausoleum entrance, which is enhanced by a portal and has a pair of maksalas. This treatment is common on facades, not in interiors.

The mausoleum walls are not straight, and inside they also show irregularities in the arrangement of the windows. The inner window openings do not correspond to the outer openings, so that the openings run obliquely through the thickness of the masonry.

The mausoleum is dated 1502/3 but the foundation deed of the madrasa has the much later date of 1521. The madrasa itself has no dated inscription, but there is no break in the masonry of the mausoleum and madrasa to suggest that they were constructed at different times.

The foundation deed of the madrasa states that it was planned for ten students who were also Sufis. Five living units under the floor of the mosque, reached from the yard, provided their lodging.

Bibliography

Mubārak. *Khiṭaṭ*, IV, p. 110.

Pl. 117. Interior of the madrasa of Amir Khāyrbak.

CHAPTER NINE

ARCHITECTURE OF THE OTTOMAN PERIOD

THE MOSQUE OF SULAYMĀN PASHA (1528)

Sulaymān Pasha's mosque is the first mosque founded in Cairo after the Ottoman conquest, but not the first religious foundation. It was preceded by the Takiyyat Ibrāhīm al-Kulshanī which was completed in 1524. The mosque is located in the northern enclosure of the Citadel which was at that time occupied by the Janissary corps of the Ottoman army. The provision that the shaykh of the mosque must be Turkish indicates its dedication to this corps.

The Exterior

The mosque's architecture owes very little to Cairene architectural traditions and its plan is entirely Ottoman. It is a rectangular building, approximately half of which is occupied by the prayer hall, the other half by a courtyard. The prayer hall is a rectangular space covered by a central dome, flanked by three half-domes. The courtyard is surrounded by an arcade covered by shallow domes. The central dome, the shallow domes around the courtyard, and the conical top of the minaret are all covered with green tiles.

This building has no facade, in the Cairene architectural sense of paneling and decorative fenestrations. Its appearance is rather introverted, and its small portal is an imitation of that of al-Nāṣir Muḥammad's mosque nearby in the Citadel, a half-dome on stalactites. The minaret stands to the left of the entrance on the south wall of the sanctuary, a high cylindrical faceted shaft. It uses a Mamluk device in the different styles of stalactite carving on the balconies, an exception among Cairo's Ottoman minarets. The profile of the dome is rounded and squat.

The Interior

There is no vestibule; the entrance leads directly into the prayer hall. The central dome rests on spherical pendentives. Its painting and that of the transitional zone have been restored. The *dikka* is attached to the upper part of the wall facing the prayer niche and is reached by an inner staircase. It is also painted. The lower parts of the inner walls are covered with marble dadoes in Mamluk style and a frieze of carved marble inlaid with paste runs above the dado.

A large marble pulpit, carved and painted, is surmounted by a conical top like that of the minaret, just as Mamluk pulpits had pavilions similar to those of their minarets.

A door in the western wall leads to a courtyard paved with marble. On the west side of the courtyard is a shrine built in the Fatimid period by Abū Manṣūr ibn Qasṭa, popularly known as Sīdī Sāryā. The shrine is incorporated into the architecture of the mosque, and covered by a dome larger than those around the courtyard. The shrine includes the tombs of Ottoman officials with cenotaphs topped with various types of turbans in marble. Until recently there was a wooden boat hanging above the cenotaph of Ibn Qasṭa; it is a popular tradition in Egypt to place boats in saints' shrines.

On the north side of the courtyard another entrance leads to a second courtyard in front of a vaulted oblong building composed of two halls. The outer hall opens to the courtyard and leads though a door into the inner hall. Both are roofed with two half domes on spherical pendentives, facing each other. According to the foundation deed, this building is a kuttāb. Its domes were covered with blue tiles; the mosque's domes are in green. The kuttāb has a prayer niche with stalactites in the conch.

Bibliography

Mubārak. *Khiṭaṭ*, V, p. 14.

THE TAKIYYA OF SULAYMĀN PASHA (1543)

The term *takiyya* (from the Turkish *tekke*) designates an Ottoman type of religious institution with boarding house functions. Its architecture, therefore, is characterized by the presence of living units for students or Sufis.

Pl. 118. The mosque of Sulaymān Pasha.

Pl. 119. The takiyya-madrasa of Sulaymān Pasha.

The takiyya is the equivalent of the khanqāh and indeed, some takiyyas had strict regulations reminiscent of the foundations of the early Mamluk period where Sufis dwelt, worshiped, and studied, following a clearly defined curriculum. Some takiyyas, such as the Sulaymāniyya and the Maḥmūdiyya (1750), are Ottoman in architecture, a courtyard surrounded by living units behind an arcade with round arches and shallow domes. The foundation deeds of later, eighteenth century, religious institutions show that Sufism was no longer part of the activities of mosques and madrasas. Instead, Sufi shaykhs pursued their rituals in the zāwiyas and takiyyas.

Sometimes, the term takiyya was simply used to designate the part of the madrasa devoted to living quarters. At the foundation of Muḥammad Bey Abū 'l-Dhahab, a madrasa for the four Islamic rites, the students' residence was called the takiyya, but no Sufis were attached to the foundation.

The inscriptions on the Takiyya Sulaymāniyya do not include the term *takiyya*, but do refer to a madrasa. Takiyya Sulaymāniyya is the popular name and also the term used by historians.

The Mamluk-style facade has a groin-vaulted portal leading through a straight, cross-vaulted passage into the courtyard. The courtyard is surrounded by a columned arcade with round arches. Behind each arch is the entrance to a cell, except on the axis of the entrance, which corresponds to the qibla. There, a domed room opens onto the courtyard and includes the prayer niche. Unfortunately, the foundation is not mentioned in the waqf deed of Sulaymān Pasha, so we do not know exactly how the madrasa functioned, or if the foundation originally included other structures. There is no mosque or minaret attached to it.

Bibliography

Mubārak. *Khiṭaṭ*, VI, p. 56; Van Berchem, *C.I.A.*, p. 606.

THE MOSQUE OF MAḤMŪD PASHA (1567)

The mosque of Maḥmūd Pasha is a free-standing building situated on the northeast side of the madrasa of Sultan Ḥasan, also facing the Citadel. Apart from its Ottoman minaret, the architecture is entirely Mamluk in style. There are even two features copied from the Sultan Ḥasan mosque: locating of the mausoleum dome behind the prayer hall to face the Citadel, and building the minaret on a semicircular, protruding buttress flanking the dome. The profile of the dome is slightly shorter and more rounded than Mamluk domes.

Pl. 120. The mosque and mausoleum of Maḥmūd Pasha.

Pl. 121. The mosque of Maḥmūd Pasha, interior view.

The minaret is a slender circular tower that appears particularly elongated because of the circular buttress on which it rests. The same feature can be seen at the nearby mosque of Sultan Ḥasan which might have inspired the Maḥmūdiyya architect. The shaft of the minaret, like the buttress, is ribbed with vertical moldings, and it has a balcony on stalactites at the roof level and another, higher balcony.

The rectangular hall's roof is supported by two pairs of columns, a feature found in the mosque of Sultan Barsbāy in the cemetery, but here the columns are ancient Egyptian granite columns and their pointed arches are not parallel to the qibla wall, but form a rectangular pavilion in the center of the mosque with a lantern in the ceiling to admit light. The side aisles are slightly higher than the central aisle. A loggia of painted wood faces the prayer niche and is reached by an inner staircase.

There is no marble decoration, but intricate stucco and colored-glass windows and a beautiful arabesque painted ceiling make this mosque particularly attractive. The fact that the mosque is free standing enhances the effect of the light coming through the windows. The dome, beyond the qibla wall, rests on pendentives and is plain. It is one of the few domed mausoleums of the Ottoman period. The mosque of Masīḥ Pasha (1575) at ʿArab Yasār in the cemetery southeast of the Citadel is similar in plan to this mosque, but its lantern is supported by piers instead of columns.

Bibliography

ʿAbd al-Wahhāb. *Masājid.*, pp. 295 f.
Williams, J. "Monuments."

THE MOSQUE OF SINĀN PASHA (1571)

This mosque is one of the most interesting in Ottoman Cairo. It was built on the Nile shore at the port of Būlāq, which was at that time separated from the rest of Cairo and closer to the river than it is today, because the river has since shifted westward.

The mosque is set askew within its enclosure to maintain the Mecca orientation. The mosque's domed chamber is surrounded on three sides by an arcade of slightly pointed arches supporting shallow domes; a minaret flanks the mosque on the south side. The enclosure does not allow the mosque a street facade. Its architecture is dominated by the central dome. The central dome's profile is rounded, and the lower part has two rows of windows, the upper ones in the shape of lobed arches. These are common on Fatimid buildings, but they are used only once in a dome, at the shrine of Sayyida Ruqayya, built more than four centuries earlier. Between the facets of the dome that include the windows, there are small buttresses or turrets crowned by onion-shaped tops, which give this dome its particular appearance. The minaret is a squat cylindrical shaft with one balcony and a conical top.

The mosque of Sinān Pasha has the largest stone dome in Cairo, with a diameter of about fifteen meters. It is a half meter larger than the dome of Barqūq.

The interior is heavily influenced by the architecture of the Fadāwiyya mausoleum. The transitional zone is set within, not above, the rectangular part of the building and is composed of trilobed squinches, each within a pointed arch. The upper arch of the squinch is decorated with stalactites. Curiously, the inner lower

Pl. 122. The mosque of Sinān Pasha at Būlāq.

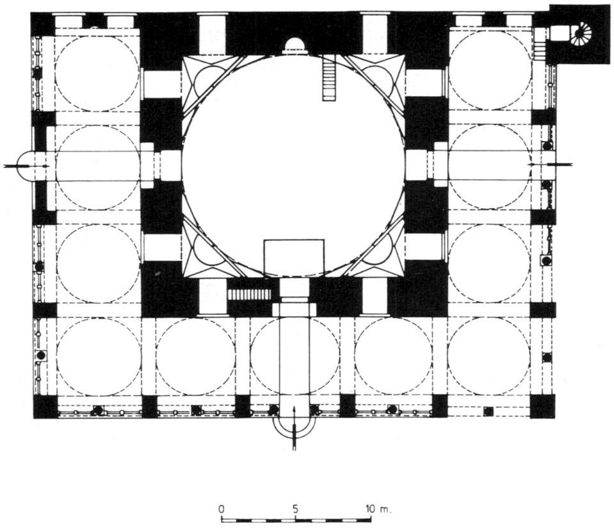

Fig. 33. The mosque of Sinān Pasha (Department of Antiquities).

windows of the dome do not have the same shape as they do on the exterior. Their exterior shape is a double arch; inside they take the shape of rosettes filled with colored glass.

The prayer niche is decorated with Mamluk style polychrome marble. Around the base of the dome runs a gallery with a wooden balustrade whose function is not evident. The *dikka* is a wooden balcony facing the prayer niche reached, like the gallery, by a staircase in the wall.

Bibliography

Mubārak. *Khiṭaṭ*, V, p. 19.

THE MOSQUE OF MALIKA ṢAFIYYA (1610)

Malika Ṣafiyya was the Venetian wife of the Ottoman Sultan Murād III. When one of her slaves, ʿUthmān Aghā, decided to build this mosque, he came up against legal problems. It was found that as a slave, he was not legally entitled either to build a mosque or to make endowments, as his properties after his death should revert to his owner, Malika Ṣafiyya. As it could not be proved that the slave had been freed before his death, nor that he had the permission of his owner to make endowments, the endowment was considered illegal. Thus the mosque and all other properties endowed to it reverted to Malika Ṣafiyya.

The mosque is built on a level much higher than the street and is reached by a long semicircular flight of steps. The exterior walls are not decorated but there are windows on two levels. A minaret flanks the building on the southeast corner. There are three entrances, one on each facade, each composed of a shallow trilobed recess framed by a molding with angular loops. They thus differ from the street entrance leading to the mosque complex, which has a trilobed groin-vaulted portal.

The plan is similar to that of the mosque of Sulaymān Pasha, with a similar courtyard. The sanctuary, however, although also covered by a large rounded dome, is flanked by small domes instead of large half-domes. The lateral small domes are supported by arches carried by columns. As at the mosque of Sinān Pasha, a wooden gallery runs around the inner base of the dome; the *dikka* is opposite the prayer niche. Three doors, the central one larger, connect the sanctuary with the courtyard. The mosque of Malika Ṣafiyya has one feature inherited from earlier architecture: a dome over the prayer niche; it protrudes at the back wall of the mosque.

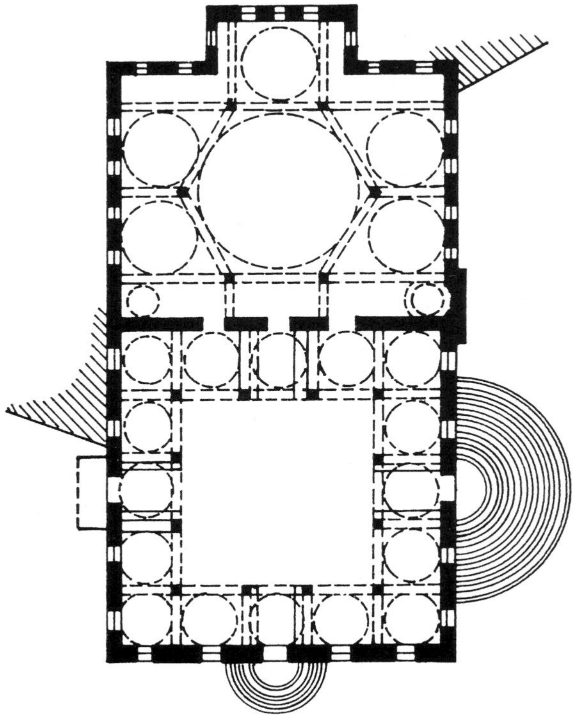

Fig. 34. The mosque of Malika Ṣafiyya (Department of Antiquities).

BIBLIOGRAPHY

ᶜAbd al-Wahhāb. *Masājid*, pp. 306 ff.
Mubārak. *Khiṭaṭ*, IV, p. 39.
Williams. "Monuments," Appendix B.

THE MOSQUE OF AMIR YŪSUF AGHĀ AL-ḤĪN (1625)

The mosque of Amir Yūsuf Aghā al-Ḥīn is located in the neighborhood of the Islamic Museum; it was built by an amir of Circassian origin. Except for the minaret, its architecture follows Mamluk traditions. A mausoleum with a dome, for the amir and his family, was attached to the building, but was demolished in the last century to make way for the construction of Muḥammad ᶜAlī street.

The mosque is a free-standing building with a qāᶜa plan, decorated with polychrome marble in the Mamluk style. The original sabīl-kuttāb can be seen on the eastern facade which also includes the portal. The other sabīl on the northwestern corner of the mosque was added in this century, when the mosque was restored after the Khalīj was filled in and replaced by a street. This new sabīl is an anachronism, as it is an imitation of the sabīl of ᶜAbd al-Raḥmān Katkhudā built about a century later than the mosque of Yūsuf Aghā.

Pl. 124. The mosque of Yūsuf Aghā al-Ḥīn, view of the interior with mashrabiyya.

Pl. 123. The mosque of Yūsuf Aghā al-Ḥīn.

The interior displays an unusual feature in the mashrabiyya occupying the western wall. The mosque was erected on the eastern side of the Khalīj and the windows were placed to allow worshipers to enjoy the view of the canal and gardens outside, as was common in residential architecture. Another interesting detail is the presence of wooden balconies that occupy the whole width of the three īwāns around the main one, and thus add a kind of upper floor to the mosque. The function of these balconies is not quite clear. It is unlikely that they all were *dikka*s for recitations.

BIBLIOGRAPHY

ᶜAbd al-Wahhāb. *Masājid*, pp. 312 ff.
Mubārak. *Khiṭaṭ*, IV, p. 102.

THE MOSQUE OF SHAYKH AL-BURDAYNĪ (1616-29)

This small building, located in the Dāwūdiyya quarter not far from the mosque of Malika Ṣafiyya, is an architectural surprise. It appears as if the architect,

Pl. 125. The mosque of Shaykh al-Burdaynī.

or the founder, tried to revive the style of Mamluk buildings of the Qāytbāy period. Lavishly decorated, its interior contrasts with that of the Ottoman buildings already described. Its founder was not a Turk, nor a member of the ruling class, but an Egyptian shaykh of the Shāfiᶜī rite.

The facade treatment is totally Mamluk. The mosque has two facades, the western one with the portal and a minaret on its right side. The minaret's first story is octagonal and the circular second section is carved. The upper part consists of a bulb resting on a balcony on stalactites, and is thus an imitation of late Mamluk minarets with a carved first story decorated with keel-arched niches framed with moldings. The two balconies rest on stalactites of different patterns. The only difference between this and Mamluk minarets is that the bulb is not carried on an octagonal pavilion, but set directly above the balcony. The quality of the carving is less refined than that of the Qāytbāy period. It is the only Ottoman minaret with an inscription band, here placed on the octagonal section. It provides the date of 1623, which is much later than that of the mosque.

The mosque is L-shaped and very small. The qibla wall is entirely covered with marble polychrome panels, and the other walls have a high marble dado. The windows have stucco and colored-glass decoration. The prayer niche, richly decorated with inlaid marble and blue-glass paste, is one of the finest examples of decoration in the Mamluk tradition, and the wooden ceiling is richly painted. Opposite the prayer niche are a *dikka* and a wooden frieze with an inscription band, also in late Mamluk style, running along the walls under the ceiling. The wooden pulpit with geometrical designs shows a successful revival of Mamluk art.

Shaykh al-Burdaynī, sponsor of the mosque, was a Shāfiᶜī Egyptian, not a Turk, and this may explain the traditional, local character of the mosque's architecture.

Bibliography

Mubārak. *Khiṭaṭ*, III, p. 64; IV, p. 65; IX, p. 16.

THE MOSQUE OF AMIR ᶜUTHMĀN KATKHUDĀ (1734)

ᶜUthmān Katkhudā, a wealthy amir, built a mosque together with residential and commercial buildings at Azbakiyya in the area which is today Opera Square. Only the left side of the facade of the mosque was visi-

Pl. 126. The mosque of Amir ᶜUthmān Katkhudā.

Pl. 127. The mosque of ʿUthmān Katkhudā, interior view.

ble from the street; the rest was surrounded by houses and a rabʿ, a ḥammām, sabīl-kuttāb and a number of shops. The structures formed a complete city quarter.

A groin-vaulted portal is in the center of the facade and a minaret stands on its left, or northwest corner. Apart from the Turkish shape of the minaret and the blue-green Turkish tiles decorating the lintel of the entrance, the facade, with its recessed panels including windows, is Mamluk in style.

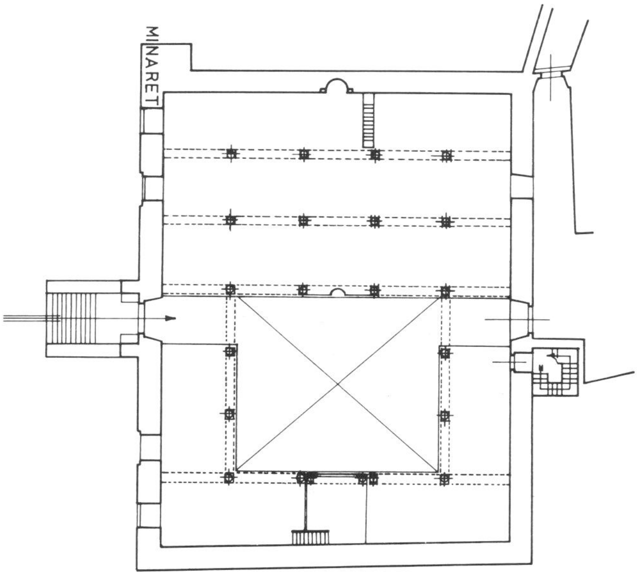

Fig. 35. The mosque of Amir ʿUthmān Katkhudā (Department of Antiquities).

The entrance leads directly into the mosque from the western side. The mosque is hypostyle in plan, with a courtyard. It is the only mosque of this period to have such an archaic layout. Marble columns support the beautiful painted wooden ceiling. The prayer niche is decorated with inlaid marble, also Mamluk in style.

Bibliography

ʿAbd al-Wahhāb. *Masājid*, pp. 323 ff.
Behrens-Abouseif. *Azbakiyya*, pp. 55 ff., 114 ff.
Mubārak, *Khiṭaṭ*, V, pp. 89 ff.

THE MOSQUE OF MUḤAMMAD BEY ABŪ'L-DHAHAB (1774)

Like the mosque of Sultan Ḥasan, that of Muḥammad Bey Abū'l-Dhahab was a madrasa for the four rites of Islamic law, but unlike the late Mamluk foundations, it had no services for Sufis.

The Exterior

Standing opposite al-Azhar in the middle of the city, it is architecturally an imitation of the mosque of Sinān Pasha at Būlāq, with slight differences. Sinān Pasha's mosque is within a garden enclosure; Abū'l-Dhahab's mosque, in the heart of the city, is surrounded by a facade wall. This wall is lower than the walls of the mosque proper, so that the arcades of the mosque are visible from outside the wall. The facade is paneled in

Pl. 128. The madrasa-mosque of Muḥammad Bey Abū'l-Dhahab.

the Mamluk style with stalactite recesses including windows. The mosque stands above shops on the east and south facades. The profile of the dome is similar to that of Sinān Pasha's mosque and it has the same width but is built of brick. The windows of the drum are the usual double-arched openings surmounted by a circular one, differing from the lobed-arch windows of the Sinān Pasha dome. Buttresses in the shape of turrets flank the sixteen corners of the drum.

The minaret also differs in shape and location. It is on the southwest corner and is an imitation of the nearby minaret of Sultan al-Ghūrī, which at the time Abū'l-Dhahab founded his mosque, still had four bulbs. The minaret of Abū'l-Dhahab has five bulbs. The portal is also Mamluk, trilobed and groin vaulted, and the windows have in their lintels bits of green and blue Ottoman style tiles.

The Interior

The portal, reached by a flight of steps, leads to a ziyāda surrounding the mosque on its east and south sides. The ziyāda results from adjusting the facade to the street alignment, making an angle with the main part of the building. To the left of the entrance is a very elaborate cast bronze grill behind which was once housed a very rich library.

Like the mosque of Sinān Pasha, this mosque is composed of a central dome surrounded on the three non-qibla sides by an arcade supporting shallow domes. The dome at the northeast corner is occupied by the tombs of the founder and his sister. The walls are paneled with Turkish and Tunisian tiles characteristically blue and yellow. The funerary corner is enclosed with a lacy bronze grill.

The sanctuary, or domed area, has three entrances leading from the three arcaded galleries through entrances enhanced by stalactite crestings. The interior has the trilobed large squinches seen at the Fadāwiyya dome and Sinān Pasha's mosque. Mother-of-pearl inlaid along with marble, an exceptional decoration for this time, is found on the prayer niche which is paneled in early Mamluk style. The inscription bands are more Ottoman in style than Mamluk, set in cartouches underneath the dome and carved in riḥānī script. They are painted and gilded. The *dikka* is a remarkable wooden balcony that projects on brackets from the wall facing the prayer niche.

On the south side of the mosque and separated from it by a wall is a two-storied complex of rooms around a courtyard. The foundation deed calls this a takiyya, and stipulates that it be used by Turkish students.

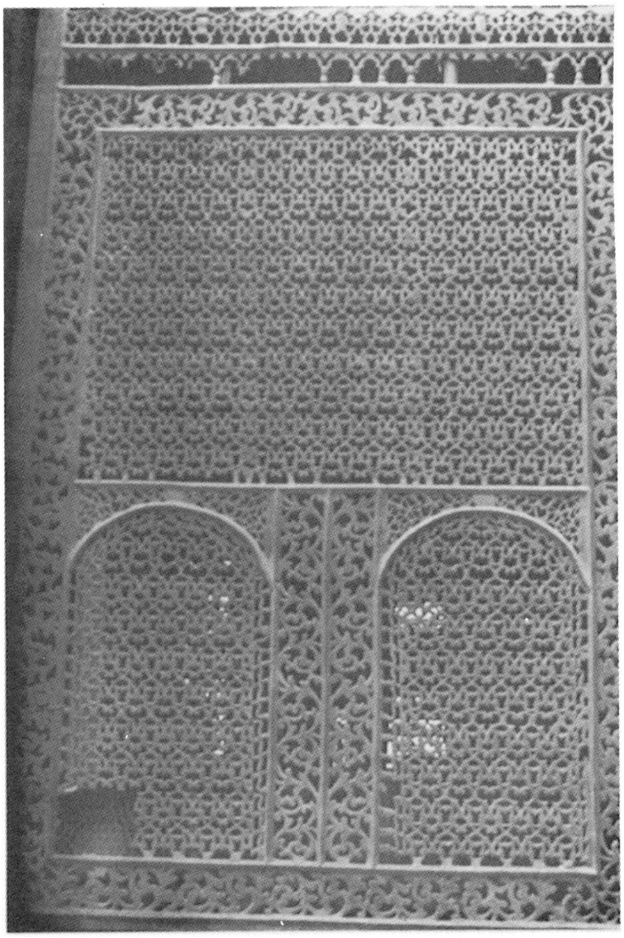

Pl. 129. Iron grill at the mosque of Muḥammad Bey Abū'l-Dhahab.

Bibliography

Mubārak. *Khiṭaṭ*, V, p. 103.
ʿAbd al-Wahhāb. *Masājid*, pp. 351 ff.

THE MOSQUE OF ḤASAN PASHA ṬĀHIR (1809)

The mosque of Ḥasan Pasha Ṭāhir was built shortly after Muḥammad ʿAli came to power by one of his officers. The building, in the Hilmiyya quarter not far from the mosque of Ibn Ṭūlūn, has a curiously hybrid character.

Pl. 130. The mosque and mausoleum of Ḥasan Pasha Ṭáhir.

The facade shows an obvious attempt to revive Mamluk architecture. It has a trilobe portal with groins and to the right is a sabīl-kuttāb. Moldings are used densely, framing carved panels. A minaret to the right of the sabīl-kuttāb is a strange imitation of Mamluk style with an octagonal first story and a circular second story with moldings. The third story carries a bulb but is a continuous circular shaft rather than a pavilion. Two balconies on stalactites are set between the three sections.

On the left side of the entrance is a mausoleum dome of peculiar architecture. Its base is below the mosque roof and the lower part has a window with a stalactite recess and moldings. The transitional zone, which is of stone though the dome is of brick, is Mamluk in style, with undulating steps. The dome itself is vertical and thin, and is decorated with moldings. Its pointed profile thus differs from Mamluk domes.

Next to this dome is another, rounded dome of even more exotic character. It was built for a brother of the mosque's founder and may have been inspired by Turkish provincial architecture.

The interior of the mosque of Ḥasan Ṭāhir is a hall whose roof is supported by three pairs of columns. There is a lantern, and the decoration is of traditional Mamluk style.

Bibliography

ᶜAbd al-Wahhāb. *Masājid*, pp. 357 ff.
Mubārak. *Khiṭaṭ*, IV, p. 87.

THE MOSQUE OF SULAYMĀN AGHĀ AL-SILĀḤDĀR (1837-39)

The mosque of Sulaymān Aghā al-Silāḥdār, not far from the al-Aqmar mosque on the opposite side of the street, exhibits all the decorative features of the Muḥammad ᶜAlī style.

The Exterior

The facade is relatively low and is composed of three sections. On the north section the mosque stands above a row of shops. An entrance at the northernmost section leads to the courtyard of the mosque. Further south is a round arched entrance between the mosque and the kuttāb, which is next to the sabīl rather than above it. The minaret, an especially elegant shaft, tall,

Pl. 131. The mosque of Amir Sulaymān Aghā al-Silāḥdār.

slender and cylindrical with an elongated conical top, stands between the madrasa and the mosque. It has one balcony on horizontal moldings.

The facade of the sabīl, a flamboyant display of late Ottoman decoration, rounded and built of marble with round arched windows, is at the southern part of the complex. Its cast bronze window grills have a very intricate lacy pattern. Above them are marble carvings imitating textile folds, a device of Italian Baroque art. Cartouches with Turkish inscriptions in nastaᶜlīq script decorate the entire upper part of the sabīl facade and above these is a repetitive motif of acanthus-like leaves. A wooden carved and painted sunshade tops the sabīl facade. There is a great similarity between this sabīl and the one facing the madrasa of al-Nāṣir Muḥammad, built in the same period (1828) by Ismāᶜīl Pasha.

Next to the sabīl of Sulaymān Aghā al-Silāḥdār is a round arch that frames the entrance on the side street leading to another entrance to the mosque through a covered flight of steps.

The Interior

The interior combines features of both Ottoman and Cairene architecture. The courtyard's rounded arcades are covered with Ottoman style shallow domes. Above the entrance to the mosque is a charming small semicircular balcony that is very Western in style. The roof of the sanctuary is carried on four identical marble columns, forming three aisles parallel to the qibla wall. They support round arches and a central lantern. The prayer niche, made of white marble, is decorated with Western style floral motifs and looks like something that might be found in a European baroque church. The *dikka* is a gallery with wooden balustrade above the entrance, communicating with the small round balcony outside. A row of horizontally pierced oval windows bring light from the courtyard into the interior.

Interestingly, and unexpectedly, the window recesses of the mosque show that the facade has been adjusted to the street alignment by progressively thickening the wall, just as in the al-Aqmar mosque and all the Mamluk mosques on the same street.

Bibliography

ᶜAbd al-Wahhāb. *Masājid*, pp. 360 ff.
Mubārak. *Khiṭaṭ*, V, p. 15.

THE MOSQUE OF MUḤAMMAD ᶜALĪ (1830-48)

In the architecture of his mosque, Muḥammad ᶜAlī Pasha, viceroy and initiator of Egypt's modern age, achieved a radical break with all traditions characterizing Cairo architecture from the Mamluk to the late Ottoman period. The break is emphasized by the choice of site.

Muḥammad ᶜAlī pulled down the remains of Mamluk palaces and their dependencies, described shortly before by Napoleon's scholars as the most impressive buildings in Cairo despite their dilapidated condition. Recent excavations show that in order to build the mosque on top of the preexisting structures, some ten meters of rubble were filled in.

Just as Ṣalāḥ al-Dīn many centuries earlier had abolished all traces of Fatimid power and status by refusing to live in their palaces and having them dismantled and parceled out to his courtiers, so Muḥammad ᶜAlī destroyed all traces of the Mamluk palaces from which Egypt had been ruled since the thirteenth century. That is why, among Cairo's wealth of historic monuments, there is not one royal palace left from these periods.

It is, however, paradoxical that while politically Muḥammad ᶜAlī acted quite independently of Istanbul, architecturally during his reign style came closer to that of Istanbul than ever before, including its Western, particularly French, influence. Muḥammad ᶜAlī's Cairo set out to abandon the oriental Middle Ages and begin the modern Western Age, in effect, to surpass Istanbul. Muḥammad ᶜAlī, who was more eager to build modern factories than religious foundations, erected this mosque, where he is buried, as a monument to himself.

Originally, the planning of this mosque was assigned to Muḥammad ᶜAlī's French architect, Pascal Coste, who probably would have built it in the local Mamluk style, judging from his interest in Cairo's traditional architecture. For some unknown reason, however, the Pasha changed his mind and an Armenian architect, whose name is not known, designed the mosque on a plan similar to that of the mosque of Sultan Aḥmad in Istanbul.

Because it is the most visible monument of Cairo, Muḥammad ᶜAlī's mosque, the least Egyptian of monuments, became a symbol of the city. Popularly known as *al-qalᶜa*, meaning citadel, it is thus confused as well with the works of Ṣalāḥ al-Dīn.

Pl. 132. The mosque of Muḥammad ʿAlī.

The long time it took to complete this monument may be due to its size, gigantic by Cairo's architectural standards. That combined with its prominent location and its profile, the domed silhouette flanked by a pair of slender high minarets, contributed to its prestige. The minarets, over eighty meters high, stand on bases only three meters wide. The architecture of the mosque is totally Ottoman, though its domes are, relative to their width, higher and less squat than those in Istanbul.

The plan is a central dome carried on four piers and spherical pendentives, flanked by four half-domes. The courtyard, as at the mosques of Sulaymān Pasha and Malika Ṣafiyya, is surrounded by rounded arcades carrying small domes.

The mosque has three entrances, on the north, west and east walls. The western entrance opens onto the courtyard, which also has a northern and southern entrance from the mosque. In the middle of the courtyard is a marble ablution fountain with a carved wooden roof on columns, the whole lavishly decorated in a style recalling the decoration of the sabīl-kuttāb facing the madrasa of al-Nāṣir on Muʿizz street built in 1828 by Ismāʿīl Pasha. The sabīl and the upper part of the courtyard facade are decorated with small oval wall paintings on which Mediterranean landscapes are represented.

On the west wall of the courtyard is an iron clock presented to Muḥammad ʿAlī by the French King Louis Philippe, with a tea salon on the upper level. Its style is a mixture of neo-gothic and oriental elements.

The entire decoration of the building is alien to Cairene traditions, and in fact, to Islamic art. There are no stalactites, geometric shapes or arabesques; only the inscription bands continue an Islamic tradition. Even the marble chosen for decoration is different from that of earlier mosques: the walls and piers of the mosque are paneled with alabaster from Upper Egypt, which is inappropriate for architecture as it deteriorates quickly.

In the southwest corner of the sanctuary, within an enclosure richly decorated with bronze openwork, is the marble cenotaph of Muḥammad ᶜAlī. In 1936 serious structural deficiencies were found in the dome and it had to be totally rebuilt. It took two years. Between 1937 and 1939 the decoration was renewed and in the mid of the 1980's the whole citadel complex was again renovated.

Bibliography

Coste, Pascal. *Architecture Arabe des Monuments du Caire*. Paris, 1839.
Mubārak. *Khiṭaṭ*, V, pp. 77 ff.
Wiet, Gaston. *Muhammed Ali et les Beaux-Arts*. Cairo, n.d., pp. 265 ff.

BIBLIOGRAPHY

THE CITY OF CAIRO

ᶜAbd al-Wahhāb, Ḥasan. "Takhṭīṭ al-qāhira wa tanẓīmuhā mundhu nashʾatihā." *Bulletin de l'Institut d'Egypte*, XXXVII (2) (1954/55), pp. 1 ff.

Abu-Lughod, Janet. *Cairo: 1001 Years of the City Victorious*. Princeton, 1971.

Amīn, Muḥammad Muḥ. *Al-awqāf wa'l-ḥayāt al-ijtimāᶜiyya fī miṣr. (648-923/1250-1517)*. Cairo, 1980.

Behrens-Abouseif, Doris. *Azbakiyya and Its Environs, from Azbak to Ismaᶜil, 1476-1979*. Cairo, 1985.

—. "Locations of Non-Muslim quarters in medieval Cairo." *Annales Islamologiques*, XXII (1986), pp. 117 ff.

Becker, C. H. "Cairo". *Encyclopaedia of Islam*. 1st ed. Leiden, 1913-36.

Blachère, R. "L'agglomération du Caire, vue par quatre voyageurs arabes du Moyen Age." *Annales Islamologiques*, VIII (1969), pp. 22 ff.

Clerget, Marcel. *Le Caire: Etude de géographie urbaine et d'histoire économique*. Cairo, 1934.

Description de l'Egypte par les Savants de l'Expédition Française. Etat Moderne. "Description de la ville et de la citadelle du Kaire," J. Jomard. Paris, 1812.

Garcin, Jean-Claude. "Toponymie et topographie urbaines médiévales à Fusṭāṭ et au Caire." *Journal of the Economic and Social History of the Orient*, XXVII, Part II, pp. 113 ff.

Goitein, S. D. "Cairo: An Islamic City in the Light of the Geniza Documents." *Middle Eastern Cities*, I. Lapidus, ed. Berkeley and Los Angeles, 1969, pp. 80 ff.

Hanna, Nelly. *An Urban History of Bulaq in the Mamluk and Ottoman Periods*. Cairo, 1983.

Hautecoeur, Louis, and Wiet, Gaston. *Les Mosquées du Caire*. Paris, 1932.

Ibn Duqmāq. *Kitāb al-intiṣār li wāsiṭat ᶜiqd al-amṣār*. Būlāq, 1314 H.

Ibrāhīm, ᶜAbd al-Laṭīf. "Silsilat al-dirāsāt al-wathāʾiqiyya. (I) al-wathāʾiq fī khidmat al-āthār (al-ᶜaṣr al-mamlūkī)." *Kitāb al-muʾtamar al-thānī li āthār al-bilād al-ᶜarabiyya*. Cairo, 1957.

Kubiak, Wladyslaw. "The Burning of Miṣr al-Fusṭāṭ in 1168; A Reconsideration of Historical Evidence." *African Bulletin* 28 (1979), pp. 51 ff.

—. *Al-Fusṭāṭ, Its Foundation and Early Urban Development*. Warsaw, 1982.

Lane-Poole, Stanley. *The Story of Cairo*. London, 1906.

Lapidus, Ira M. *Muslim Cities in the Later Middle Ages*. Cambridge, Mass., 1967.

Massignon, Louis. *La Cité des Morts au Caire. Qarafa — Darb al-Ahmar*. Cairo/London, 1958.

al-Maqrīzī, Taqiyy al-Dīn Aḥmad ᶜAlī Ibn ᶜAbd al-Qadir Ibn Muḥammad. *Kitāb al-mawāʾiẓ wa'l-iʿtibār fi dhikr al-khiṭāṭ wa'l-āthār*. Būlāq, 1306 H.

Mubārak, ᶜAlī. *al-Khiṭaṭ al-Jadīda al-Tawfīqiyya*. Būlāq, 1306 H. IV, pp. 3 ff.

Nāṣir-i-Khusraw. *Relation du voyage de Nassiri Khosrau*, Charles Shefer, ed. Paris, 1881.

Rāğib, Yūsuf. "Al-Sayyida Nafisa, sa légende, son culte et son cimetière." *Studia Islamica*, XLV (1977), pp. 27 ff.

—. "Un Oratoire Fatimide au Sommet du Muqaṭṭam." *Studia Islamica* LXV (1987), p. 51 ff.

Ravaisse, P. "Essai sur l'histoire et la topographie du Caire d'après Makrizi." *Mémoires de la Mission Archéologique Française au Caire*, I:3 (1881-84).

Raymond, André. *Grandes Villes Arabes à l'Epoque Ottomane*. Paris, 1985.

—. "Essai de géographie des quartiers de résidence aristocratique au Caire au XVIIIème siècle." *JESHO*, VI (1963), pp. 58-103.

—. "Cairo's Area and Population in the Early Fifteenth Century." *Muqarnas*, 2 (1984), pp. 21 ff.

—, and Gaston Wiet. *Les Marchés du Caire. (Traduction annotée du texte de Maqrīzī)*. Cairo, 1979.

Salmon, Georges. "Etudes sur la topographie du Caire: Kalᶜat al-Kabch et Birkat al-Fil." *Mémoires de l'IFAO*, VII (1902).

Scanlon, G. T. "Housing and Sanitation; Some Aspects of Medieval Public Services." *The Islamic City*, A. H. Hourani and S. M. Stern, eds. Oxford, 1970, pp. 179 ff.

Wiet, Gaston. *Cairo, City of Art and Commerce*. Seymour trans. University of Oklahoma, 1964.

Williams, John Alden. "Urbanization and Monument Construction in Mamluk Cairo." *Muqarnas*, 2 (1984), pp. 33 ff.

THE ARCHITECTURE OF CAIRO

ᶜAbd al-Laṭīf al-Baghdādī. *Kitāb al-ifāda wa'l-iᶜtibār fī umur al-mushāhada wa'l-ḥawādith al-muᶜāyana bi arḍ miṣr*, Sylvestre de Sacy, ed. Paris, 1810.

ᶜAbd al-Wahhāb, Ḥasan. *Tārīkh al-masājid al-athariyya*. Cairo, 1946.

Ahmad, Muhammad. *The Mosque of ᶜAmr Ibn al-ᶜĀṣ at Fusṭāṭ*. Cairo, 1939.

Aḥmad, Yūsuf. *Jāmiᶜ Sayyidna ᶜAmr Ibn al-ᶜĀṣ*. Cairo, 1917.

Ali Ibrahim, Layla. "Mamluk Monuments of Cairo." *Quaderni dell Istituto Italiano di cultura per la RAE*. Cairo, 1976.

—. "Middle-class Living Units in Mamluk Cairo." *AARP*, 14 (1978), pp. 24 ff.

—. "Residential Architecture in Mamluk Cairo." *Muqarnas*, 2 (1984), pp. 47 ff.

—. "The Transitional Zones of Domes in Cairene Architecture." *Kunst des Orients*, X (1/2), 1975, pp. 5 ff.

—. "The Zāwiya of Shaikh Zain al-Dīn Yūsuf in Cairo." *Mitteilungen des Deutschen Archäologischen Instituts Abteilung Kairo*, 34 (1978), pp. 79 ff.

Amīn, Muḥammad Muḥ. ed. Waqf of Qalāwūn's Hospital published as appendix in: Ibn Ḥabīb. *Tadhkirat al-nabīh fī ayyām al-Manṣūr wa banīh*. Cairo, 1976-86. I, pp. 295 ff.

—. ed. Waqf of the madrasa of Sultan Ḥasan published as appendix in: Ibn Ḥabīb. *Tadhkirat*, III, pp. 349 ff.

Behrens-Abouseif, Doris. "Change in function and form of Mamluk religious institutions." *Annales Islamologiques*, XXI (1985), pp. 73 ff.

—. "Fêtes populaires dans le Caire du Moyen-Age." *Quaderni dell'Istituto Italiano di Cultura per la R.A.E.* Cairo, 1982.

—. "Four Domes of the Late Mamluk Period." *Annales Islamologiques*, 17 (1981), pp. 157 ff.

—. "The Lost Minaret of Shajarat al-Durr at Her Complex in the Cemetery of Sayyida Nafisa." *Mitteilungen des Deutschen Archäologischen Instituts Abteilung Kairo*, 39 (1983), pp. 1 ff.

—. *The Minarets of Cairo*. Cairo, 1985.

—. "The Northeastern Expansion of Cairo under the Mamluks." *Annales Islamologiques*, 17 (1981), pp. 191 ff.

—. "The Qubba, an Aristocratic type of Zāwiya." *Annales Islamologiques*, 19 (1983), pp. 1 ff.

—. "Quelques traits de l'habitation traditionelle dans la ville du Caire." *La Ville Arabe dans l'Islam, Histoire et Mutations*. Tunis, 1982, pp. 447 ff.

Bloom, Jonathan M. "The mosque of al-Ḥākim in Cairo." *Muqarnas*, 1 (1983), pp. 15 ff.

Casanova, Paul. *Histoire de la Citadelle du Caire*. Mémoires publiés par les Membres de la Mission Archéologique Française au Caire, VI, Cairo, 1894-97 (Arabic transl. Darrāj, Ahmad. *Tārīkh wa waṣf qalʿat al-qāhira.*, Cairo, 1974).

Čelebi, Evliya. *Seyahatnamesi X, Mısır, Sudan, Habeş*. Istanbul, 1938.

Coste, Pascal. *Architecture Arabe des Monuments du Caire*. Paris, 1839.

Crecelius, Daniel. "The waqfiyya of Muḥammad Bey Abū al-Dhahab." *Journal of the American Research Center in Egypt*, XV (1978), pp. 83 ff.; XVI (1979), pp. 125 ff.

Creswell, K. A. C. *A Brief Chronology of the Muhammadan Monuments of Egypt to A.D. 1517*. Cairo, 1919.

—. "The Evolution of the Minaret with Special Reference to Egypt." *Burlington Magazine* (March-June), 1926, pp. 1 ff.

—. *The Muslim Architecture of Egypt (M.A.E.)*. Oxford University Press, 1952-60.

—. *Early Muslim Architecture (E.M.A.)*. Oxford University Press, 1932-40.

Darrag, Ahmad. *L'Acte de Waqf du Sultan al-Ashraf Barsbay*. Cairo, 1963.

Ebeid, Sophie. "Early Sabils and Their Standardization." M. A. Thesis, American University in Cairo, 1976.

Fabri, Félix. *Le Voyage en Egypte* (1483). Cairo, 1975.

Fernandes, Leonor E. "The Evolution of the Khanqāh Institution in Mamluk Egypt." Ph D. Thesis, Princeton University, 1980.

—. "Three Sufi Foundations in a 15th Century Waqfiyya." *Annales Islamologiques*, 17 (1981), pp. 141 ff.

Flury, Samuel. *Die Ornamente der Hakim und Ashar Moschee; Materialen zur Geschichte der aelteren Kunst des Islam*. Heidelberg, 1912.

Garcin, J. C., Maury, B. R., Revault, F., Zakarya, M. *Palais et Maisons du Caire I: Epoque Mamelouke, XIIIe-XVIe Siècle*. Paris, 1982.

Ghaleb Bey, K. O. *Le Miqyas ou Nilomètre de l'Ile de Rodah*. Cairo, 1951.

Goitein, S. D. "A Mansion in Fustāt: A Twelfth Century Description of a Domestic Compound in the Ancient Capital of Egypt," in H. Miskinim, ed., *The Medieval City*. New Haven, 1977, pp. 163 ff.

—. "Urban Housing in Fatimid and Ayyubid Times as Illustrated by the Cairo Geniza Documents." *Studia Islamica*, 47 (1978), pp. 5 ff.

Grabar, Oleg. "The earliest Islamic commemorative structures." *Ars Orientalis*, 6 (1966), pp. 27 ff.

Grotzfeld, Heinz. *Das Bad im Arabisch-Islamischen Mittelalter. Eine kulturgeschichtliche Studie*. Wiesbaden, 1970.

von Harff, Arnold. *The Pilgrimage of Arnold von Harff, 1496-99*. Transl. Malcolm Letts. London, 1946.

Herz, M. *Die Baugruppe des Sultans Qalawun*. Hamburg, 1910.

—. *La mosquée du Sultan Hassan au Caire*. Cairo, 1899.

—. "La mosquée d'Ezbek al-Youssoufi." *Revue Egyptienne*, I (1899), pp. 16 ff.

Ibn al-Hājj, Abū ʿAbd Allāh Muḥ. Ibn Muḥ. al-ʿAbdarī al-Fāsī. *al-Madkhal*. Cairo, 1981.

Ibn Iyās, *Badāʾiʿ al-zuhūr fī waqāʾiʿ al-duhūr*. Ed. M. Mustafa. Cairo/Wiesbaden, 1961-83.

Issa, Ahmed. *Histoire des Bimaristans (Hôpitaux) à l'Epoque Islamique*. Cairo, 1928.

Kessler, Christel. *The Carved Masonry Domes of Medieval Cairo*. Cairo, 1976.

—. "Funerary Architecture within the City." *Colloque International sur l'Histoire du Caire*. Arab Republic of Egypt, Ministry of Culture. Cairo, 1969, pp. 257 ff.

—. "Mecca-Oriented Urban Architecture in Mamluk Cairo: The Madrasa-Mausoleum of Sultan Shaʿbān II." *In Quest of an Islamic Humanism*, A. H. Green, ed. Cairo, 1984, pp. 97 ff.

Lane, E. W. *An Account of the Manners and Customs of Modern Egyptians, 1833-1835*. The Hague, 1978.

Lézine, Alexandre. "Les salles nobles des palais mameloukes." *Annales Islamologiques*, X (1971), pp. 72 ff.

—. *Trois Palais d'Epoque Ottomane*. Cairo, 1972.

—. "Persistance des traditions pré-islamiques dans l'architecture domestique du Caire." *Annales Islamologiques*, XI (1972), pp. 1 ff.

Makdisi, George. "Muslim Institutions of Learning in Eleventh Century Baghdad." *Bulletin of the School of African and Oriental Studies*, XXIV Part 1 (1961), pp. 1 ff.

Maury, B., Raymond, A., Revault, F., Zakarya, M. *Palais et Maisons du Caire II: Epoque Ottomane, XVIe-XVIIIe Siècle*. Paris, 1983.

Mayer, L. A. *The Buildings of Qāytbāy as Described in His Endowment Deeds*. London, 1938.

Mehren, A. F. *Câhira og Kerafât*. Copenhagen, 1869.

Meinecke, Michael. "Das Mausoleum des Qalāʾun in Kairo. Untersuchungen zur Genese der Mamlukischen Architekturdekoration." *Mitteilungen des Deutschen Archäologischen Instituts Abteilung Kairo*, 27 (1971), pp. 47 ff.

—. "Die Mamlukische Faiencedekorationen: Eine Werkstätte aus Tabriz in Kairo (1330-1355)." *Kunst des Orients*, XI (1976-77), pp. 85 ff.

—. "Zur mamlukischen Heraldik." *Mitteilungen des Deutschen Archäologischen Instituts Abteilung Kairo*, 28 (1972), pp. 213 ff.

Meinecke-Berg, V. "Osmanische Fliesendekorationen des 17. Jahrhunderts in Kairo." *IVème Congrès International d'Art Turc*. Aix-En-Provence, 1971, pp. 153 ff.

Misiorowski, Andrzej. *Mausoleum of Qurqumas in Cairo: An Example of the Architecture and Building Art of the Mamlouk Period*. Warsaw, 1979.

Mostafa, Saleh Lamei. *Kloster und Mausoleum des Farag Ibn Barqūq in Kairo*. Glückstadt, 1968.

—. "Madrasa, Hanqā und Mausoleum des Barqūq in Kairo mit einem Beitrag von Felicitas Jaritz." *Abhandlungen des Deutschen Archäologischen Instituts Abteilung Kairo, Islamische Reihe*, 4 (1982), pp. 118 ff.

Muḥammad, ʿAbd al-Raḥmān Fahmī. "Bayna adab al-maqāma wa fann al-ʿimāra fī al-madrasa al-saʿdiyya." *Majallat al-majmaʿ al-ʿilmī al-miṣrī*, 52 (1970-71), pp. 39 ff.

Pauty, Edmond. *Les Hammams du Caire*. Cairo, 1933.

Pedersen, J. "Masdjid." *Encyclopaedia of Islam*. 1st ed., Leiden, 1913-36.

Popper, William. *The Nilometer, Studies in Ibn Taghribirdi's Chronicles of Egypt* (Part 1). Berkeley, 1951.

al-Qalqashandī, Abū al-ʿAbbās Aḥmad Ibn ʿAlī. *Subḥ al-Aʿshā fī Ṣināʿat al-Inshā*. Cairo, 1963 III, pp. 337 ff.

Ragib, Y. "Les sanctuaires des Gens de la Famille dans la Cité des Morts au Caire." *Rivista Degli Studi Orientali*. Vol. LI Fasc. I-IV (1977), pp. 47 ff.

Raymond, André. "Les constructions de l'émir ᶜAbd-Rahman Katkhuda au Caire." *Annales Islamologiques*, 11 (1972), pp. 235 ff.

—. "Les fontaines publiques (Sabil) du Caire à l'époque Ottomane." *Annales Islamologiques*, 15 (1979), pp. 5 ff.

—. "The Rabᶜ: A Type of Collective Housing in Cairo during the Ottoman Period." *The Aga Khan Award for Architecture. Architecture as Symbol and Self-Identity, Proceedings of Seminar IV (1980)*.

Rogers, J. M. "Evidence for Mamluk-Mongol Relations 1260-1360." *Colloque International sur l'Histoire du Caire (1969)*. Cairo, pp. 385 ff.

—. "al-Ḳāhira." *Encyclopaedia of Islam*, 2nd ed. Leiden, 1960-.

—. "Madrasa." *Encyclopaedia of Islam*, 2nd ed. Leiden, 1960-.

—. "Seljuk Influence in the Monuments of Cairo." *Kunst des Orients*, 7 (1970-71), pp. 40 ff.

—. "The Inscription of the Cistern of Yaᶜqub Shah al-Mihmandar in Cairo." *Fifth International Congress of Turkish Art*. Budapest.

Shāfiᶜī, Farīd. "The Mashhad al-Juyūshī: Archeological Notes and Studies." *Studies in Islamic Art and Architecture in Honor of Professor K. A. C. Creswell*. Cairo, 1965, pp. 237 ff.

—. "West Islamic Influences on Architecture in Egypt." *Bulletin of the Faculty of Arts*. Cairo University XVI, Part II (December 1954), pp. 1 ff.

al-ᶜUmarī, Ibn Faḍl Allāh. *Masālik al-abṣār fī mamālik al-amṣār*. Cairo, 1985, pp. 79 ff.

Van Berchem, Max. *Matériaux pour un Corpus Inscriptionum Arabicarum*. Mémoires publiés par les Membres de la Mission Archéologique Française au Caire, Tome XIX (I-IV). Cairo, 1894-1903.

Van Ghistele, de Joos. *Le Voyage en Egypte, 1482-83*. Cairo, 1976.

Whelan, Estelle. "The Origins of the *mihrab mujawwaf*: A Reinterpretation." *International Journal of Middle East Studies*, 18 (1986), pp. 205 ff.

Wiet, Gaston. "Les inscriptions du mausolée de Shafiᶜi." *Bulletin de l'Institut d'Egypte*, 15 (1933), pp. 167 ff.

—. *Muhammed Ali et les Beaux-Arts*. Cairo, n.d.

—. "Sultan Hasan." *La Revue du Caire*, June 1938, pp. 86 ff.

Williams, Caroline. "The Cult of ᶜAlid Saints in the Fatimid Monuments of Cairo. Part I: The Mosque of al-Aqmar." *Muqarnas*, I (1983), pp. 37 ff.

Williams, John A. "The Monuments of Ottoman Cairo." *Colloque International sur l'Histoire du Caire*. Arab Republic of Egypt, Ministry of Culture. Cairo, 1969, pp. 453 ff.

Yūsuf, Aḥmad. *Jāmiᶜ Ibn Ṭūlūn*. Cairo, 1917.

Zakarya, Mona. *Deux Palais du Caire Médiéval: Waqfs et Architecture*. Paris, 1983.